D1417821

Experience the Message

Experience the Message

How Experiential Marketing Is Changing the Brand World

Max Lenderman

CARROLL & GRAF PUBLISHERS
NEW YORK

Experience the Message
How Experiential Marketing Is Changing the Brand World

Carroll & Graf Publishers
An Imprint of Avalon Publishing Group Inc.
245 West 17th Street
11th Floor
New York, NY 10011

AVALON
publishing group incorporated

Copyright © 2006 by Max Lenderman

First Carroll & Graf edition 2006

Library of Congress Cataloging-in-Publication Data is available.

ISBN-10: 0-7867-1536-7
ISBN-13: 978-0-78671-536-7

9 8 7 6 5 4 3 2 1

Interior Design: Susan Canavan
Printed in the United States of America
Distributed by Publishers Group West

To my mother and father,
Dina and Yefim Lenderman

Contents

ntroduction : *Making Friends with Brands*

My marketing career began as a cofounder of a "youth marketing" agency in Montreal, Canada. In fact, my partners and I had earlier started an online portal for North American students called uPath.com. Our mission was to be authentic to the students' needs and relevant to their lifestyles. I was the editor in chief and creative director of the portal. I had to make sure we gave students a voice. In doing so, we began supporting student causes, clubs, and local bands. We encouraged and supported young writers, and paid them like we meant it. We also began sponsoring campus events and off-campus concerts. To reach our target market, we needed to be where they were and to provide them with a head-turning branded experience. Our success on campus did not go unnoticed. Our clients stopped asking for banner ads. They wanted to be there physically with us instead. Our access to student lifestyle venues across the country—earned through our grassroots efforts—allowed us to begin building brand experiences for our clients' young consumers.

Access to campus and youth venues also allowed us to start deploying street teams to support our event marketing. We began to

1

offer "guerrilla marketing" solutions to clients who did not have the deep pockets to afford the advertising and venue fees that come with event marketing or sponsorships. Our form of guerrilla marketing had a specific ethos to it: it had to be based on some form of relevant experience associated with the brand we were marketing. We didn't want to add to the clutter; our target audience was too marketing-savvy for that. Smart kids can smell a marketing come-on from a mile away. The guerrilla marketing we chose to wage, in all its manifestations, cut through the ad clutter by invoking a powerful sensory or cognitive consumer response. Our guerrilla marketing campaigns revolved around the idea of providing a consumer experience with the brand. Instead of creating ads and writing copy, we were creating unconventional branded experiences for our audience with hundreds of our own brand guerrillas, whom we called our Gears. We named the company Gearwerx.

Our marketing battles weren't being waged on TV screens and in magazine spreads. They were fought on the streets, in the bars and nightclubs, in malls and movie theater lobbies, at beaches and ski hills, in the downtown cores and on leafy university campuses. We were taking brands directly to the people. In doing so, we engaged them in a form of dialogue that was simply not possible with mass marketing and advertising. We used personal interactions between our Gears and consumers to develop trust and empathy. Our Gears "spoke the language" of our target market. They dressed the same. They believed in the same things. Many of our Gears heard about the company from their friends who had worked for us, but we made it a priority to constantly recruit new guerrillas with specific skill-sets, abilities, and passions. If we were marketing an alternative sports brand, we would recruit skaters and boarders. If it was a beauty product that was about to launch, we would find aestheticians to join the guerrilla teams. If we needed to reach the student audience, the teams were deployed to campus to get the message out. Our guerrillas were authentic to the brands they were marketing. When they spoke to consumers, they meant what they said.

Creating unconventional brand experiences with our Gears won the company eager clients looking to reach an elusive and ad-savvy youth audience. In the summer of 2003, a major hair care company was introducing a hair gel called Hard into the Canadian marketplace. (You can probably guess the name of the company.) This gel was targeted squarely at the teen and young adult market. Their advertising was edgy, their models were edgy, the name was edgy, and so were their target consumers. But the target consumers are also edgy enough to ignore traditional advertising. They are prone to laugh at the models on the screen or page, and actually care how well a product works before buying it. Most importantly, this target consumer needs to be shown—directly and in their face—how well a product named Hard can stand up to their lifestyle and hairstyle choices.

We worked closely with GMR Marketing to create the Hard Truck and Crew, a head-turning and fully branded bright green Hummer H2 that pulls up in front of a concert venue. Out of the truck fly six punk-rock guys and girls, their outfits and hair reflecting the postgrunge punk-pop ethos. The crew proceeds to set up a couple of industrial-grade fans right in front of the truck. All concertgoers passing through the fans on their way into the concert are struck by a blast of air from the fans. Instantly, their edgy coiffed hair gets tussled. Can their hair product stand up to the Hard Challenge? Hundreds of punks and hard-core concertgoers go head to head with the Crew to see whose hair can "stand up" to industrial-strength wind tunnels. Losers get free Hard product. Winners—and there are a few of them—get massive bragging rights with their friends for days to come.

Or imagine Reading Week on campus: bleary-eyed students stagger with their jumbo-size coffee mugs from their dorms to class to the library to the campus center. This is their daily pattern for weeks leading up to their final exams, until a little fun comes roaring onto the quad, thanks to DaimlerChrysler Canada. The company hired Gearwerx to develop and execute a Jeep-sponsored national campus tour to reconnect the brand with the student market. We rolled three vibrantly colored Jeep TJs onto campus right in the middle of exams, right in front of the main student campus center. Taking a cue from runaway hits such as "American Idol" and "Popstars," we customized one of the Jeeps with a state-of-the-art mobile karaoke machine and propped up the experience with a mobile soundstage—a PA system, large screens, karaoke DJ and MC—to let the kids blow off some steam and belt out a couple Mariah Carey or Metallica ditties and sappy duets.

Kids would pile into the back of the Jeep—sometimes eight at a time—grab a microphone and start singing their favorite pop songs. If anything would convince a potential consumer that a Jeep can take all sorts of punishment, it is the sight of eight freshmen in a Jeep jumping up and down in unison to a Green Day anthem. All these performances are videotaped and edited by Gearwerx. A personalized e-mail is then sent to the students a few days after the event with his or her clip attached. The e-mails also prompts the users to share the clip with their friends in other schools across the country. Long after our Jeep-brand guerrillas left the campus, karaoke clips were being spread across Canada virally from one student in-box to another, and the Jeep site was receiving thousands of visits of students watching their clips.

Our "Gear-illas" were so effective at reaching our intended audiences, and the personal interactions and connections they were able to achieve between brand and consumer were so meaningful, that our form of experience-based guerrilla marketing began to spread positive word of mouth within the communities we were speaking with. We quickly learned that good brand experiences created incredible word of mouth and buzz. Bad brand experiences, conversely, spread bad buzz much more quickly. Nevertheless, it became clear that staging brand experiences ignited the best and most compelling form of marketing: consumer recommendations to fellow consumers.

I didn't really internalize how vital word of mouth is to a brand's success until one of my Gears explained to me how she thought that what my company was doing was really making friends with brands. I was puzzled and asked her to explain her rationale. After she was through, I hugged her and asked her if I could use her analogy in my pitches to clients, and now I'll share it with you.

"You market brands the way we make friends," she said. She was twenty-one at the time.

"What do you mean?" I asked.

"You start buzz about a brand, then you send in the guerrillas to the street to hype that brand, and then you organize these underground events and concerts sponsored by the brand. That's just the way we would make friends."

"Huh?"

"C'mon, you're not that old! You remember how your earliest friendships were made! You're sitting in a college dorm room or a friend's flat, doing whatever"—she then winked at me mischievously—"and someone says, 'Do you know Katie? She lives on the third floor. No? You should. She's into what you're into, and I hear that she's pretty cool, everyone likes her,' etc. That's word of mouth, Max. A friend has recommended a friend to me, and because I like and respect my existing friends, this recommendation goes pretty far."

"That's how I met most of my good friends, through other friends," I agreed.

"Okay. Now imagine you're walking to class or a bar or something with your friends, and you run into Katie on the street. Your friends introduce her to you. You exchange some friendly banter, laugh a bit, dish out some gossip, have a good experience . . . and if you like her style and attitude, you would probably make some sort of tentative plans to hang out together sometime soon. That's guerrilla marketing. You bring a brand (friend) into a natural and unexpected environment and introduce the brand (friend) to someone willing to meet it and hang out."

"Go on," I jumped in. "This is awesome."

"Then you meet Katie at a bar or concert or whatever. Or maybe you already made plans with her when you first met, or during a couple of subsequent chance meetings. However you got there, you have a great time at the event. You dance your pants off at a club, or laugh yourself silly at a comedy show, or just have a great time hanging out together in an apartment watching *Melrose Place* reruns. That's it! You two are good friends now. Maybe even for life."

I was impressed. Very impressed. My Gear understood more about the modern state of marketing than most CMOs or ad agency execs. She got it, and she made me get it, too. It is no surprise, therefore, to find that a large number of experiential marketing firms have started out just like Gearwerx—as youth marketers who appropriated guerrilla, event, and word-of-mouth marketing to reach their target audiences. Small guerrilla agencies started to call their services "experiential," because the guerrilla teams were able to provide a personal branded experience for the consumer.

San Francisco–based Swivel Media is one such agency that progressed from youth marketing initiatives to experiential marketing campaigns.

Since then, the company's founder and creative director, Erik Hauser, has emerged as a leading voice in experiential marketing circles. He says he started his business "organically" by working for guerrilla marketers, passing out flyers at age seventeen. His entire marketing career has been based on connecting with the consumer personally. Hauser started Swivel Media after witnessing firsthand the disconnect between a brand's fabulously produced TV commercial, and that same brand being represented by an apathetic and disengaged twenty-year-old handing out flyers on the street—not to mention the sixty-something sampler in the grocery store sticking toothpicks into the product.

"What Swivel Media tries to do is to put the living, breathing embodiment of the brand in the field, who is well trained and is great at interacting with consumers, giving them the same impression that they would if they saw a commercial on television," Hauser explained to me one day at a conference in Chicago. "We are all social creatures. Humans connect with humans. They don't hug TV screens or radios. If you can interact with a human in a live brand experience and form a connection with that person, and then walk the consumer through an experience with a product or brand, this greatly increases the meaning and relevance of the brand. The ultimate medium for marketing is people, and to reach them involves giving them a fantastic brand experience. They then will do the marketing for you."

At the tail end of 2003, Erik founded and launched the International Experiential Marketing Association (IXMA). I was fortunate enough to be one of the association's founding board members. While working to grow the association to represent over ten thousand members in more than sixty countries, we recognized that the notion of providing a marketing experience to consumers went far beyond event, guerrilla, and word-of-mouth marketing. The various types of marketers who flocked to the association proved to us that providing a branded experience encompasses an incredible array of marketing methodologies: promotional marketing, public relations, direct marketing, sponsorships, store design and merchandising, product placement, mobile marketing, retailtainment, Internet marketing, packaging, product innovation, and trend seeding—just to name a few. Whatever our field of marketing expertise was called, all of us at the association understood that providing consumers with meaningful experiences was the new way to market to them.

I proposed to Erik that we write a manifesto for the association, and working with a number of members, we announced it to the marketing world in the summer of 2004 on our Web site, www.ixma.org. "Markets have undergone a profound transformation after decades of top-down corporate messaging. As you read this, the marketing world is changing, and with it the way business will be conducted for decades to come," we proclaimed. "This change is being demanded by the enlightened and empowered consumer—the so-called prosumer—who no longer responds to a media-propelled 'brand essence.' Most current advertising still relies on obsessive proliferation of the brand through mass media that seek economies of scale—the more eyeballs, the better. But consumers want more than mass messages sent to eyeballs. They want respect, recognition, and relevant communication, and they've indicated that the best way to give it to them is through experiences that are personally relevant, memorable, sensory, emotional, and meaningful. Consumers have changed dramatically, and the brand world must change to meet their needs and desires, or lose them to those that recognize the unique influences shaping the evolving marketplace."

Customers expect product quality and a positive brand image, we posited, but what they demand is products, communications, and marketing campaigns "that dazzle their senses, touch their hearts, and stimulate their minds—that deliver an experience. It is those companies that can deliver the right experience to customers that will succeed in the global marketplace today. Businesses will live or die not by the attributes they promise, but by the experience they offer customers at every touch point—in the store, at the Web site, with the product, and through events and advertising."

We created the IXMA to share insights with freethinking business leaders in preparing for profound changes about to challenge traditional advertising and marketing. The IXMA became a forum for "radically new thinking about how brands are introduced and sustained. The IXMA shows how experiential marketing (XM) uses credible voices, sensory experiences, and respect for the consumer to bring brands—and their essence and benefits—to life, and to create direct and meaningful connections between companies and their customer." To us, "the question isn't which industries will be transformed by the focus on customer experience, but only which will be first. Companies who do not recognize this change will perish. Those who see the necessity for change and embrace XM will be embraced in turn by the most empowered consumer base in the history of the world."

We knew that the power of experience is the new marketing paradigm, but defining experiential marketing was less clear-cut. Agencies and the press were already using the term interchangeably with event marketing, guerrilla marketing, promotions, mobile marketing, and sponsorships. Anything "alternative" in the marketing world, such as product placements, trend seeding, and buzz marketing, was also becoming categorized as experiential marketing. Because our own members came from a wide array of marketing and advertising disciplines, it was no surprise to us that their definitions would vary as well.

Still, a number of common themes—particularly concerning our duty to consumers—quickly became evident. The idea that the marketing message had to be as beneficial to the consumer as the product or service being marketed was at the core of the accumulated definitions. IXMA members described experiential marketing as the opposite of product-centric marketing, as a marketing tactic that provides something meaningful to the individual consumer. They talked about provoking the senses in the consumer, in wrapping her or him up in a brand to instill an inherent understanding of the brand's value in the consumer's life. They saw experiential marketing as an integral part of "customer experience design" or "consumer experience management." In other words, experiential marketing is a marketing strategy that seeks to intentionally bring to life and animate the brand promise for consumers through staged experiences they have with the brand before they buy, during the buying process and at all touch points they may have with it thereafter.

The rise of experiential marketing is a result of the consumer desire to be connected to brands through memorable communication, and the need for marketers to break through the ad clutter and counteract the growing ineffectiveness of mass marketing. Consumers do not want their time wasted on marketing, but they still love an incredible idea or experience. Experiential marketing delivers the brand message when and where the consumer is most responsive to it, and allows the consumer to interact with the brand or product. They want to do this personally. They want to try before they buy, and a dialogue with a brand ambassador is imperative to their understanding of the brand.

Consumers need to internalize the brand, product, or service as individuals and to understand its place in their lives. Experiential marketing encourages sensory and emotional brand connections during this trial and interaction, much more so than traditional advertising. By giving consumers the tools to engage with the brand, and by enhancing that experience, experiential marketing campaigns are extremely effective at influencing purchase. Furthermore, a positive brand experience gets consumers talking about the brand to their friends. They may even become brand ambassadors, and bring the brand message into their everyday conversations with other consumers. Most importantly, experiential marketers keep the needs of the individual consumer to heart and strive to reach her or him with relevant, resonant, and memorable marketing experiences.

Perhaps a real-life scenario can best illustrate the ethos of experiential marketing. Because experiential marketing has been so closely linked with event marketing, let's take an example of how interactions with consumers at events can be transformed into a great example of experiential marketing. Imagine the typical summer concert or festival. The day is hot. Beer tents at the fairgrounds hawk the title sponsor's libations. Servers in the tents put on a good experience, with DJs and scantily clad brand ambassadors. Next to the tents, a major soup company is giving away samples of homestyle chili in small branded bowls. A major wireless company has set up a dozen X-Box game console stations and lets festivalgoers play to their heart's content. An automaker has rolled in a fifty-three-foot semitrailer to showcase the latest models, encouraging consumers to get a picture taken next to the machines and sign up for a test drive at a local dealership. Consumers appreciate these types of brand outreach and participate enthusiastically. To most, these interactions complement the festivalgoing experience.

Are the companies participating in creating a brand experience? Yes they are. The consumer enters a branded environment to be entertained and educated by a staff of brand ambassadors, at a venue where they are relatively open to the marketing pitch. In the mind of the typical consumer, brand presence at events has become a common sight. Getting inside the latest Corvette at the event is much more valuable and resonant to him than simply seeing a Chevrolet logo above the stage and on his ticket. In that sense, the company's presence at the event is indeed experiential. But is it memorable? Will it get consumers chatting? Does it viscerally connect the consumer to the brand? Does it evoke emotional attachment that's beyond reason? Does it cut through the clutter?

Experiential marketing tries to create a bit of magic for the consumer. This magic is the experience itself. Much like groundbreaking advertising creative, experiential marketing strives to hit an emotional and/or intellectual chord in the individual consumer. It creates a direct and meaningful connection between the consumer and the brand or product being marketed through marketing experiences that go deeper than any form of marketing deployed today.

Manchester, New Hampshire–based Gigunda Group went beyond typical event marketing executions to provide consumers with a magical brand experience at events and festivals for client Procter & Gamble and its Charmin brand. Working with his creative team at Gigunda, CEO Ryan Fitzsimmons came up with an idea he quickly termed Potty Palooza. The cornerstone of the Potty Palooza campaign is a twenty-seven-room traveling bathroom facility mounted on the trailer of an eighteen-wheeler and painted sky blue with big, fluffy clouds that could be seen from a mile away. All the rooms feature flushing porcelain toilets, hardwood floors, air conditioning, aromatherapy, skylights, changing stations, a "Little Squirts" stall for kids, and an LCD video screen. Each room is also individually staffed by a brand ambassador, who welcomes guests and makes sure the experience has not been, um, soiled by the last visitor. Put the Potty Palooza next to the lime green Porta-Johns that are typical to a concert or event. Who would choose not to do their thing in the Potty Palooza? It's the ultimate comparison test, and to the consumer, it's no contest.

Consumers lined up for the Charmin-sponsored bathrooms for twenty minutes at a time, while the regular bathrooms went vacant. During the lineups, Gigunda deployed a dancing Charmin bear—a nod to Charmin's television and print advertising—to entertain concertgoers and their kids. With Potty Palooza, Gigunda was able to own and direct the entire experience of the interaction between the consumer and the Charmin brand. Furthermore, it allowed the brand to greatly enhance the concertgoing experience for their customers, making the Charmin brand into a positive and relevant memory that enables them to talk about it to their friends for weeks to come. By entering the Potty Palooza environment, the consumer is immediately surrounded by the brand message. Ingeniously, Potty Palooza openly uses other Procter & Gamble cleaning products in front of consumers, further establishing the company as an experience enhancer while showing firsthand the efficacy of these products.

In 2003, Potty Palooza was experienced by over 2 million consumers at more than twenty events in the United States, including the Super Bowl in San Diego. Procter & Gamble's research showed that Charmin sales increased by 14 percent among consumers who participated in the campaign. This convinced the company to build another Potty Palooza unit to reach twice as many consumers at twice as many events. The company also began making over public restrooms at state fairs, donating time, money, and products to make the bathroom experience wholly Charmin-branded. Overall, more than 30 million consumers experienced Charmin and interacted with its brand ambassadors in just one year. Potty Palooza gave Procter & Gamble the ultimate captive audience, and in turn gave that audience the ultimate branded experience.

Experiential marketing can be as complex as creating Potty Palooza or as simple as encouraging salespeople at car dealerships to pretune a new car's radio to the same stations programmed in the customer's trade-in car radio, as Dallas-based Sewell Automotive Companies do. To some marketers, experiential marketing efforts are tactical in nature, and are increasingly being integrated into the overall marketing mix. To others, the consumer experience is the centerpiece of an overall brand strategy where all aspects of the experience are managed—what Columbia University professor Bernd Schmitt terms Customer Experience Management—and experiential marketing is more a large-scale strategy than an individual tactic. Professor Schmitt, who is also the CEO of the Ex Group and a fellow IXMA founding board member, sees Customer Experience Management as "the process of strategically managing a customer's entire experience with a product or a company."[1]

Schmitt points to Singapore Airlines as a company that provides a great customer experience through exceptional service, and Starbucks as a "fast food" chain that uses store design, sensory stimulation, and an innovative product line to deliver a unique consumer experience. We can, as consumers, all point out certain companies and their brands that offer us a meaningful experience. Think of Apple, Amazon, Nike, or Jeep. Some companies are using a great brand experiences with their customers to drive their competitive advantage. According to Schmitt, companies like these "have a real understanding of the customer experience and use that to provide service, products and communications that are relevant to the customer's lifestyle and deliver a consistent experience."[2]

This book is about experiential marketing, or put another way, this

1. Bernd H. Schmitt, "Competitive Advantage Through the Customer Experience," The Ex Group, 2003.
2. Ibid.

is a book on how to market so that the consumer's experience with the brand is the centerpiece of the campaign. In an article published in late 2004, *Advertising Age* editor in chief Scott Donaton wrote that "the advertising business is transformed into the marketing business" and that the "definition of marketing is broadened."[3] If this is the case, then experiential marketing can really be viewed as the next level in advertising as well.

Marketing and advertising started out as tools for consumers to make choices regarding the countless new lifestyle products that were hitting the marketplace in an overproductive industrial revolution. In this climate, as Naomi Klein posits, "competitive branding became a necessity of the machine age—within a context of manufactured sameness, image-based difference had to be manufactured with the product."[4] The idea of the brand was invented to meet this need. And as the industrial economy was necessarily made obsolete by the service economy in advanced capitalist markets, advertising and marketing became even more necessary to connect the consumer to the brand. As you read this, this brand paradigm is changing, and changing along with it is the way business will be conducted for decades to come. This change is being demanded by the enlightened and empowered consumer—the *prosumer*—because the traditional concept of the brand and the mass media that propagate it simply do not work anymore. What the consumer needs is "brand experience," and this need is presently inaugurating what Joseph Pine and James Gilmore call the Experience Economy.

All marketing in the future will be based on some form of consumer experience. It's already happening. The mass marketing paradigm is over. Consumers have had enough. People don't want to be spoken to anymore;

3. Scott Donaton, "Lunch with the Million-Dollar Brain," *Advertising Age,* October 4, 2004.
4. Naomi Klein, *No Logo: Taking Aim at the Brand Bullies* (New York: Picador, 2000), p. 6.

they want to engage in conversations. Millions of us are bombarded by messages and media that are contradictory at best and misleading at worst, messages meant to control and stimulate the impulse to buy. Many of us, however, are no longer part of the passive consumer base—those who are most susceptible to being swayed by advertising and marketing programs. Rather, we are brand atheists and purchase resisters who no longer respond to twentieth-century marketing strategies. Or no longer respond the way traditional marketers would like us to.

Experiential marketing is poised to change all that. As a marketer or advertising professional you will have to come to terms with the fact that you need to know about experiential marketing to survive and thrive. As a consumer you will come to recognize experiential marketing as a direct reaction—even an antithesis—to the way you are being marketed to right now.

The IXMA manifesto was a shot across the bow for traditional marketers, one that signaled this paradigm shift toward experience-based marketing. When we wrote and released it, we attached an eight-point directive for marketing in the so-called Experience Economy. This book is a wide extension of those eight points. It uses IXMA's eight-point declaration as a primer for experiential marketing principles. It is a guideline for experiential marketers worldwide.

In this book you will read about some of the most forward-thinking marketers, academics, grassroots activists and social commentators who are trumpeting a new course in marketing. The book will immerse you in groundbreaking case studies and outrageously successful experiential marketing tactics. It will discuss the latest trends in marketing—such as product placements, buzz, subviral marketing, roach marketing, text marketing (SMS), flash mobs, pop-up retail, and causal marketing—as manifestations of the experiential marketing revolution.

Through case studies of leading companies' experiential marketing strategies (both their profound successes and their ugly failures) and interviews with leading experiential marketers and experience economy academics, *Experience the Message* hopes to augur in a whole new discussion among marketing professionals. It also presents practical strategies and tactics for marketers and executive to jettison their obsession with the status quo. It will encourage all of us to not only think differently, but act differently as well. This book will try to unveil the story of how everything in marketing has changed—and *is* changing, even as you read these lines. It's a brave new marketing world. Enjoy the experience.

Chapter 1	**Experiential marketing** campaigns should clearly deliver a meaningful benefit to the consumer.

What kind of world do we live in where something called "ass-vertising" is a tried and true marketing method? Seasoned marketing veterans, with MBAs tucked away in their pockets, have raised a collective thumbs-up to putting their companies' logos on the business end of skimpy panties, which are then flashed by curvy beauties on the streets and in the malls of America. They have paid teenagers to paint logos onto their foreheads and walk around campuses, drawing stares and heckles from their peers. There are ads on vomit bags and tray tables in airplanes, and there are ads on toilet paper. There is eggvertising (yeah, ads on eggs!), and there are ads on the back of corporate pay checks. In 2004 a USA Network campaign for a show called *Traffic: The Miniseries* affixed fifty thousand one-dollar bills with peel-off stickers stamped with air date, time, and channel. The bills were then introduced into circulation at bars in New York and Los Angeles.

Experiential marketing is practically the opposite of these marketing ploys. For experiential marketers, consumers expect products, communications, and marketing campaigns that dazzle their senses, touch their hearts, and stimulate their minds. In other words, consumers expect marketing to deliver them an experience, not just another marketing message. Experiential marketing uses credible voices, sensory experiences, and respect for the consumer in its tactics and strategies, and it is employed to create direct and meaningful connections between companies and their customers. Yet most traditional marketers continue to bombard the consumer instead with base marketing. You can get your wedding sponsored by a brand. You can wrap a seventy-story office tower with mesh fabric to make it look like a Pepsi bottle. A twenty-two-year-old Illinois man named Jim Nelson auctioned off "ad space" on the back of his head off of eBay last year. The winning bidder, Web hosting firm CI Host, was granted a five-inch square on the back of Nelson's noggin, which he permanently tattooed with the company's logo and tagline. His contract with the firm stipulates that he must keep the tattoo visible for at least five years. The successful sale of head space promoted one company to offer tattoo advertising to hundreds of corporate clients. According to the Web site for TatAd, a company specializing in something called "tattoovertising," the company is "revolutionizing advertising and the relationship between customer and company. Tattooing is the perfect way to do it. It's that simple, we're all walking billboards anyway so why not get paid to do it?" The company specializes in matching people, based on where they live and their lifestyle choices, with marketers who are interested in getting their logos and icons permanently tattooed on strangers. So far, about one thousand people have offered up skin space on the site. If you can brand the human body, you can brand anything.

Thirty years ago, the average American was targeted by 560 daily ad messages. Today the average consumer is exposed to 3,000 to 4,000 marketing messages, from billboards and blimps to TV ads and online pop-ups. These numbers (which, in my estimation, are significantly higher for younger consumers) are growing every day. Consequently there's too much commercial noise in our lives—the white noise of marketing blitzes and advertising overkill. This white noise is called clutter. Clutter is why TiVo was invented: to get rid of all the crap we don't really want to see but that shows up on TV anyway. Clutter is why there are pop-up blockers. Clutter is why the U.S. Congress imposed a "do not call" law on telemarketers. Clutter is why social pundits and the anti-establishment vehemently assert that corporations control our cultural landscape and the media jungle.

Marketers haven't run out of ideas or media; they're just thinking of new and radical ones at breakneck speed. Often they are overzealous and truly tasteless. A local campaign for a twenty-six-restaurant pizza company in Oregon and Washington State called Pizza Schmizza, for instance, paid homeless people in Seattle to hold up signs that read "Pizza Schmizza paid me to hold this sign instead of asking for money." The Associated Press quoted advertising industry watchers as pronouncing the campaign a "first of its kind," citing the perennial mantra of ad clutter to explain the imperative need for alternative marketing channels.

Even the toilet—probably the last bastion of privacy—is no longer a refuge from the ad-weary consumer. Marketers are buying ad space on stall walls and urinal mats (yes, urinal mats!) to attract an audience that is "captive to its biological needs." The Indoor Billboard Advertising Association estimates that North American revenues from bathroom advertising is still relatively small—$50 million in 2004, compared to the $5.5 billion spent on outdoor advertising—but the practice is on the rise, up 14 percent from 2003, which rose 12 percent over the year before. It seems that brands don't mind if they're pissed on, as long as someone sees the logo.

Even if no one sees it, marketers are anxious to brand it. In 2003 the

Russian space program launched a sponsored rocket emblazoned with a thirty-foot Pizza Hut logo. Who knows? Maybe E.T. loves deep-dish pepperoni and cinnamon sticks.

Consumers are inundated with brands at every turn, even in the cosmos. Now, with alarming frequency, consumers are being branded by their news. Not a day goes by without some mention on the nightly news of a publicity stunt, or PR-driven human interest, pop culture, or celebrity "news" reporting. The power and prevalence of PR and the publicity stunt have never been greater. Film releases, magazine cover stories, album sales, news cycles, and product launches desperately rely on PR and stunts like a drowning man reaching for a life preserver. The axiom for these campaigns is simple: the more outrageous the story, the greater the coverage.

For instance, a PR stunt had guys across this continent dripping with lusty machismo when gambling site GoldenPalace.com (which reportedly sees daily action grossing more than $5 million) slathered its URL on a B-list porn star and paid her to streak topless across the eleventh hole in the final round of the 2003 U.S. Open. Earlier that year, another branded streaker emblazoned with the casino's online coordinates took a sprint through the French Open; the same guy did a buff victory lap at the UEFA Cup soccer final in Spain. The "streaker as advertising" medium worked so well in getting the attention of a slack-jawed press that the company continues to expose itself through publicity stunts during global sporting events, most recently the 2004 Super Bowl and at the Athens Olympics, when a man in a purple tutu outwitted terrorist-obsessed security guards and dove into the Olympic swimming pool in front of the world's cameras.

The year 2004 was also permanently marked by the mother of all PR stunts when Justin Timberlake ripped the bodice off of a performing

Janet Jackson and bared her right breast during CBS's Super Bowl half-time show. A few days later, search-engine company Lycos released statistics that may possibly be the first clue to the end of the world: Internet search activity after Jackson's "wardrobe malfunction" set a new record for activity. Prior to this stunt, the most-searched event in the history of the Lycos 50 survey over a one-day period was the September 11, 2001, terrorist attacks. Janet's boob had beaten al-Qaeda.

Despite all denials, Jackson's flash was a premeditated publicity stunt. It's no coincidence that Janet's new—and desperately needed—album was about to drop into the market within the month. A single from her upcoming record was unsurprisingly released early, a day after the boob made headlines. The brouhaha forced broadcaster CBS to impose a five-minute delay for the Grammys, making it company policy for any live telecasts. Later that year, the Federal Communications Commission reported that no TV event has ever elicited as many complaints from the American public, slapped the network's owner, Viacom, with a record $550,000 fine for the flash. A maximum $27,500 fine was imposed on the twenty CBS affiliates that are owned by the network, while affiliates with separate owners were exempt from the wrist slap. And a wrist slap it was: the entire fine could be paid with 7.5 seconds of Super Bowl ad time.

Advertising Shell Shock?

The Janet Jackson incident raised some serious questions in the PR industry, foremost being how to top it. If there was any soul-searching in the offices of PR flacks, it was how to get their clients to do more stunts, not less. After all, the halftime show attracted 2 million more viewers than the game itself, and the day following the infamous Super Bowl, Viacom's stock actually went up. And Janet—"Ms. Jackson if you're nasty"—didn't fare badly at all. According to research firm CARMA International, she garnered twice as many U.S. press mentions as the Super Bowl commercials in the four days following the event. With attention-grabbing wins such as these, it's no wonder that the practice of PR shock and awe continues to pervade our cultural landscape. Interestingly, Janet Jackson's album actually tanked on the charts, after an initial spike directly after the Super Bowl. Apparently no amount of shock value can sell a bad album.

So why do companies choose to assault an already marketing-savvy (and weary) consumer with a blitz of senseless marketing? Surely after dozens, if not hundreds, of such assaults make the front pages and nightly newscasts each year—and after enough pundits decry the moral decrepitude of our social fabric while an equal-strength of marketing execs dictate the need to be "edgy"—these types of campaigns do nothing but calcify the consumer into a mistrustful and even negative reactionary force to creative marketing.

The incursion of advertising and marketing into every facet of our daily lives is reaching absurd proportions, and only a handful of leading marketing and advertising experts are calling for *less* clutter. The news media often resemble infomercials, as businesses rely on outrageous PR stunts to get on the nightly newscasts. The cumulative result is consumer mistrust converting into utter contempt for intrusive marketing. If everything has been co-opted into a marketing pitch, you can't really trust anything you see or hear in the media, and you certainly don't buy what the ads are selling. After all, how can a consumer reasonably trust a company from an ad tattooed on a guy's head? Of course, the outrageous ploy will generate headlines (pun intended) and spikes to CI Host's business. But what then? What else would CI Host need to do outrageously to get the consumer to pay attention?

And just exactly how many more products can be integrated into our movies and shows before they morph into feature-length commercials? Marketers have already devoted an entire movie to introduce a car into the cluttered marketplace, with last year's *USA Network with Pontiac and General Motors Present: The Last Ride.* That's really the name of the movie, which stars Oscar-nominated actor Dennis Hopper and the 2004 Pontiac GTO. General Motors took a page out of its own history. Decades ago it packaged shows such as *The Dinah Shore Chevy Hour* on NBC. But this movie took the practice of product placement to its ultimate end: a feature-length movie scripted, produced, directed, and edited by a corporation. And what will top the Janet Jackson stunt, because we can all rest assured that it will be topped? Some would say that the purple tutu guy at the Olympics already topped the breast-baring antics of the Super Bowl. Is there more to come?

It's no wonder that the modern-day consumer is shell-shocked by all the base hoopla. Worse still, these prevailing marketing and advertising ploys are all characterized by an impersonality that is tellingly out of touch with the desires of the consumer. There is no emotional connection to their tactics. There is no inherent consumer respect of their strategies. There is no resulting interaction after they have been deployed. There is no conversation between consumers and brands. There is only more white noise.

The Pauper King

We as marketers must listen and proactively respond to the consumers' dissatisfaction with intrusive marketing. In fact, a landmark survey published by Yankelovich Partners in 2004 found that 65 percent of consumers feel that more regulations and limits should be imposed on marketing because "they are constantly bombarded with too much advertising," and 61 percent feel that advertising is "out of control." The recent spate of intrusive marketing such as clutter, product placement, and publicity stunts is the primary reason for this dissatisfaction, leading 60 percent of poll responders to state that their view of advertising is "much more negative than just a few years ago." These figures are hard to ignore, and yet so many marketers continue to ignore them. If consumers are cynical about our messages and put up ever higher barriers, marketers reason, then ever more extreme efforts are needed to break through.

Consequently, the marketing and advertising industries are "caught up in a death spiral of disrespect," according to Gary Ruskin, executive director of Commercial Alert. "In its desperate clamor to claim the attention of potential shoppers, the industry invents a new intrusive ad mechanism almost every week, until citizens are driven nuts by all . . . of it. As for the bromide that the 'consumer is king'—well, no one harasses a real king."

Present-day traditional marketers can hardly be said to be giving the consumer the royal treatment. If consumers are cynical about advertisers and marketers, it is not surprising to find marketers and advertisers getting increasingly cynical about consumers' needs and brand habits. J. Walker Smith, president of Yankelovich Partners, points out that his company's survey found "69 percent of the consumers interviewed don't say that they're getting new technologies so that they can have a better relationship with marketers, they're trying to opt-out, block, and skip advertising. We have to find a way to combat that." At a 2004 industry conference where these figures were presented to a ballroom full of marketing execs, Smith audaciously floated an idea to combat the consumer's attempts to block out advertising: advertisers will need to *pay* people to look at their ads. "The thing is that consumers want some sort of reciprocity," he said. "Pretty soon we're going to get to the point where we're going to have to pay people to watch our ads. And I do mean cash money."

So instead of issuing a call to reconnect with the consumer and rediscover a dialogue between marketers and consumer, the industry cynically determines reciprocity to mean money changing hands. It is telling of how much disrespect the marketing and advertising industry has for the typical consumer, and how out of touch they are with their certain demise.

It is obvious that the consumer is dead tired of the intrusion of marketing and advertising in our cultural landscape. Studies all suggest a deep-rooted hostility to more clutter, yet traditional marketers continue unabated. If folks don't respond to thirty-second spots, they'll embed products in the TV shows instead. If that doesn't seem to work either, they'll get the products on the news. If people turn off their televisions, they'll call them at home. They'll get you at work, at play, at the restaurant, at the hospital, at university, at the wedding, and at the funeral. Like a nightmare salesman, they will intrude and infiltrate and invade until you notice. They will keep at it until you buy something, anything, to get them to stop. And then, pointing at the blip on their sales charts, they will declare their tactics a success and renew their efforts with cynical vigor.

But who told them they can do that? Who allowed these marketers and advertisers to take over the consumer's discretion? Who invited them in?

The awful truth about marketing, according to Doc Searls, is that "it broadcasts messages to people that don't want to listen. Every advertisement, press release, publicity stunt and giveaway engineered by the marketing department is colored by the fact that it's going to a public that doesn't ask to hear it." No wonder that present-day marketing is failing. Much marketing fails to provide a surprise, let alone a benefit. Some would argue that head tattoo advertising is experiential because it is shocking. It is not experiential. Some would argue that streaking at Wimbledon is experiential because it provokes a knee-jerk press with ample chatter to contribute to public fascination. But who is this benefiting?

Enter Experiential Marketing

Experiential marketing is a consumer-focused discipline. There certainly needs to be reciprocity in advertising and marketing, but that reciprocity shouldn't be financial, as Smith suggested, it should be personal. XMers predicate our marketing campaign on the elements of conversation, a dialogue that is based on one-to-one dynamics. Even if that dialogue is conducted with millions of consumers, the same rules and social graces of personal conversations are inherent in the strategies and tactics we employ. Experiential marketing is therefore a discipline of personal voices. It is a methodology based on human interaction, even if that same interaction is repeated hundreds, thousands, and millions of times.

It is therefore no coincidence that the rise of XM methodologies comes at exactly the time when commercial intrusiveness is at an all-time high. Ruskin and Commercial Alert are pushing the idea that consumers "are hungry for acts of heroism and principle in the advertising arena." The tenets of experiential marketing, ones that will hopefully be appropriated by marketers worldwide, are based on such principles and always bear the consumer's benefit in mind. One of the basic notions in experiential marketing is that it shouldn't intrude on the consumer. Rather, it should enhance his or her experience with the brand or product message.

Take, for instance, the experience of going to the movies. A recent form of marketing called cinema advertising—ads that appear before movies, not ads that promote movies or movie theaters—is becoming one of the fastest-growing forms of ad-supported media. Right before the cool quick-cut movie trailers appear, moviegoers are subject to a number of long-format commercials, much like the ones they see on TV. Never mind that the experience of going to the movies is loved because it leaves the TV commercials at home. For modern marketers, the movie screen is becoming one giant TV screen anyway, without the remote control.

The problem with cinema advertising is, of course, that no one really likes it that much. Consumers see cinema advertising in the same light they see advertising in other media: they want to avoid it like the flu. Research from Insight Express shows that 91 percent of moviegoers say they "notice" the commercials in movie theaters, but 53 percent stress that movie theatres should stop showing them! Furthermore, 27 percent said they plan to attend *fewer* movies as a result of growing cinema advertising. Now, here's research that clearly shows how marketers are not delivering a meaningful benefit to the consumer. In fact, they are adulterating, if not wholly ruining, the moviegoing experience.

Why would any rational marketer—or a theater operator, for that matter—want to use cinema advertising? There is only one reason: the audience is captive. No one wants to miss the previews, those awesome gems of cinema editing that get people talking at the water cooler. Cinema marketers have shown their clients that cinemas have tracked down an audience that has been fleeing TV, and now that the audience is captive, marketers can throw the intrusive ads people have been avoiding right back into their faces. This is the type of cynical and disrespectful *Weltanschauung* that traditional marketers are used to. They *know* that their audience hates the ads, so they produce and screen even more of them.

From an experiential marketer's perspective, this is absolutely ludicrous and unacceptable. If there is no meaningful benefit to a marketing foray, it is not and cannot be experiential marketing. How can the simple fact that an audience is "captive" be ample justification for ruining the consumer's experience? To experiential marketers, a dubious practice such as cinema advertising is an outcome of not putting a consumer's positive experience with a brand or product first and foremost in importance. More bluntly, cinema advertising is *stupid* advertising. Marketers are not thinking enough about the consumer, and only thinking about the consumer's glazed-over eyeballs.

But if marketers could only concentrate on a positive consumer experience, and think like Seth Godin would want them to think—like a Purple Cow, man!—then marketing in a movie theater is an experiential nirvana. Consumers are already there for an experience. Why not enhance it? For instance, Gearwerx worked together with GMR Marketing in Canada to brainstorm and create a theater program for Vaseline Hand Lotion marketed by Unilever, which was testing a platform called "Touch." The notion was to show that having soft hands, and soft skin in general, was a perfect catalyst for touch, bringing people together in intimate and friendly proximity to each other. In other words, touching can make us feel better. I suppose that a clever or touching (pun intended) sixty-second cinema ad could have been the easiest way to reach the captive audience. Vaseline could have spent a few million on stellar creative, found a Hollywood actress to star in a big-budget commercial, and screened them in movie theaters around the country. That's how it's usually done. Scott O'Hara at GMR Marketing convinced the brand managers and directors to think differently, to think of a benefit—small as it may be—to add to the moviegoing experience.

We wanted to make the intimate moments of touch come to life in a movie theater. So we proposed installing dozens of two-person couches—branded with Vaseline creative—into a number of downtown cinemas, just in time for the release of a number of romantic holiday movies. What better way to communicate touch in a theater than to allowing couples—or parents and kids—to sit together on a comfortable and lush love seat and enjoy a feel-good film? Brand ambassadors acted as "touch ushers" and would invite couples and moms to sit on the "touch couch" during the movie. If they agreed, they would be personally escorted and seated. Upon exiting the theater, all moviegoers would receive a movie-themed postcard and sample of hand lotion. For those who experienced the movie from the comfort of a couch—and those who would look forward to sitting on one for another movie—the simple idea would become an instantly meaningful benefit. The couch experience would become synonymous with the movie experience, enough so that when anyone asked them about the movie, or when they would talk about it at the water cooler, the Vaseline Touch Couch would be top of mind.

Experience as Benefit; Benefit as Transformation

Of course, this is only a small example of experiential marketing that benefits the consumer—a simple way to bring people together. The notion of beneficial marketing is at the core of experiential marketing for a very simple reason: people like positive and meaningful experiences. This experience—the consumer experience—is the next competitive business battleground. The consumer, however, is not a pushover and not at all receptive to traditional marketing. Yankelovich Partners research suggests that 37 percent of consumers give up one hour of sleep to get more time back into their lives. Why would they want to waste fifteen minutes watching commercials at a movie theater—an experience for which they had neglected precious REM?

Simply put, a marketing experience that doesn't deliver an inherent benefit to the consumer—physically, emotionally, viscerally, or mentally— is not experiential marketing. It's just more white noise and clutter. More importantly, if consumer experiences are the next big battleground for customers and their loyalty, then companies cannot afford to engage in nonbeneficial experiences. Adding to the clutter will only turn more people off.

The inundation of impersonal PR stunts, cheap marketing gimmicks, and lowest-common-denominator advertising has inexorably unleashed a consumer backlash. The companies and brands that recognize this consumer shift are the ones most likely attracting and keeping their customers. Those who add to the clutter are most likely to flounder like fish out of water. The future of marketing must therefore be based on an experience that provides something more than just a commercial pitch, marketing message, or transactional solicitation. Pine and Gilmore note in *The Experience Economy* that "as economic activity shifts further and further away from goods and services, those companies which stage experiences alone—without considering the effect these experiences will have on the participants and without designing the experiences in such a way as to create a desired change— will eventually see their experiences become commoditized."[5] In other words, there is no real distinguishing value to the experience. A

5. B. Joseph Pine II and James H. Gilmore, *The Experience Economy: Work Is Theatre & Every Business a Stage* (Boston: Harvard Business School Press, 1999), p. 165.

marketing experience alone is not enough. It's certainly safe to presume that mass marketing has become commoditized. TV ads all look the same. Substitute one brand's commercial with another brand and you won't notice the difference. If the consumer experience doesn't deliver a benefit to the consumer, it, too, will become commoditized. And if experiential marketing doesn't do the same, it simply won't work.

Take, for instance, a simple and time-honored practice of cereal marketing: the toy inside the box. Kids, and some adults still, find the lick-on tattoos and special decoders a great little value-added when buying our favorite cereal. Surely when the first trinket was placed in cereal boxes, kids across the land were marveled by the experience of a new little toy that came with their cereal. These days, however, the cereal toy is an extremely commoditized practice. A trinket is a trinket. There is no distinguishable value to a cheap prize inside a cereal box. Recently, however, Kellogg Canada was able to transform this simple idea into a memorable experience by providing a clear benefit to the consumer.

The company was able to make the toy inside the cereal box a positive experience once again—this time for adults—by placing eight hundred thousand pedometers in boxes of Special K cereals. These step counters, which retail at $15 each, were distributed nationally in a company-sponsored initiative to help Canadians fight obesity. The packaging on the boxes encouraged Canadians to clip on their pedometers to calculate their physical activity levels and to donate their steps online to a national organization that monitors the effectiveness of step counters in increasing physical activity. When confronted with a company that cared about their personal health, and the health of the country, an adult Special K consumer could be as surprised as a six-year-old fishing his or her first plastic robot out of a cereal box. As I write this, Canadians have donated 679,170,854 steps so far to Canada on the Move.

When a clear benefit to the consumer is evident and intended, a simple toy-in-the-box program can transform itself into an experiential marketing coup. At the heart of the transformation is an authentic corporate or brand interest in delivering a benefit to the consumer through the marketing they do. For instance, sampling has been a mainstay in consumer packaged goods marketing for decades. And much like cereal box toys, sampling has long been a staid and often intrusive marketing practice. Nothing can embody today's sampling campaigns better than grocery store sampling, where dispirited samplers dole out cubes of cheese on splintered toothpicks. And how many times have you passed by a disinterested college kid handing out samples of gum, soda, razors, perfume strips, or cheese puffs? Most sampling campaigns, sadly, are relegated to more fodder for the clutter.

For Stonyfield Farms, an upstart yogurt brand launched in the mid-1980s, sampling was at the core of their marketing strategy—because it was all the company could afford. Company cofounders Gary Hirshberg and Samuel Kaymen had incorporated altruism and corporate philanthropy from the outset—10 percent of Stonyfield Farms profits are donated to charity, mostly environmental causes—and they incorporated that altruism into their sampling tactics. Instead of sampling on street corners and in grocery aisles, Stonyfield harnessed their activist roots and turned sampling into a transformational experience. They would sample at rallies and marches in Washington, D.C., and at high schools and colleges for Earth Day events. They would drive their sampling trucks into the middle of antinuclear rallies, "in a field with 4,000 protestors, handing out cups of yogurt," Hirshberg explained in an online interview with *Reveries Magazine*.[6] Stonyfield Farms steadily

6. Interview. *Reveries Magazine*, www.reveries.com, June 2002.

developed a devoted consumer base, almost exclusively relying on experiential sampling and corporate altruism. "People came away knowing,
not only that this was great yogurt, but also that Stonyfield is a company
that truly cares. . . . There was always an environmentalist edge to it."

Even when the company blossomed to the number-four yogurt
brand in the United States in 2001 with more than $100 million in
annual sales, and when Groupe Danone SA purchased a 40 percent
stake, the company continued to rely on experiential sampling campaigns to engage with the grassroots consumers. In a one-of-a-kind
sampling campaign, Stonyfield Farms partnered with the Chicago
Transit Authority to sample their yogurt throughout the city using
public transportation as an experiential platform. According to Hirshberg, the idea to sample to commuters was brilliantly simple. "People
riding trains and buses in the morning think they're going to work, but
really they're practicing environmentalism in the purist and most powerful way. So we went to the Chicago Transit Authority and told them
we'd like to stand on their train platforms, hand people cups of yogurt,
and thank them for riding the trains. They said, 'Excuse me? You want
to do what?' They had never before allowed food to be served on their
platforms. But we reached eighty-five thousand people in three days and
bumped our market share three points."

Experiential Humanism

In the same interview, Hirshberg recalls a *Wall Street Journal* interview
with then-Danone chairman and CEO Frank Riboud, who interrupted
an asset-obsessed reporter to remind him that Stonyfield Farms had
become much more than a balance sheet acquisition for Groupe
Danone. The company "represents an ethic, and it's an ethic that we at

Groupe Danone have to adopt if we're going to be successful in the twenty-first century." This societal ethic, according to Hirshberg, has positioned Stonyfield as a company whose environmental cause "is not just limited to our marketing. We're more accurately a cause-related company and our marketing is just a reflection of that."

More and more, companies and brands are beginning to stand for something—environmentalism, health research, antipoverty, anti-globalization, etc.—and their stances are the main driver of their marketing. Many refer to them as cause brands, and their marketing as causal marketing. In some cases, the cause alone is enough for consumers to buy the product. For instance, 100 percent of profits from Athena Water go directly to breast cancer research. In fact, the CEO of Athena Partners didn't start the company to market water, she started it to help out a very personal cause: as a breast cancer survivor, she wanted a way to raise money for research and prevention. Water as a product was just an afterthought. By choosing a commodity like water, Athena Water's cause becomes the focal point. The cause becomes the brand. After launching in mid-2003, the water is now available in 75 percent of markets in the Washington State area and growing. Consumers have made Athena Water a success not because of how it tastes or is packaged, but what it means and stands for on a much deeper and personal level. By purchasing Athena Water, a consumer purchases a piece of altruism that is much more refreshing and cool than the liquid itself.

After the September 11 tragedy, many marketers and economists began talking about charity and community in earnest, not just as a marketing ploy but also as a realignment of corporate values. Writing in *Marketing* magazine shortly after the attacks, business ethics consultant John Dalla Costa declared that "all of our learning about brand equity has taught us that great brands are not the product of marketing alone, but of operations and culture, of designers and manufacturing people, of sales and service support. Brands live in companies, express their companies to customers, and are carriers of vision and values. If companies are going to become as focused on human development as on profits, and on social impacts as on competitive positioning, then by necessity if not by default brands, too, will become catalysts for human development and conduits for community building."[7] If brands are to assume this stance, then the marketing of these brands must do the same.

Dalla Costa reduces the history of brand marketing into five periods: in the 1960s, branding was characterized by *awareness* and *convenience;* in the 1970s, branding evolved into *parity* and *pricing;* in the 1980s, it was all about *quality* and *status;* the last decade of branding is generalized by *technology* and *globalization,* "and it looks like branding will now be about *human development* and *community building.*" Dalla Costa is pointing toward the importance of beneficial and humanistic marketing in the decades to come.

At the heart of the rehumanization of branding and marketing is the notion that experiential marketing should be predicated on the dynamics of one-to-one interactions. A personal marketing interaction or dialogue is instinctively humanistic. That in itself is a form of marketing that delivers a benefit; it makes marketing better for the consumer. Therefore a dialogue between a consumer and brand ambassador is one of the most simple and compelling methods of branding that is focused on human development and community building. "The task now is to grow our capacity for dialogue," Dalla Costa argues. "Dialogue is that process of encounter and exchange [by] which we create a genuine sense of 'we' . . . Discussion marketing is

7. "What Really Matters Now," *Marketing Magazine,* January 7, 2002.

based on the premise that brands will make a difference to consumers and customers. Dialogue marketing is based on the premise that brands, too, will be transformed by the interaction with customers."[8]

Causal XM

Successful brands exist and sustain their relevance by discerning, understanding and delivering what consumers value, appreciate, and prioritize. It should not be surprising, therefore, that causal marketing and corporate giving are on a steep rise. According to an October 2004 Conference Board report, corporate giving in the United States rose 24 percent in 2003 to reach $3.88 billion. Brands are responding to and joining in causal programs that address the social concerns of consumers because social concerns are more relevant than ever. Issues such as environmental protection, breast cancer awareness, and research, fair trade, Third World debt, literacy, and AIDS and other fatal illnesses all have brand champions supporting them. Often the connection between brand and cause is so deep that an entire marketing platform is established to support them. For instance, the Ronald McDonald House Charities—which provides homes away from homes for families of seriously ill children receiving treatment at nearby hospitals—has become a causal institution and an integral part of McDonald's corporate philanthropy. In the days prior to World Children's Day each November, McDonald's donates a dollar from every purchase of a Big Mac to Ronald McDonald House. In 2003 McDonald's raised more than $15 million. In 2004 the goal was to break the $20 million threshold.

Certainly, McDonald's corporate philanthropy is transferred into

8. Ibid.

their marketing, primarily through heavy PR, celebrity endorsements, print and TV advertisements, and in-store signage. But does a causal program that uses a dollar donation for every Big Mac purchase make it experiential? By responding to marketing that derives from a charity campaign, the consumer certainly gets a benefit—namely, the feel-good factor. And unless you are directly affected by the efforts of Ronald McDonald House Charities, the connection between the consumer and a cause usually ends with that—the feel-good factor. Plus, she now has a Big Mac in her hands. Causal marketing has done its job, but that doesn't make it experiential or humanistic.

Avon, the world's largest direct seller of beauty and related products, has been recognized as a top corporate citizen by a number of magazines. The company has a staggering 4 million sales representatives in 100 countries, and posts annual revenues that top $2 billion worldwide. *Fortune* magazine named Avon one of the top 100 most valuable global brands and one of the most admired companies. The cosmetics giant's corporate philanthropy covers a number of important social issues regarding women through the Avon Foundation, including women's empowerment and domestic violence programs. Yet it is the company's efforts to raise awareness for breast cancer issues that take center stage.

The Avon Breast Cancer Crusade is a U.S. program created by the Avon Foundation in 1993 to raise awareness and funds for access to care and finding a cure for breast cancer. Avon also supports breast cancer programs in nearly fifty countries worldwide. The Avon Walk for Breast Cancer is the flagship philanthropy program that has so far raised more than $300 million for the cause. Unlike McDonald's, the company's main Web site barely mentions their philanthropy outreach programs, but in 2003 Avon gathered about twenty times the amount of donations collected by Big Mac and company.

The key to Avon's philanthropy efforts is its sales force—the women (and some men) who make the actual sale in direct interaction with the consumer. Avon's philanthropy campaigns are experiential because they are predicated on a one-to-one interaction and dialogue between marketer and consumer. The volunteer sales force, when out selling to the consumer, also sells Pink Ribbon products, a line of inexpensive beauty-related products designed with a pink ribbon motif, the symbol for breast cancer awareness. Ranging from $4 to $8 per item, the net proceeds from cosmetic cases, candles, teddy bears, and umbrellas, along with limited-edition lipsticks and pins, are fully donated to organizations that finance breast cancer research. With each product the customer receives a pamphlet complete with information on how to fight and prevent breast cancer and the organizations with which Avon collaborates.

Most recently, Avon has re-created the experiential elements to another cause-related effort, the Avon Heart of America Children's Charity, established to help the children of the September 11 tragedies. Avon representatives offer a special commemorative pin for $4 when out on sales calls. One hundred percent of the proceeds went directly to the charity. Moreover, Avon has fully embraced the "think globally, act locally" mentality of their sales associates. The company's Associate Giving Program encourages the sales force to become involved in causal programs in their own neighborhoods. Each year the sales associates run their own giving campaigns to raise money for local charities. Whatever the sales associates themselves donate to the cause, Avon matches the donations dollar-for-dollar. In this manner, more than $500,000 was raised in 2002 for children's charities, shelters, environmental and literacy programs in local markets. These types of activities, the company's Web site says, "instill a culture of giving at Avon and stimulate associates' understanding and commitment to philanthropy and community service."

This type of corporate interaction is reminiscent of a minor case study described in Malcolm Gladwell's *The Tipping Point: How Little Things Can Make a Big Difference,* a story about Georgia Sadler. Ms. Sadler is a nurse from San Diego who began a grassroots campaign to raise awareness for breast cancer and diabetes in the African-American neighborhoods around the city. She at first focused her prevention and education movement in the churches, but didn't see any success. Her message to the women in these churches was not tipping into mass reception or buzz. She needed a better, more experiential way to deliver a message, and she needed to deliver that message where women were most receptive and comfortable receiving it. She needed to get out of the churches and into the hair salons.

And that's exactly what she did. Sadler recruited a number of hair stylists to become her "brand ambassadors" and trained them to present information on breast cancers in a compelling way—and in their own words. Most hair stylists are naturally friendly and conversational. A majority of them are seen as trusted friends and sources of relevant information. The information about breast cancer and diabetes that was being delivered to women—who often spend an entire day at a hair salon—had to be natural and storylike, following the natural conversational patterns of a crowded salon, as well as one-on-one dialogue.

Sadler therefore brought in a folklorist to help train the stylists. Sadler also "kept up a constant cycle of new information and gossipy tidbits and conversation starters about breast cancer flowing into the salons, so that each time a client came back, the stylist could seize on some new cue to start a conversation."[9] Ms. Sadler was marketing experientially. And by relying on experiential methods and ethos, she began

9. Malcolm Gladwell. *The Tipping Point: How Little Things Can Make a Big Difference* (Boston: Back Bay Books, 2002), p. 255.

to change the attitudes and habits of women in her neighborhoods. Her message had been tipped into grassroots buzz.

"American" Altruism

As will be evident throughout this book, word-of-mouth contagion is an intrinsic element in experiential marketing. In this day and age, a well-executed and relevant causal campaign is truly compelling to consumers, and marketers are keenly aware of the power of investing in communities and physically helping people. The more experiential the campaign—personal interaction, relevant messaging, nonintrusive intercept, authenticity, innovation, engagement—the more that campaign has a propensity for buzz. To reach a new kind of consumer—one who demands and responds to experiential marketing tactics—some new upstart companies are marketing altruism as experience. By making causal marketing hip again, they are tapping into a youth-led movement for humanism and corporate philanthropy. For American Apparel—a much-buzzed-about and very profitable T-shirt company—altruism is an entire experiential marketing platform. By combining altruism with sexy trendiness, American Apparel delivers an unrivaled experience.

Their mission statement makes it clear that their value proposition isn't only about high quality, but also the fact that their manufacturing methods don't rely on cheap labor, and that everyone who works for American Apparel receives a decent income much higher than the industry standard. Without overmouthing it, they also make it clear that they are in the business of making money, but that the means justify the ends.

Shopping at their retail outlets is evidence enough that they intend to let their consumers know that part of their offering is what happens within their company premises in downtown L.A., and that their employees are more than satisfied with everything they receive. Their intended message is clear, altruistic, and experiential: buy our T-shirts and feel good about it; you're helping society.

Founder Dov Charney's vision was to create a company committed to making clothing of the highest quality while pioneering industry standards of social responsibility in the workplace: "Our goal is that everyone touched by the business process has a positive experience."[10] American Apparel is a youth-directed company founded without the assistance of institutional investors. Having no political ties, the company has rejected established norms on all sides. "We've dismissed both the corporate right and the politically correct left in favor of something new," Charney claims. American Apparel is the product of a business model that he refers to as "hyper capitalist-socialist fusion."[11]

When Charney turned American Apparel profitable four years ago, he didn't do it by selling boxy, mass-market T-shirts. Instead American Apparel weaves thin-fiber cotton yarn into styles favored by urban trend-seekers in cities such as San Francisco and New York. Much of the company's business comes from small, independent designers who buy the shirts wholesale, embellish them with original touches, and resell them in boutiques for twice the price. Rather than follow seasonal trends, American Apparel offers an expansive year-round line to which new styles and colors are continuously introduced. Priority is on quality and fit, with the company frequently turning back to their customers for feedback and ideas.

From an idea to a living, breathing concept, American Apparel has transformed itself into one of the world's giants in the apparel industry and has won acclaim from both social responsibility advocates and the business community at large. In fact, American Apparel now stands as the

10. From the Web site: www.americanapparel.net.
11. Ibid

third-largest T-shirt manufacturer in the United States, behind Hanes and Fruit of the Loom.[12] How, in such a short time, has Dov Charney managed to achieve this level of success? How did a company come to dominate an industry with such an apparently unorthodox business model? How did it grow so fast without airing one TV commercial, and only once advertising in a magazine with a circulation over 100,000?

According to Charney, the answer to those questions is very simple. It is a matter of how you treat people—not only employees, but also all those within the sphere of influence of the company, including suppliers and, of course, customers. In an industry sometimes known for exploiting its workers, this may seem unique. Given the workings of American business in the past decade, it probably is. The reality is that corporations can succeed without having to exploit people or the environment, and Charney is using his company to prove it.

The business model is simple and proposes that "it is possible to combine innovation, profitability, and social responsibility."[13] American Apparel is a vertically integrated manufacturer and retailer of clothing for men, women, kids, and dogs (yes, dogs!). This means that every stage of the production process is consolidated under one roof at a downtown Los Angeles factory—from the cutting and sewing of the garment right through to the photography and marketing.

This production model is what differentiates American Apparel from its competitors. American Apparel produces more than 1 million pieces a week at its 800,000-square-foot factory in downtown L.A. In addition to the oft-quoted "sweatshop-free" claim, the company employs 2,250 people with a waiting list 1,000 names long for factory jobs that pay as

12. Interview. M Publications. Kimberly Lloyd. 2003; http://www.americanapparel.net/ presscenter/articles/2003mpublication.html.
13. Dov Charney at the Idea City Conference in Toronto, 2003.

much as $18 per hour. In fact, Charney runs the single largest garment factory in the United States, mainly because his competitors have opted for offshore labor markets.

It should be made clear that Charney does not confuse what he and any sincere businessperson believes; that "the ultimate purpose of business is to make money, but in doing so, raising the well-being of society."[14] He has a mission to prove to corporate America that his model works and works well. To prove that with no subcontracting, no off shoring, and with competitive wages, benefits, and employee development programs, not only can an American manufacturer succeed, he also can win. By "bringing dignity back to the workplace of apparel," Charney believes that you can learn to exploit human potential and develop more productive employees.[15] The model is simple, and Charney claims it is not difficult to understand. Unfortunately, in spite of the fact that issues concerning workplace ethics are very simple, Charney believes that the business community fails to understand them. Companies go overseas—for example, to escape regulation—and often end up paying more in other costs, such as quality control, than would be the case if a sustainable model would be followed. As Charney puts it, "workplace ethics with no sustainable business model is meaningless. You have to have a business that will last, that will make money. It has to be profitable or you are in trouble . . . and by profit, I don't necessarily mean in the short term but also in the long term."[16] More importantly, the company's overall message is one of its fundamental

14. Interview. M Publications. Kimberly Lloyd. 2003; http://www.americanapparel.net/presscenter/articles/2003mpublication.html.
15. Ibid.
16. Prentice Hall Management Series 2004: Social Responsibility. Taken from www.americanapparel.net.

selling points: giving the consumers a feeling of social responsibility when purchasing their clothes. If not, their T-shirts wouldn't be able to sell at their current premium.

Little Things That Help

The core customer who finds Charney's vision compelling is the same one who keeps a vigilant eye on a variety of altruistic concerns, such as the environment, globalization, poverty, and human rights. American Apparel hits on a couple of altruistic heartstrings: patriotism, social values, ecofriendliness, and value to a price-sensitive youth marketplace. In addition, they make a really good T-shirt. To the kids who shop in his stores, this brand approach speaks directly to their political consciousness and the emotional bond with the company. To them, buying an American Apparel T-shirt provides a benefit to the world. The feelings that come with that—pride, satisfaction, devotion, altruism—are clearly benefits to these kids.

In its own altruistic endeavor, electronics maker Philips took its medical technology to shopping malls in Argentina, Chile, Brazil, and Mexico and invited all pregnant women in the area to come in and receive three-dimensional ultrasounds. The images were captured and sent off by e-mail to family and friends. To some, this may seem like a cynical marketing campaign. But consider that most women in these developing countries probably never had an ultrasound, and had never seen their own babies. They had for the first time experienced what we take for granted in North America. Of course, Philips was there to market their technology and increase brand awareness, but did it not provide a clear benefit to those women in Latin American malls?

Or what about Commerce Bank's ten-minute rule? The New Jersey–headquartered bank's operating hours are normally 7:30 A.M. to

8 P.M., seven days a week. Already, the bank provides a valuable service by staying open for more hours than any other bank. But as a company-wide rule, the branches open ten minutes early in the day and stay open ten minutes later than closing time. Just recall the feelings we've all had when we run just a bit late to the bank, only to see the clerks locking up with 4:59 P.M. showing on their watches. Doesn't something as simple as the ten-minute rule provide a clear consumer benefit?

Another little thing that makes a big difference in Commerce Bank branches—which the company calls "stores," because they "don't like to think like bankers"—is the bright red Penny Arcade found in every store's lobby. When other banks were getting rid of their coin-counting machines, or were charging customers to exchange their coins, Commerce spent millions to install their Penny Arcades, which are free for all to use. Anyone can come in and dump their coins into the arcade, receive a receipt for the total amount, hand it to the teller, and get the cash. This is more than mere convenience for the consumer, although a free service like this is clearly beneficial to the bank's customer. The real value comes from the fact that the Penny Arcade is fun. Kids come in and break open their piggy banks in front of amused customers. Teens come in to scrounge up a few bucks for the movies with the change in their pockets. And, of course, when someone comes in with their lifetime collection of coins in huge coffee jars, the entire place gathers around the Penny Arcade to yell out their guesses for the total amount. It's fun, and it's a unique benefit to the customer, a form of differentiation from the staid and money-hungry banks across the street. It drives foot traffic as well. In 2001 the Penny Arcades handled 750,000 transactions that totaled over $71.7 million.[17]

17. Grant Delin, "Customer Service: Commerce Bank," *Fast Company,* May 2002.

The Lego Company routinely rolls out a holiday event to benefit Habitat for Humanity International in malls during the Christmas season. Malls would feature the Lego "Build an Ornament" centers next to the ubiquitous mall Santa's Village. For a dollar donation, kids can create their own ornaments using Lego elements, which are tagged with their names and ages and hung on a huge Christmas tree in the mall.

Ben & Jerry's ice cream donated dozens of winter coats to the homeless in Amsterdam. The company had donated some money to a group of Augustinian nuns who ran a number of shelters for the homeless in the city. The homeless men and women volunteered to wear the branded jackets as a personal thank you to the nuns and the company that supports them. How different this approach is to paying homeless people to hold up signs shilling pizza!

In Canada, IKEA invited students into their stores in exchange for doing their laundry. Citing student polls that say doing laundry is their least favorite chore, IKEA offered to do up to ten pounds of dirty laundry for them. A mall in Virginia responded to a survey showing that women are increasingly interested in experiential gifts such as facials and spa treatments at the top of their wish list, saying that destressing and having fun are very appealing in their hectic life schedules. So the Fashion Center at Pentagon City came up with a program called Simon Mall for You, where busy local women are invited to take a break and enjoy free pampering such foot massages, makeovers, fashion tips, and relaxation techniques. The event's cosponsors included Diet Coke, Cotton Incorporated, and *Self* magazine.

Environmentalist and entrepreneur Paul Hawken writes that "in a postindustrial age, the critical shortages are time and meaning. And people will only give up their time for meaning. It follows, then, that one of the challenges facing American business is to add meaning to commercial life. . . . A lot of companies have lore; they have history; they have tradition; they have huge markets; but they have no meaning. 'Why are we here on Earth? What am I doing? Who benefits from this?' These are valid questions for businesspeople to ask—and answer, with no words over three syllables and no business terms. When you look at your business with these questions in mind, it looks very different."[18]

Marketers need to ask the same questions, and look at their campaigns and tactics with this different perspective. It is imperative that they do so, because their customers are already asking these questions for them. Experiential marketing needs to provide some of the meaning they desire. Consumers are looking at marketing campaigns with the same critical eye that they use to choose their brands and make their purchases: features and benefits. Marketers can start thinking of the business and process of marketing as just another product category. Consumers would pick and respond to marketing campaigns directed at them in the same way they would pick brands, products, and services. In effect, brand marketing itself should have its own features and benefits, because consumers will "pick" the marketing methodologies that are most relevant and meaningful to them just as they would choose products on the shelf. If the marketing shows meaning and benefit—either directly for the consumer or in a more abstract, altruistic manner—then it will break through the cluttered marketing landscape that considers something like "ass-vertising" a viable option to engage the consumer.

18. Anita Sharpe, "Thought for the day," *Worthwhile Magazine*, October 4, 2004, www.worthwhilemag.com.

	Experiential marketing will
Chapter 2	be predicated on a one-on-one
	personal interaction between a
	marketer and a consumer.

I n late September 2004, conferencegoers and jaded New Yorkers were surprised to see a giant bloodshot eyeball standing tall in Times Square. The bloodshot eyeball was part of *Ad Week*'s Madison Avenue Walk of Fame, where consumers voted on the best ad characters in the history of advertising. Tony the Tiger, the M&M characters, the Aflac duck, Mr. Clean, and the Pillsbury Doughboy paraded around Times Square, to the delight of many onlookers and ad execs. Yet it was the giant bloodshot eyeball that got most of the attention. No one really knew what to make of it. Was it a new mascot for a yet-to-be-launched product, or was it the symbol of the conference itself?

The eyeball, it turned out, was a publicity stunt to hype the initial *Advertising Week* in New York conference, a mascot imagined by ad execs to pump up the media hoopla for an ad exec conference. With a seemingly innocuous mascot like a bloodshot eyeball, the creative department at Euro RSCG Worldwide in New York unwittingly symbolized everything wrong with the state of advertising and marketing today: it's all about eyeballs. Advertisers and marketers are still fixated on reaching tired, overworked, bloodshot eyeballs.

Mass media marketers are unconcerned about meaningful, humanistic interaction with consumers because, to marketers, consumers aren't human. They are merely a pair of giant eyeballs. The need to get a brand or a product in front of them isn't judged by how many times a consumer has *experienced* the product or brand, but how many times she has *seen* it. This is why to some marketers, something like *ass-vertising* is a viable option. Present-day advertising amounts to the obsessive propagation of the brand, and the desire to reach eyeballs. Mass media is the preferred conduit for distribution, and much like the driving ethos of a corporation, mass media seeks to achieve economies of scale: the larger the number of eyeballs, the better.

Five years ago in the Internet world, success was measured by how many eyeball "impressions" a site or a banner ad received. Anything less than a million a day was unacceptable. This type of tally wasn't invented by online operators, it was simply copied from the tabulating norms of mass media: how many eyeballs saw an ad, how many households watched a show, how many Web surfers clicked on. Hindsight makes it pretty clear how successful these impressions were. Experiential marketing rejects this eyeball-counting formula. An impression for an experiential marketer can mean only one thing: a personal interaction between consumer and brand to create a memorable experience that is nothing less than *impressive*. Experiential marketers aren't as concerned about eyeballs as they are about the entire human being. To us, the best way to deliver a marketing message to a person is to do it physically, face-to-face, and in the language both parties understand. This one-on-one personal interaction and engagement between a business and the consumers it serves is at the core of experiential marketing because it delivers on the humanistic principles that are instrumental to the future of marketing practices. Experiential marketers hone their strategies and tactics for a consumer brand *experience,* not merely a brand *impression.* This in itself is revolutionary in the current marketing world.

Millions of us are bombarded by messages and media that are contradictory at best and misleading at worst, messages meant to influence and stimulate the impulse to buy. It's no wonder, therefore, that advertisers see us as inert consumers with bloodshot eyes. Watching television—and viewing the ads—is a passive experience. Listening to the radio—and hearing the ads—is also passive. The only active part of reading a magazine is flipping past the ad pages. Conversely, experiential marketing is everything but passive. It makes a connection with the consumer that hasn't been achievable with traditional marketing. It's not about reach, it's about depth. It's not mass-based, it's personal. It's not about gimmicks, it's about relevancy. Experiential marketing can thus be viewed as a new marketing promise to the consumer: you will not be spoken to; we will listen. Consequently, experiential marketing is a marketing philosophy that views the typical consumer as everything but a set of eyeballs.

Experiential marketing uses a strategic series of events or encounters (or a singular event or encounter) that seeks to elicit personal consumer involvement, which in turn will help foster a positive brand or product experience. This in turn helps to enable the consumer to become an advocate for the brand or product in other forums and conversations. Think of Dov Charney's vision for American Apparel, and how it is at the center of the American Apparel experience, and how that experience generates buzz among his youthful customers. The ethos of XM is not to push a consumer to purchase with a deluge of ads, product placements, and PR stunts, but to pull her willingly into a brand world where a meaningful dialogue with a marketer can take place.

"Companies need to come down from their Ivory Towers and talk to the people with whom they hope to create relationships," claim the authors of *The Cluetrain Manifesto: The End of Business as Usual.* "Companies that don't realize their markets are now networked person-to-person, getting smarter as a result and deeply joined in conversation are missing their best opportunity." Experiential marketing is a response by nontraditional marketers to take part in the new marketplace of P2P networks, increasingly sophisticated consumer conversations and respectful dialogue demanded by today's consumer.

A large reason for the existence of the new marketplace is undoubtedly the Internet, which has opened up a myriad of channels for dialogue, and taught consumers how to talk again. That talk is the germination of buzz, which has always been important to companies but is even more important to marketers in the twenty-first century. Experiential marketing takes advantage of the consumer's increasing tendency to spread buzz person to person—favorably or not—about a brand or product. By staging dynamic and personal interactions, experiential marketers aim to invite and involve the consumer in an enjoyable experience that passive marketing can never hope to accomplish.

An experiential marketing campaign comes with an invitation to the individual consumer to participate in a conversation. The invitation is a direct antithesis to the invasion of traditional marketing. Because of the increasing interconnectivity among consumers and marketers who serve them, experiential marketing seeks to establish an interaction with the consumer that is impossible with a TV or print ad, product placement, or PR stunt. Furthermore, marketers need to learn from these conversations, not just spark them. A one-to-one interaction is the ideal learning environment, so totally removed from the focus group and survey environment, and the mentality of traditional marketing.

Certainly not all marketing can be feasible or cost-effective through one-on-one methodologies, but each experiential campaign should strive to achieve and make use of them. This is the crux of experiential marketing. We need to market personally, because the marketplace has become individualized and better connected at the same time. Every decade, it seems, companies and marketers choose to rediscover the individual consumer, and with each period of rediscovery, a new paradigm shift is announced to anoint the individual consumer as the savior of the increasingly competitive marketplace. In fact, a few weeks after the *Advertising Week* conference in New York, a clarion call to reconnect with the individual consumer came from one of the biggest mass marketers in the world. At the Association of National Advertisers' conference in October 2004, McDonald's global chief of marketing announced the end of mass marketing and advertising. "Mass marketing today is a mass mistake," declared Larry Light.[19] According to him, McDonald's used to spend two-thirds of its ad budget on network television prime time. That figure is now less than one-third.

Getting Individualized

The explosion of postwar consumption in the 1950s was the first catalyst for marketers to discover the individual consumer. In 1954 Peter Drucker published *The Practice of Management*, which proclaimed that the customer determined what a business is. "What the business thinks it produces is not of first importance," he wrote. "What the customer thinks he is buying, what he considers 'value,' is decisive."[20] Marketing was seen

19. Scott Donaton, "Adjusting to the Reality of a Consumer-Controlled Market," *Advertising Age*, October 18, 2004.
20. Shoshana Zuboff and James Maxmin, *The Support Economy* (New York: Penguin Books, 2002), p. 247.

as instrumental in ascertaining the needs and desires of the consumer, and what the consumer considered to be of value. In response, this new thinking led to the invention of brand management and the use of market research techniques—surveys, focus groups, test marketing—to hone market-segmentation strategies. Yet by the 1970s, it was clear that the consumer-focused revolution did not really change the way business was conducted, and marketing became entrenched as a management function, not a customer-focused advocacy for individualism. The job of marketing continued to be "to sell what the factory could produce."[21]

The notion of "total quality management" of the 1980s failed to meet the needs of the end consumer, as corporations simply established their own internal standards, which were never consumer-focused anyway. The notion of corporate "reengineering," introduced in a 1990 article in the *Harvard Business Review* by Michael Hammer, led U.S. businesses to spend $30 billion in 1994 on reengineering, with plans to spend another $50 billion by 1996. By 1995 more than 80 percent of the *Fortune 500* companies had embarked on some form of reengineering activities.[22] But the only thing reengineering really did was force companies to cut costs and downsize their workforce. The result was overworked and stressed-out employees doing more work and leaving less time for customer concerns. Lately companies have embarked on "mass customization" for their products and services to meet the needs of millions of individual consumers. The individualism of the new consumer, it is assumed, would be assuaged by increased product variety and more choice. Between 1984 and 1989, for instance, the number of new products grew by 60 percent, to reach 12,055 new products introduced each

21. Ibid., p. 249.
22. Michael Hammer, "Reengineering Work: Don't Automate, Obliterate," *Harvard Business Review*, July–August 1990, pp. 70–91.

year in the United States alone.[23] One only has to visit the supermarket to see product choice in action.

Modern marketing has become a battle for individual customer loyalty, and Customer Relationship Management (CRM) has become the holy grail of relating to the increasingly fickle consumer. CRM was in full swing when the Gartner Group estimated sales from customer relationship management projects at $20 billion in the United States in 2000. Implementation costs added another $30 billion to that number. Just one year later, CRM sales increased by $5 billion in 2001, and were expected to top $64 billion by 2005.[24]

Managing customer relationships may have started out as a way to ensure customer loyalty, and the way to ensure that loyalty may have been thought of as a one-on-one relationship practice. In effect, most CRM has been anything but personal or individualized. Instead, CRM relies on increased capacity to store data and the price associated with storing it. Further technological improvements, such as data capture at point of sale, bar codes, loyalty cards, and the increased reliance on analysis tools and technology have positioned CRM as a number-crunching practice, not a customer-focused paradigm shift.

Getting Personal

Marketing tactics today, therefore, "rely on database technologies to integrate and track customer data. These efforts may result in personalized letters, using the customer's name during a call center transaction, price incentives, personalized Web content, frequent-user programs,

---

23. Shoshanna Zuboff and James Maxmin, *The Support Economy,* p. 249.
24. Ibid., p. 265.

preferred-customer programs, customer-referral benefits, invitations to product-oriented parties and seminars, or customization efforts"[25] These tools are, however, mostly developed for the benefit of sellers to track customers and upsell them on more services or packages. They are not consumer-focused efforts that enable valuable support for today's individual consumers. The result is that end consumers do not have a relationship with people, but with databases.

From the end user's perspective, CRM and relationship marketing look more like junk mail than a conversation. Furthermore, this lack of conversation does nothing but exacerbate the relationship between consumer and marketer. A *Marketing Magazine* survey stated that "what is meant to be a dialogue with customers is all too often one-way. . . . Customers were badgered by companies for more personal data, while they saw no return on their investment of time and information, and they complained about the 'one way' nature of the so-called relationship."[26] The researcher concluded that the consumer's experience with CRM was characterized by "loss of control, vulnerability, stress and victimization."[27]

This is exactly what experiential marketers seek to avoid. Experiential marketing is a methodology that goes far beyond CRM software and database management. These marketing tools simply record a consumer's transactional history and the contact she has had with the company. The contacts are recorded only at certain company touch points, such as call centers, e-mail exchanges, or at point of purchase. CRM software and databases can't trap and evaluate the nonverbal information that is critical to the customer experience, nor can they capture key insights at other customer interface points that CRM cannot reach.

25. Ibid., p. 263.
26. Ibid., p. 264.
27. Ibid.

Experiential marketing guru Bernd H. Schmitt points out that "to provide a truly satisfying experience for their customers, companies need to go beyond what CRM offers."[28] He positions three types of customer interface that are instrumental to an experiential campaign: face-to-face, personal-but-distant, and electronic. For experiential marketers, the face-to-face interaction is extremely important to develop, because it is the face-to-face interface that is most tailored to the individual customer. This is the backbone to a successful marketing effort to reach an elusive consumer.

A face-to-face or one-on-one interface can include in-store exchanges and interactions; in-field marketing; service personnel; and offerings such as consulting, counseling, and entertainment. "All these exchanges and interactions offer opportunities to connect with customers, delight them, provide them with the right information efficiently, and enrich their lives."[29] How much different this seems from the vulnerability, stress, and victimization that traditional customer interfaces such as CRM seem to cause.

Moreover, experiential marketing predicated on one-to-one interactions is a highly dynamic practice. Traditional mass media advertising and marketing rely on features-and-benefits positioning, branding, packaging, logos, and retail spaces to push their products and services. These practices are generally static in nature, and passive in terms of consumer interaction. Conversely, the one-on-one interface—at a store, on the street, at a hotel check-in, during a sales visit, and even online—is highly dynamic and intangible. The voice, attitude, style, empathy, and appearance of the marketer are some of the most obvious intangibles. These elements, and

28. Bernd H. Schmitt, *Customer Experience Management* (Hoboken, NJ: John Wiley & Sons, 2003), p. 142.
29. Ibid., p. 154.

the added effects of sensory stimuli and memorable interaction, are at the heart of a successful experiential marketing program.

Checking In

These intangibles offer up a major advantage to an experiential one-to-one interaction: the ability for customization. This time, however, we are not interested in customizing a product. We are devoted to customizing a marketing experience. The reason is simple. By customizing the experience, and by staging a series of them that speak directly to the individual consumer, companies can escape the me-too trap and begin delivering meaningful marketing experiences. "When you customize an experience, you automatically turn it into a *transformation*."[30] If done right, a personal marketing experience will leave the consumer different from before. She would be delighted, touched, or inspired. Her perception of the brand or company will be transformed, because she herself has somehow been transformed also.

A quick reference to the hotel industry can shed some light on the needs and successes of personal, customizable, and highly experiential marketing tactics. For instance, the housekeeping staff at the Walt Disney hotels transforms a child's stay into a special experience. Each day the staff will reposition a child's toy—whether it was brought by the child or bought at the Disney store—throughout the room. One day, a Mickey Mouse is seated in front of a television, with the channel set to the Disney Channel (of course). The next day, Mickey will be repositioned, this time in the bathroom with a toothbrush nearby. Adults may understand that it's the staff who is doing this, but for the kids it's nothing less than magical.

30. Ibid.

Last year, Fairmont Hotel and Resorts launched a highly experiential pilot campaign at ten of their forty-three resorts worldwide that transformed a simple hotel stay into a memorable and lasting experience. The hotel chain partnered with Hewlett Packard to offer their guests use of the latest HP Photosmart digital cameras and printers during their stay. Anyone staying at the hotel—honeymooners, family vacationers and conference attendees—can test HP's products and discover hands-on the benefits of digital photography. Guests check out an HP R707 camera from the hotel concierge or front desk, snap pictures throughout their stay, and instantly print the photos when they get back to the hotel on a photo printer. HP representatives are on hand at each hotel throughout the campaign to provide personal guidance to each guest who wants to use the service. HP and Fairmont are therefore able to provide a relevant experiential campaign in a nonintrusive way that is sure to be remembered and appreciated by each satisfied guest.

Westin Hotels and Resorts used an experiential campaign to introduce its now famous "Heavenly Bed" in 1999. After conducting preliminary research of more than six hundred business executives, the company found that 63 percent of respondents said that getting a good night's sleep was the most important service a hotel could provide. So when it was time to announce the launch of the Heavenly Bed, Westin pulled off an experiential coup by lining up thirty of the downy beds in front of the New York Stock Exchange for business travelers to take a plop on it. Next to the beds were teams of practiced Westin brand ambassadors who encouraged the surprised Wall Street exec with an invitation to stretch out on the bed and experience the comfort for themselves. Commuters in Grand Central Station also tested twenty of the beds in the station's main hall. Westin representatives were on hand throughout the promotion to explain the bed's features, as well as hyping the upcoming improvements Westin was making for the benefit of the weary business traveler.

Ritz-Carlton has for years been practicing a form of one-to-one interaction that morphs a simple transaction into a transformative experience. First, employees at the hotel chain address their guests by their first names. Each day the doormen and concierges at the hotel chains are given a guest check-in manifest, which they learn or memorize. When a guest arrives at the hotel's doors, he is greeted personally by the staff. After a day of travel, being greeted personally makes for a great first impression. Moreover, by relating to guests on a one-to-one basis, Ritz's employees learn the intimate habits and demands of each individual guest. With each stay, the hotel associates observe the preferences of the individual—favorite type of pillow, preferred radio or TV station, late night snacks, Pepsi instead of Coke—and enter that information into a database to form a "learning relationship" with individual guests."[31] The more frequently someone stays in Ritz-Carlton hotels, the more the company learns, and the more customized goods and services it fits into the standard Ritz-Carlton room, thereby increasing the guest's preference for the hotel over others."[32] This type of learning relationship is made possible, however, not by the databases that are created but by the insistence on one-to-one interactions between a hotel associate and an individual guest.

An excellent example of how a database can be transformed into an exceptional and memorable interaction is when a "lucky ambassador" greets a Harrah's Hotel and Casino guest at a video poker machine. This "lucky ambassador" calls the player by name, much like the Ritz-Carlton concierge, wishes her a happy birthday, and offers a couple of tickets for

31. Ibid., p. 69.
32. Ibid.

a Las Vegas show. The reason the "lucky ambassador" can do all of this is because of Harrah's multimillion-dollar database that tracks each guest at any of its twenty-eight properties through a loyalty card that guests opt in to receive. Every time a customer slides her loyalty card into a slot machine, uses it to pay for dinner, or shows it to a baccarat dealer, Harrah's knows each move the player makes. When the database sees that the guest is losing badly, a "lucky ambassador" will quickly approach the guest with some hotel perks to assuage the sting of losing. This is experience-making through CRM at its finest, says *Fast Company* magazine. "While many companies struggle to employ CRM success-fully, gathering massive amounts of data without using it to benefit customers, Harrah's is building on its mastery."[33]

Similarly, Starwood Hotels and Resorts entered into an experiential marketing program with Volkswagen in early 2004 at four W Hotels in the United States. W Hotels in New York, Chicago, Los Angeles, and San Francisco were each provided with seven new Phaeton cars to promote intimate test drive experiences for their guests. The cars were given to the hotel chain to be used as complimentary guest shuttles before they even hit the general marketplace. The interior of the Phaetons were customized to reflect the W Hotel aesthetic and ethos, and a personal driving tour was given to every guest who used the shuttle while riding to their destination. "Exclusive, virtually unfettered access to the new luxury Phaeton is the type of experiential opportunity our guests have come to expect when staying at a W Hotel," remarked Ross Klein, CMO at W Hotels Worldwide. The guests were able to experience a sensory-rich marketing environment—the new-car smell, the supple leather seats, the soothing surround-sound stereo playing—that was made more

33. Jena McGregor, "Customers First," *Fast Company,* October 2004, p. 88.

memorable and personalized by a friendly marketing chauffeur, who naturally became a brand ambassador for Volkswagen.

Knowledge Is Power

What we learn from one-to-one marketing cannot be underestimated, not just to create customized and personal future interactions, but also to acquire qualitative knowledge that is impossible to achieve with traditional research methodologies. Again, the emphasis with one-to-one marketing rests squarely on an interaction that elicits a dialogue between marketer and consumer. A conversation is a two-way street, or at least that is what conventional wisdom suggests. Yet for traditional advertisers and marketers, their dialogue with the consumer has never been about reciprocity.

A dialogue presupposes it is done *with* someone (or something). How apt is it to find that marketing is done *to* someone, as in, "companies are marketing *to* the Nexus generation" or "we resent being marketed *to*." Have we ever seen a sentence such as "Our products are marketed *with* the Nexus generation" or "We respect being marketed *with*"? Of course not. By inventing the verb "to market," traditional marketers and advertisers have jettisoned the dialogue and taken over the conversation.

Companies have hijacked this conversation at their own peril. Without listening to the consumer, a beneficial consumer experience is impossible to achieve. Writing in *Customer Experience Management,* Schmitt notes that "traditional marketing strategy is product-based, not customer-based. . . . Most marketing departments are organized around product categories and focus on pushing as many units of the same product as possible to any kind of customer. Because repeated selling of desirable products to a specific customer segment is not a primary objective, traditional marketing is not really interested in an indepth understanding of customers."[34] Experiential marketing, however, is interested because experience usually elicits a response. From a marketing perspective, that response better be positive. If it is not, then the experiential platform is flawed. Marketers who use experiential strategies are able to gauge any and all flaws almost immediately, because they will be visible on the faces of their customers.

Furthermore, one-on-one dialogue and interaction is a better way of understanding the needs and desires of the consumer. The focus on a personal and customizable interaction is in direct antithesis to the standard and accepted practice of focus grouping and surveying the consumer. Gerald Zaltman, the Joseph C Wilson professor of business administration at Harvard Business School who wrote *How Customers Think: Essential Insights into the Mind of the Market,* posits that something like the ubiquitous focus group does little more than study all kinds of human biases. "Ninety-five percent of human cognition is unconscious. The 5 percent cognition that is conscious is not necessarily verbal," he says. People cannot readily explain their thoughts, actions, and emotions in words, especially in a group setting. Furthermore, not only do focus groups fail to get to the true consumer insight and draw transformative conclusions, they also offer no competitive advantage and can be misleading if misinterpreted.

Gaining knowledge about the consumer therefore rests on experiential transactions between an individual marketer and an individual consumer. According to Zaltman, "many researchers [say] that one-on-one interviews are superior to focus groups. That is, even a few conventional one-on-one

34. Bernd H. Schmitt, *Customer Experience Management*, p. 37.

interviews yield essentially the same data as several focus groups. Additionally, there is now a lot of evidence that personal interviews yield deep insights that can't be obtained from focus groups. So, my preference is to conduct in-depth, one-on-one interviews. . . . Often, the result of such interviews can be used to design more comprehensive surveys. And properly designed surveys, when subjected to careful statistical analyses, can yield further insights into unconscious consumer thinking."[35]

Zaltman describes a unique research project conducted by General Motors for designing vehicles, advertising, and dealership appearances by asking consumers to bring objects expressing "optimism" to a one-on-one interview. One participant brought in an image of a champagne flute, explaining that the image represented the dawning of a new day. GM's designers then used this understanding—however intangible—to convey optimism in their car designs. In another metaphor-elicitation project, GM designers asked consumers to rank photos of "friendly" watches. The prominent design features of the selected watches included a large face, easily legible numbers, and a nonindustrial feel. The design team also learned that slight changes in design would alter the metaphor drastically. That's why, according to Zaltman, GM's research "uses in-depth one-on-one interviews rather than focus groups to probe deeply and figure out why a subtle change in design produces a major change in the metaphors used to describe one design option versus another."[36]

Rather than relying on the groupthink that inevitably arises from focus groups, marketers are increasingly using experiential platforms to conduct their research. For instance, Procter & Gamble sent research teams to observe the consumer doing her laundry at home. When asked

35. Manda Mahoney, "The Subconscious Mind of the Consumer," Harvard Business School Working Knowledge Series, January 13, 2003.
36. Ibid.

by the team if she had any problems doing her laundry using P&G's detergent, she said no. Then the team saw her use a screwdriver to open the box of detergent, and poke a stick into the wash to dissolve the powder. When asked about these actions, she replied, "I didn't think about it." A focus group would never have caught this anomaly.

In 2004, *Fast Company* magazine profiled a baker's dozen of companies that were leaders in "putting the customer first," unwittingly repeating a mantra intoned by Drucker sixty years ago. Wachovia Bank, one of the profiled companies, stood out for its insistence on a one-to-one relationship between the individual consumer and its tellers to drive consumer knowledge. The magazine reports that "when Wachovia surveys customers—an impressive 25,000 every month—for feedback on its service experience, it doesn't just collect the results branch by branch. Rather, the bank asks customers about individual employees and uses those answers in one-on-one staff coaching. A recent 20-minute coaching session at a Manhattan branch made clear how this feedback—each customer surveyed rates 33 employee behaviors—can improve service. The branch manager urged an employee to focus on sincerity rather than on mere friendliness, to 'sharpen her antenna' so she'd listen to customers more intuitively, and to slow down rather than hurry up. That focus on careful, sincere, intuitive service has paid off: Wachovia has held the top score among banks in the American Customer Satisfaction Index since 2001."[37]

People Matter

San Francisco–based Swivel Media practices a form of personal interactive experiential marketing that it calls Brandshake Marketing. The practice is

37. Jena McGregor, "Leading Listener: Trader Joe's," *Fast Company,* Issue 87, October 2004, p. 82.

based primarily on establishing warm and inviting human intimacy between marketer and consumer from the first instant of interaction. The company's founder, Erik Hauser, believes that "the key to a successful XM program is to have a highly targeted (almost intimate) experience with the consumer. I have always felt that this can be done best by using humans as the key delivery tool for the product/service messaging—no matter how big or small the event is. Humans are social creatures. We want to be social and interact with others like us. Employing people in XM programs to connect with the consumer is the most important thing—period."[38]

The intimacy created by using real people to connect with other real people may not seem to be revolutionary, but when measured against the prevalent forms of intrusive marketing increasingly deployed by traditional marketers, it is clear how something like the notion of Brandshake becomes an extraordinary tool to reach and influence the consumer. "Anytime someone enters into a live event, a connection should immediately be made with a staffer/ambassador," Hauser explains. "This ambassador is a great first touch with the consumer. Then, as the well-trained ambassador begins to walk around and showcase the product or service they can show off the products/services attributes that the consumer had expressed interest in. This makes the experience much more relevant and meaningful. So, not only have we formed a human bond, we have made sure that the consumer had a great tour guide to make sure that they had all of their questions answered in a soft, non-saleslike way. Having a conversation to find out about what the consumer likes or dislikes is so very vital. To me, this is the most powerful thing in the world."

38. Interview with Erik Hauser, combined with online postings on the Experiential Marketing Forum message boards.

Whether virtual or physical, interaction is inherently personal and often intimate. Experiential marketers are keenly focused on establishing a higher level of intimacy than traditional marketing. For instance, my company was called in by the Canadian division of Bristol-Meyers Squibb to sample their Keri brand of hand lotion. Traditionally, the giant pharmaceutical concern had relied on print and television advertising to market Keri Lotion, and sampling had always been something of an afterthought. For the Christmas shopping season, the company decided not to take chances with their growing competition. They wanted to bring the product directly to the consumer. Still, I was not convinced that simple sampling would do the trick in connecting with the core consumers, who are primarily married and working women who don't have the luxury of buying boutique brands, but still expect something beneficial from a trusted brand such as Keri Lotion. Simple sampling was not intimate enough. It didn't connect. So we decided to give thousands of women a free hand massage on the winter streets of Canada.

We provided our Keri ambassadors with hand warmers and mufflers so their hands would always be very warm to the touch. Then we deployed these trained masseurs and masseuses to intercept our consmers at outdoor bus shelters, metro stations, office lobbies, malls, and Keri Lotion retailers. Imagine the look of surprise on the faces of tens of thousands of women turning into sublime pleasure as they received a warming, luxurious, and relaxing hand massage before and after work. During the experience, our brand ambassadors engaged in simple and lighthearted conversation while delivering product information and offering coupons, if requested. Everyone came away from the experience with not only a sample of the product for home consumption, but also a memorable experience.

Word of mouth was immediate, as women who received a massage went back to their offices and sent their coworkers down to the teams on the street to get their own hand massage. Soon local reporters were getting hand massages as well, and contributing to unpaid media placements for Keri Lotion in the press. By "experientializing" simple sampling and adding an intimate interactive element to the campaign, we were able to connect deeply with the consumer. Not only did we provide immediate sales success during the holiday season, we also kept the brand in the collective memories of Canadian women for months, if not years, after the campaign.

Perhaps more importantly, we heard stories—stories that were told to our masseurs and masseuses by the consumers themselves. These stories were about their experiences with the Keri brand, and their experiences with other brands as well. Consumers would divulge when and how they like to apply hand cream, how that made them feel, and how it made their partners feel when they touched their skin. Through the thousands of hand massages given to Canadians across the country, the brand ambassadors would learn deeply personal and insightful information, which was promptly relayed back to the company. Even more importantly, the brand ambassadors were able to respond. The focus of the hand massages was not entirely to deliver a targeted features-and-benefits message to the consumer. Instead, we laid emphasis on the warm and sensuous feeling of the hand massage, the friendly conversations between consumer and marketers, and simple humanism based on friendliness and kindness. Marketers "need to shift efforts from collecting data on customers to actually influencing how they think about the firm and its products and services," and customer interaction is an excellent approach to connecting with customers.[39]

---

39. Dave Ulrich, Jack Zenger, and Norm Smallwood, excerpt from "Results-Based Leadership: How Leaders Build the Business and Improve the Bottom Line," Harvard Business School Working Knowledge Series, October 12, 1999.

At its most basic, the one-to-one interaction is two human beings coming together. From this interaction, both individuals can share mutual empathy and have a chance to learn something they did not know before the one-on-one. One-on-one interactions also lead to marketer empathy, a crucial component of customer service. If experiential marketing is based on these interactions, and meaningful dialogue between a marketer and consumer, then empathy is bound to grow for the consumer's needs and desires. Marketing invariably becomes more relevant and therefore more effective.

At Fairmont Hotels and Resorts, employees in training are sent out as travelers to experience firsthand what customers themselves experience. The program began after the company's research indicated that guests were deeply impressed with "empathy" as a service differentiator. The company has since added empathy to the traits it screens for when interviewing recruits. At Petsmart, potential employees are interviewed on the sales floor, not in the manager's office, to screen them for one-on-one rapport and empathy with customers. Managers, with recruits in tow, walk the floor and start a conversation with a customer. They then bring the recruit into the conversation, step back, and observe the interaction. The idea is to witness that recruit's personal interest in the customer's needs and his or her level of empathy to the customer's experience.

One on One with Influentials

In the traditional marketing world, humans are divided into catch-phrases and slogans. The latest research and literature on how to market effectively all mention the "80–20 rule," where marketers desperately search for 20 percent of the consumer population to start 80 percent of the buzz on a product, brand, or service. The art of buzz has received ample attention with the publication of Gladwell's *The Tipping Point* or Rosen's *The Anatomy of Buzz*. What these works plainly illuminate is that buzz—that word-of-mouth contagion—is the most natural form of one-on-one marketing, one that is dependent solely on the 20 percent of consumers.

Some marketers put the figure lower, to about 10 or 15 percent. They are at a frenzy to find ways to reach and engage them, giving them monikers such as "alphas," "early adopters," "mavens," or "influentials." These titles reflect a consumer base that is at the top of the pyramid, the types of personalities who can spark and spread buzz that the masses listen to. To modern marketers, influentials are like consumer rock stars. They are the ones with knowledge, with expertise, and a cool, critical eye. Coupled with another group of buzzmakers, the "connectors" or "bees," who are characterized by their sociability and connectedness, and you have the recipe for reaching the "tipping point."

The problem is that influentials—and to a slightly lesser degree the connectors—do not respond to traditional marketing. According to *Marketing Magazine*, a report commissioned by Arnold Worldwide in Canada showed that influentials "are not looking forward to hearing from [marketers] . . . and are not pro-advertising."[40] Influentials have an acutely low tolerance for hype, with 53 percent stating that they actively avoid buying products that overadvertise. More than 74 percent of them feel that "there are just too many commercial messages to pay attention to anymore."[41]

The experiential notion of one-to-one marketing is an ideal method

40. Lynn Fletcher, "The Buzz on 'Buzz'," *Marketing Magazine*, August 23, 2004.
41. Ibid.

to connect to the influentials. Because influentials see themselves as deeply knowledgeable, sophisticated, and unconventional, traditional marketing and advertising are regarded as "beneath them." Paradoxically, because of their disdain for traditional marketing and their status, influentials are the inspiring link to get connectors to spread buzz. In fact, connectors are at least twice as likely as any other consumer cluster to recommend a brand to seven or more friends or colleagues.[42] The Arnold study, echoing the pronouncements of Rosen and Gladwell, shows that the way to get connectors to talk about a brand is to get the influentials talking about it first. Since they don't respond to traditional mass marketing and advertising, one of the only ways to reach the influential consumer is through one-on-one marketing.

Moreover, reaching them may not be enough. They need to be inspired by the brand, product, or service. And they need to be inspired by the marketing. An experiential approach—one that emphasizes a personal and sensory interaction—is proving to be the best way to reach the elusive influentials and connectors, who "like the unconventional" and "appreciate creative efforts to be entertaining" in marketing. They are more likely to spread buzz when confronted with a brand ambassador, rather than targeted by a commercial or magazine advertisement. They are more likely to be inspired by a sensory experience that surrounds that interaction, which enhances the memorability of the campaign. Equally important to inspiring the influential is the product itself, and an experiential marketing campaign will often position the product front and center through hands-on demonstrations and sampling like the Keri hand massages.

42. Ibid.

Take, for instance, the phenomenon of the Apple stores in the United States. Almost as an afterthought, Apple decided to install a number of tech ambassadors—the company calls them, perhaps presumptuously, Geniuses—behind a sleek, barlike counter in most of the more than one hundred stores in the United States. The Geniuses are clad in cool black uniforms and offer anyone who walks in the store—Mac or PC users—technical service and advice. So far, according to a *USA Today* dispatch, more than one hundred thousand people visit the Geniuses every week. And the stores represent nearly 50 percent of Apple's retail sales. The stores are setting a scorching pace for revenue growth. Apple stores were on track to generate $1.2 billion in 2004, compared to Apple's $8.3 billion fiscal revenue.[43] Fascinatingly, Apple serves only about 3 percent of the computing public.

The genius of the Genius marketing lies in the experiential aspects of customer service. The Geniuses are one-to-one ambassadors who engage in friendly, almost neighborly, interactions with a consumer who is deeply interested in the product and brand. "Half of the people who walk into the stores are Windows users," the *USA Today* story says, quoting an analyst. "They come in not because they want to switch but because the stores are different and so inviting. Do they walk out with a Mac? Probably not. But they do leave with an iPod, which they might not have done otherwise."[44]

The stores themselves are an experiential marketer's wet dream. All Apple products are available for hands-on play. Kids are allowed to play games on a number of plasma screens, and aficionados can relax in an upstairs theater and watch presentations on digital photography, moviemaking, or music production. Some stores have DJs

43. Jefferson Graham, "Apple Reboots into Retailing,"*USA Today,* November 11, 2004.
44. Ibid.

broadcasting music from their iPods. Other stores offer educational courses . . . taught by celebrities. For instance, Spike Lee was asked to teach an in-store course on film editing, and Moby has come in to talk about music.

But the biggest attraction is the bar with the Geniuses behind it. Not coincidentally, the idea of the Genius Bar came from the Ritz-Carleton experience. Apple's senior vice president of retail and a team of marketers watched management at Ritz-Carleton open up two new hotels, and out of that the Genius Bar was born. The focus was on personal interaction between brand and consumer, an inviting and open experience that ensured that the interaction was predicated on a one-on-one basis. The Genius Bar "[reaches] out to the other 97% who don't use Macs," Johnson is quoted in the article. "The idea of free face-to-face support in your neighborhood is a critical difference between us and the Windows world."

Influentials think they're smart, so brand ambassadors need to be smarter. By hiring and training a highly qualified force of brand ambassadors, and giving them a one-on-one forum to service and market to a sophisticated consumer, Apple's stores are impressing the influencers. Moreover, the stores are a point of inspiration. For instance, Dell and HP charge $35 to get postwarranty tech support over the phone. Apple itself charges $49 for telephone tech service. But an interaction with a Genius is the store is always free. This is an eye-opening, jaw-dropping experience for customers who expect so much less and get so much more. That inspirational encounter leads to return visits, buzz, and sales. It's no wonder that each Apple store averages about $15 million in sales each year.[45]

45. Ibid.

Redefining Samplers

Another store experience setting benchmarks for one-on-one interaction and highly knowledgeable ambassadors is Wegmans. The sixty-six-store chain is primarily located in the northeastern and mid-Atlantic states. In an industry that sees Wal-Mart as the fastest-growing food retailer, Wegmans thrives on offering food products that "require knowledge in terms of how you use them . . . anything that requires knowledge and service gives [them] a reason to be."[46] It's the type of company where a typical store offers more than four hundred types of cheese. With choice such as this, it is imperative that store ambassadors interact with consumers to determine their needs and expectations, and to know specific information about all the products available and how to serve them. Training, therefore, is paramount. Ambassadors in the meat or fish departments must pass a thirty- to fifty-five-hour "university" program.[47] Many of the stores' managers are sent overseas to work and learn from French patisseries or to tour the Italian countryside to learn about specialty cheese and meat products. The specialization, and the emphasis on personally interacting with the consumer, lead to what the company calls "telepathic levels of customer service."[48] Consequently, revenues grew 9 percent in 2003, to $3.3 billion in just sixty-six stores.

Just think how different a Wegmans store experience may be from a typical grocery store visit. How many times have we entered a grocery store to be greeted by unenthusiastic elderly part-time samplers giving out bits of food stabbed with a toothpick? Many marketers are too comfortable

46. Michael A. Prospero, "Customers First," *Fast Company,* October 2004, p. 88.
47. Ibid.
48. Ibid.

with the way they sample, thinking it is an easy and uncomplicated tactic when compared to more traditional and mass-based brand-building programs. Actually, sampling has always been one of the best methods to introduce and sustain a product on the consumer's radar screen. For twenty years, the Donnelley/Cox Survey of Promotion Practices ranked sampling at or near the top of "most popular" marketing tactics.[49] But when done wrong or ineffectively, sampling can be a disaster for a product or brand. Most often the problem isn't the product. It's the people sampling it who push away the consumer. Sampling at grocery stores is a perfect example of how disregard for the human dynamic, and the messages that come out of that interaction, can do more harm than good. "Not only do substandard marketing programs fail to accomplish the immediate goal of converting a trial into a purchase, they can turn off shoppers to the point where a return trip to the store falls into doubt."[50]

Consequently, recruiting high-quality, well-trained people as in-store brand ambassadors may be the single most important thing retailers and manufacturers can do to ensure a shopping experience that converts shoppers into customers.[51] Grocery store samplers, and samplers at retail in general, are often overlooked as the main ingredients to customer satisfaction. Most often, samplers are recruited from small local agencies and are not deployed based on their credentials or to the way they fit the brand's or product's image. Instead, they are hired based on availability and hourly rates. Based on these criteria, in-store sampling suffers because retailers and manufacturers forget that the strongest

---

49. Chain Reaction Study, "Brand Ambassadors: Three Steps to Brand Activation at Retail," *Reveries Magazine*, January 2003.
50. Ibid.
51. Ibid.

relationships are personal. "In today's economy, consumer trust and confidence are at historic lows. Now is the time for leading retail companies to take what they know about customers' likes and marry them to in-store strategies that put people into the equation."[52]

The right kind of brand ambassadors—trained, motivated, career-driven, and personable—offer retailers a great point of differentiation from their competitors. Furthermore, they are well poised to gain essential insights into and knowledge about their customers, to turn shoppers into consumers. One of the most important roles for a brand ambassador—besides enhancing a particular experience—is to observe the consumer and ascertain her likes and dislikes about the particular experience she is having. For stores that are interested in improving the shopping experience, customer feedback can be gathered by encouraging brand ambassadors to record customer opinions and comments on a sheet of paper, computer, or handheld PDA. It may even be more subtle. Brand ambassadors can be taught to keenly observe customer behavior. Customer feedback can be gleaned in casual conversations with the brand ambassadors, or it can be acquired through more formal dialogue, such as interviews and surveys. This information is indispensable for experiential knowledge, because it is knowledge that is acquired while the shopper is in the store and is actually shopping.

Trained brand ambassadors such as Apple's Geniuses are becoming increasingly integral to a company's total marketing mix. More than 83 percent of respondents to a survey on event marketing from Jack Morton, Inc., said that the presence of an on-site representative they can talk to about a product or brand is extremely or very important to them. The focus on quality face-to-face conversations between a

52. Ibid.

highly trained and dedicated brand ambassador and consumer is a key component to one-on-one marketing, and to experiential marketing in general. So much is dependent on the people who represent the brand, yet so many marketers forget this simple reality. But sampling programs—and the events, promotions, and awareness campaigns that may accompany them—are the all-important touch points where the target consumer actually interacts with the brand or product. What good does a Super Bowl commercial do when the consumer has recently experienced a lackadaisical and irrelevant interaction with a sampler?

Allied Domecq Spirits, the world's second-largest liquor marketer, chose to stop ignoring their sampling programs in 2004 and fundamentally rethought their marketing efforts. When chief executive Philip Bowman declared to shareholders that Allied Domecq will become a marketing-led company—as opposed to its current reputation as a sales-driven company—he clearly had sampling and consumer interaction in mind. Allied Domecq conducts more than fifteen thousand on-premise events each year in North America for dozens of its brands in five thousand accounts spread across thirty markets. These on-premise sampling programs—where both brand-building and volume-driving are at the core of the executions—were switched from Allied Domecq's traditional focus of discounting to more experiential aspects of sampling that pull (instead of push) consumers toward one of the company's brands.

First, the typical teams of shooter girls were replaced with brand ambassadors. According to Simon Hunt, Allied Domecq's executive vice president of marketing for North America, "having attractive guys and girls handing out free shots no longer provides the ROI we're looking for. Traditional sampling is simply not enough anymore. We need to create a real brand experience that sparks a connection."[53] Second, typical on-premise signage was replaced by props and sets to enhance the experience of sampling. "Part-timers were replaced by full-timers, and quantity-based nightlife marketing was turned into quality-based on-premise theater."[54]

For instance, rum-flavored spirit Malibu was sampled through the company's "Caribbean Cops" program in which models in police uniforms "raid" a bar or club to write up tickets to anybody "taking life too seriously." These culprits were handcuffed, read their rights, brought to the bar, and given a drink with Malibu. Allied Domecq samples its Stolichnaya brand through its Cold Truth campaign, which literally freezes clubs with ice slides, sculptures, and actual frost. In effect, sampling events such as this become live translations of the specific brand. In marketing circles this is called "bringing a brand to life." In the ultimate form of live one-on-one marketing, Allied Domecq has rolled out its "It Girl" tour for the Midori brand, which featured a mobile tour to clubs for free makeovers for the ladies at popular nightclubs in eight major U.S. markets. A twenty-four-foot truck pulls up in front of a location, and a team of brand ambassadors invites the women to the environment. There the consumer is pampered and made over by professional stylists. Once made over, the brand ambassadors stage a mini photo shoot for the dolled-up consumer, and the images are then posted online.

Since Allied Domecq has redefined the way it conducts its sampling and on-premise marketing, the company's brands are growing in awareness and sales. In fact, execs predict that "2005 will be a defining year" at the company.[55] By adding a more personal dimension to their sampling

53. "Cover Story: Below the Line," *Event Marketer Magazine*, October 4, 2004.
54. Ibid.
55. Ibid.

activities, and by concentrating on using trained and motivated brand ambassadors instead of part-time samplers, the company is seeing big sales lifts from most of its core brands.

One-on-one interaction is clearly the catalyst for the growth spurt. Swivel Media's Hauser has seen similar results for a nonalcoholic brand: "I created an event marketing campaign last summer for our Twisted Tea Hard Iced Tea. All events had sampling, but some had sampling and interactive games," he explains. "The accounts with events with both sampling and interaction saw an average sales increase of 49 percent over those with just sampling. The best part: these volume increases were maintained three months after the event happened."

Closing the Loop on CRM

People, not improved databases and better number-crunching, are the keys to CRM in the future of the retail business. Retailers and manufacturers must evolve their definitions of customer relationship management to a new, higher level—the human level. In other words, emphasis will be on the "R" instead of the "M" in "CRM." This is the true promise of CRM and its *raison d'être* for connecting and reconnecting with the consumer. Yet many analysts and initial proponents of CRM methodologies have lost faith in the practice. In fact, the growth forecast for CRM initiatives has dropped significantly in 2005, with the International Data Corporation predicting that CRM services through 2006 will reach only $10.5 billion, with a five-year cumulative annual growth rate of 5.2 percent. CRM's reputation isn't faring any better. "CRM has been over-hyped, over-promised and over-sold," wrote Deloitte consultants Mark Whitmore and Jonathan Copulsky in an editorial in *Marketing Magazine*. "More than one of our clients has, in fact, decreed that the term CRM will no longer be used, given the bad reputation that it now enjoys."[56]

What happened to connecting with the consumer and serving her needs seamlessly? For one, many corporate executives and their marketing cohorts relied much too heavily on the technological aspects that accompany CRM initiatives. "Many companies were so focused on getting the enabling CRM technology in place that they neglected some of the work required to get their employees on board. . . . Maybe the term CRM will go underground, but taking care of customers effectively is more important than ever in an environment where growth cannot be achieved through price increases and increased demand. So call it what you will, but businesses and their customers need what CRM is promising."[57] The new cadre of marketers is calling "it" experiential marketing.

Information technology and database management have hijacked the premise of CRM and transformed it into a predominantly troublesome endeavor for most companies. Companies need to stay clear of this trap. Instead, they should focus on acquiring information about customer experiences and interactions instead of their e-mail addresses. "It's a question of thinking more about capturing the interactions already taking place that by definition are building the relationship, and integrating them together so as to be able to extract insight about how I need to be managed, as opposed to finding new opportunities for the technologies to create a new interaction that hasn't yet taken place," says Harvard Business School professor Susan Fournier. "That's where I like to think of creating value."[58]

This is music to experiential marketers' ears: a CRM consultant

56. Mark Whitmore and Jonathan Copulsky, "CRM RIP?," *Marketing Magazine*, April 7, 2003.
57. Ibid.
58. Manda Mahoney, "It's Time to Reinstall the R in Your Customer Relationship Management Programs," Harvard Business School Working Knowledge Series, July 1, 2002.

placing interaction in front of technology. Of course, the more personal the interaction, the better the information being gathered. This notion is gathering momentum among CRM experts and the CEOs who depend on them. According to an online publication devoted to CRM studies called SearchCRM.com and Stamford, Connecticut-based consultant group Gartner, Inc., the "voice of customer departments are beginning to make a comeback in boardrooms and corporate organizations around the world."[59] The customer departments generally represent the needs, experiences, and satisfaction metrics of a company's customer base, and report these experiences to the board or high-level executives. Some departments get only twenty minutes each quarter to make the customer's voice heard in the sacred top floors and boardrooms. Yet other customer departments are getting more face time with the honchos, and are getting more creative in stating their case for better consumer interactions. "Some firms are using multimedia presentations with video footage of a customer's shopping experience, or call center recordings. Others are taking the board out [into the field] and giving it a hands-on customer experience. Many are moving away from analytical feedback to more experiential."[60]

According to Gartner, industries such as banks, high-tech firms, and telecommunications industries are driving the move toward experiential CRM. Another driver for the voice of the consumer, and their experiences with the product or brand, are systems integrators and consultants such as Accenture and IBM Global Services, who are pushing customer experience management (CEM) within large organizations. The reemergence of the focus on consumer experience is poised

59. Barney Beal, "Voice of the Customer Departments Making a Comeback," *CRM News*, January 10, 2005.
60. Ibid.

to drive the practice and methodology of CRM into new realms, mostly because this focus is increasingly customercentric.

Firms often measure their customers' reactions to what they already produce or service, not what products or services their customers really want or need. If a brand ambassador engages a customer one on one, through informational conversation at an event or through an on-site survey at the store, both the customer and the brand ambassador have an opportunity to learn something from each other. This exchange happens every day during thousands of interactions between a brand ambassador and consumer. From store clerks to call center operators, brand ambassadors interact with consumers enough to begin influencing consumer behavior. If the interaction stinks every time, then nothing is being learned and the customer goes away This has been the bane of CRM for too long. By making it more experiential, and by implementing customer feedback quickly and efficiently back into a company's operations and offerings, CRM will be more than just number crunching or surveying. It will become a customer experience benchmark and facilitator. CRM can actually improve a company's product and enhance the brand.

For instance, at software developer and marketer Intuit, the customer service people who answer the phone to field consumers' questions and problems are part of the product development team. After encountering a consumer complaint, they are expected to immediately report the complaint or comment to the software engineers. This ensures that the next patches and full suites of software will seamlessly integrate a much higher and relevant amount of solutions that the engineers may not have thought of. Consequently, the software products are remarkably easy to use and glitch-free, because they have incorporated answers to a plethora of customer questions and complaints. This has allowed Intuit to preemptively act on customers' problems and concerns and to eliminate the software glitches that cause them. The company "has made customer service excellent by removing most of the need for it."[61]

Tech-supplier CDW, based outside of Chicago, emphasizes personal interaction over technical and database tools. That's right: a tech and IT company is eschewing the typical CRM disciplines to get back to the "relationship" in its customer management initiatives. The twenty-year-old company, started at a kitchen table by Michael Krasny, sells about $5 billion worth of computer equipment and services each year, acting as a middleman for companies such as HP, Microsoft, IBM, and Apple. Of course, the company's clients can go directly to these manufacturers, but CDW's selection, speed, and service win over its more than 400,000 small-business clients. In particular, the success of its 1,880-member sales force rests squarely in the personal interactions and relationships they establish with their clients. In an industry that sees IT prices continue to decline, margins steadily narrow, and keeping customers is more important than ever, CDW is flourishing because of a simple yet incredibly powerful principle: "people do business with people they like."[62]

Customers say CDW's sales and customer retention philosophy is based firmly on a "one-on-one relationship with account managers."[63] Interestingly, this one-on-one relationship occurs primarily over the phone. CDW's customer-management software (CRM), compensation, training, and culture are designed to encourage unusually close and

61. Martha Lagace, "Your Customers: Use Them or Lose Them," Harvard Business School Working Knowledge Series, July 19, 2004.
62. Chuck Salter, "The Soft Sell," *Fast Company*, January 2005, p. 72.
63. Ibid.

long-lasting partnerships with clients. According to the company's new CEO, John Edwardson, who previously headed United Airlines, "account managers get more training than some pilots: six weeks of orientation, then six months of sales training in CDW Academy, then another year of monthly training sessions in the masters program. . . . New hires start with the basics, the traits that make account managers successful: enthusiasm, empathy and responsiveness."[64] There is no script to the sales calls, just a personal and deeply committed relationship to keep customers happy.

Just how personal do they get at CDW, and just how happy are CDW's clients? Well, one customer invited his CDW contact to his wedding. Clients and sales personnel share season hockey tickets. Clients know their sales reps' family and pet names, hobbies and interests, and vice versa. Account managers are trained to think like their clients and try to anticipate their needs and problems. For instance, right before hurricanes slammed the Florida coasts, sales reps e-mailed their Sunshine State clients with battery and backup storage solutions. Personal efforts and interactions like these are at the heart of experiential sales and marketing. CDW is "not just selling," says one client, "but getting into people's lives."[65] This type of effort, culture, and marketing point of differentiation is as experiential as it gets.

The one-on-one marketing experience is also genuine, more so that a typical commercial or billboard, because marketers who care about their customers are greatly more forthright than the typical marketing pitch and come-on. People who interact with each other instinctively pick up on clues that may expose half-truths or omissions. Consumers can query a marketer one on one until they are satisfied with the level of authenticity

64. Ibid.
65. Ibid.

and candor that the marketing provides. This achievement of authenticity is critical to providing a positive experience in a marketing campaign. If people can readily smell the BS in a typical marketing campaign, they can do so even faster with a one-on-one interaction.

Chapter 3

Experiential marketing will be authentic. This will mobilize the marketplace.

In the past few years marketers have seen the rise of a number of new tactics used to get the attention of increasingly weary consumers. From roaching to buzzing, from viral to subviral, not all have sought a sincere relationship with consumers. Others, such as certain guerrilla efforts, have had a profound effect on the development of experiential marketing. Those methods that help create the give-and-take of a dialogue between consumer and marketer can be used to help build strong relationships and can take their place in an experiential campaign.

When I would present guerrilla marketing strategies and tactics at conferences and seminars, I began by featuring two portraits flashed onto the overhead screen: Mao Tse-tung and Sean "P Diddy" Combs. These two, I would say, are the godfathers of guerrilla marketing. This usually received a collective chuckle from the audience, but the juxtaposition of the two when describing guerrilla marketing was oddly compelling: Mao—and later Ernesto "Che" Guevara—codified strategies and tactics for guerrilla warfare and spread these methodologies throughout the world in wars for national liberation; P Diddy used these tactics in the ghettos of New York City to launch a multimillion-dollar music, media, fashion and luxury goods empire that has become serious competition for traditional ad agencies.

There's a distinct ethos that these two men bring to the concept of guerrilla marketing, and that ethos informs the two fundamental tenets that I use to define guerrilla marketing. First, guerrilla marketing is "populace-friendly." It is based on people and winning these people over to the cause, "because guerrilla warfare basically derives from the masses and is supported by them, [and] it can neither exist nor flourish if it separates itself from their sympathies and cooperation."[66] Once the populace is on the side of the guerrillas, revolution will inexorably grow. Second, guerrilla marketing is "street-friendly," which means that the guerrilla marketing revolution is not fought on billboards, thirty-second TV spots, or fancy magazine spreads. It's fought in the streets, where the consumer works, lives, plays, and purchases.

Combs's hip-hop roots instinctively drew him to the street-friendly aspect of guerrilla marketing. Realizing that New York City ghettos didn't have HMV megastores for his potential consumers to sample his new artists—and discovering that commercial radio wasn't willing to break unknown rappers from the 'hood—Combs used guerrilla tactics to attack his market with a fleet of trucks outfitted with huge speakers. He would spin his artists' records on corners and at block parties himself. If the street wasn't going to come to him, he was going to come to the street. This ethos is especially palatable to the youth demographic—the present and future consumers who are idealistic enough to believe in the power of the individual, street-savvy enough to understand the power of grassroots activism, and jaded enough to develop deep immunity to traditional mass marketing.

66. Gabriel Stricker, *Mao in the Boardroom* (New York: St. Martin's Press, Griffin, 2003), p. 174.

The brave new world of media overload, word-of-mouth frenzy, and the white noise of commercialism is fertile ground for guerrilla marketing that uses unconventional means to bring the message where it will be received. Not surprisingly, guerrilla marketing has taken its place in this world as a methodology for companies and marketers to break through in a sea of competing messages and commercial pervasiveness, especially when targeting the younger generation of marketing-savvy consumers.

To Be a Guerrilla

According to Jay Conrad Levinson, the oft-described "father of guerrilla marketing," the practice called guerrilla marketing is "a body of unconventional ways of pursuing conventional goals. It is a proven method of achieving profits with minimum money."[67] Guerrilla marketing is a new way of marketing goods and services, relying on time, energy, and imagination rather than the bottomless marketing budget.[68] Whereas the initial beneficiaries of guerrilla marketing were small businesses with even smaller budgets, the practice has evolved into a proven methodology pursued by the likes of Virgin Mobile, Nike, Microsoft, and Coca-Cola. In fact, virtually every major youth brand has by this time rolled out at least one guerrilla marketing campaign. From sampling street teams to celebrity seeding to underground parties to viral word-of-mouth, guerrilla marketing is proving an effective means to spread buzz and distribute product.

Very often, the strategies employed by guerrilla marketers closely mirror those of "traditional" guerrillas, the small armed groups of

67. Taken from Levinson's Web site: www.gmarketing.com.
68. Jay Conrad Levinson, *Guerrilla Marketing Attack* (Boston: Houghton Mifflin, 1989), preface.

fighters who wage unconventional warfare against a much larger foe. The term "guerrilla" originated in Spain during the Napoleonic wars, when peasant fighters harassed an army with hit-and-run raids and acts of sabotage. By adding the diminutive suffix *(-illa)* to the Spanish word for war *(guerra),* these tactics introduced the notion of a "little war" into military lexicon. In fact, guerrilla warfare can trace its roots to biblical narrative, when Judas Maccabeus led a revolt against the Syrians between 166 and 158 B.C.[69] Classical historians have pointed out a number of revolts against Rome that had all the telltale signs of guerrilla strategies and tactics, which have been utilized for centuries.

Guerrillas have always needed to possess local knowledge of the terrain, as well as the support of the local population. Guerrilla units were generally more mobile than their counterparts, which led to hit-and-run tactics that would hurt their opponents and, more importantly, prolong the struggle. Guerrillas inherently understand that there are no decisive battles, because of the superiority of their opponents. The battle needs to be continuous and unrelenting.

By the eighteenth century, guerrilla tactics were recognized by conventional armies as an invaluable tool to support conventional campaigns, just as present-day corporations have been increasingly implementing guerrilla marketing into their marketing mix to support their conventional mass media campaigns. Irregular units were organized to operate on the flanks and behind enemy lines to harass the enemy and infiltrate the populace for valuable intelligence. Prior to the twentieth century, however, few military theorists made any direct correlation between guerrilla warfare and political change.[70] Until Mao Tse-tung's guerrilla theories were promulgated and emulated across

---

69. Ian F. W. Beckett, ed., *Encyclopedia of Guerrilla Warfare* (New York: Facts on File, 2001), p. xi.
70. Ibid., p. xii.

the globe, guerrilla warfare continued to be waged along traditional military lines.

Mao's fusion of traditional guerrilla hit-and-run tactics with political objectives—with the addition of political, socioeconomic, and psychological measures and the mobilization of the population—to enhance military tactics marked the emergence of a new style of guerrilla warfare as a means by which a small minority can gain political power. Military historians have called Mao's form of guerrilla warfare an "insurgency movement," which relies on a combination of guerrilla action, propaganda, subversion, and political mobilization. Following the doctrines of insurgency guerrilla warfare is seen as an effective means of achieving power and influence in a state, or of bringing a particular cause to the notice of the national or international community.[71] According to Mao, "basic guerrilla strategy must be based primarily on alertness, mobility and attack. It must be adjusted to the enemy situation, the terrain, the existing lines of communication, the relative strengths, the weather and the situation of the people." Remarkably, this strategy is as equally applicable to marketing as it is to warfare.

In his excellent book called *Mao in the Boardroom,* Gabriel Stricker asserts that most major brands and companies built their empires using Mao's basic guerrilla strategies, citing behemoth companies such as Coca-Cola, Nike, Virgin and Apple. Conversely, their smaller upstart competitors are now using the same strategies to win market share away from the giants. How? Guerrillas are more alert and in touch with their core populace/consumer than their competition; guerrillas are quicker to react to fluid market changes and are more mobile in their attacking patterns than their competition; guerrillas are constantly on the attack and bring the

71. Ibid., p. xiii.

battle to their turf, where the competition is out of its element and taken by surprise.

Moreover, guerrilla marketing is as much a state of mind as it is a tactical exercise. Successful marketing is no longer perceived as being the loudest. Being the smartest is what really counts. Guerrilla marketers are not bound by media boundaries. The imperative for the underdog is to continue the fight, in any way possible. Consequently, as more guerrilla marketers perfect the basic tenets of guerrilla strategy—alertness, mobility, and attack—victory in battle will inexorably begin to fall to the guerrillas. According to Mao's principles, if "we make war everywhere and cause dispersal of the competition's forces and dissipation of its strength, the time will come when a gradual change will become evident . . . and when that day comes, it will be the beginning of our ultimate victory."

Support of the People

However, victory is impossible without the support of the populace. "Because guerrilla warfare basically derives from the masses and is supported by them, it can neither exist nor flourish if it separates itself from their sympathies and cooperation. . . . The moment that this war of resistance disassociates itself from the masses is the precise moment that it disassociates itself from hope of ultimate victory."[72] Likewise, a guerrilla marketing campaign is successful only if it has the support of the consumer. If consumer support is lacking, guerrilla marketing campaigns run the risk of looking like terrorist marketing instead. Perhaps even worse, guerrilla marketing can look like a drive-by shooting.

We are all familiar with the annoyed feeling we get when we return to

72. Mao Tse-Tung, Samuel B. Griffith II, tr., "On Guerrilla Warfare," *Selected Works of Mao Tse-Tung* (Champaign, IL: University of Illinois Press, 2000), p. 44.

our parked car and find the windshield covered in flyers. This form of marketing would be considered guerrilla marketing—nontraditional, grassroots, and wild media distribution if we all loved the idea of getting flyers on our windshields. But we don't, which transforms an apparent guerrilla foray into a terrorist attack. The same could be applied to menu drop-offs or coupon circulars, which find themselves unread and in the recycling bin. In Montreal, for instance, a company called Publi-Sac delivers a plastic bag stuffed with coupons, circulars, and pamphlets each week to the doorsteps of thousands of Montrealers. In late 2004, the amount of waste contributed by consumers discarding the Publi-Sacs led to a public outcry to ban the practice. It was estimated that each year more than eleven thousand tons of paper were wasted by unwanted circulars, a number equal to fifty-four thousand destroyed trees.[73]

Equally distanced from the sympathies and cooperation of the people is the moronic sampling campaign that features dozens of slack-jawed part-timers distributing irrelevant products at high-foot-traffic spots such as subway stations and busy intersections, slowing down pedestrians and commuters already too stressed to listen to a marketing pitch. Many marketers get ecstatic about guerrilla marketing when faced with unaffordable multimillion-dollar price tags for TV commercials or magazine spreads. So they flood the streets with teams and collateral, happy with thoughts of cost savings, targeted market saturation, and direct marketing distribution that a guerrilla campaign can effectively deliver. But just because a marketer uses guerrilla tactics does not make the campaign a populace-friendly foray. Consequently, the campaign fails and the guerrillas are defeated by consumer apathy and commercial overkill.

Ill-conceived and "unfriendly" guerrilla marketing campaigns often

73. CBC Radio report, December 9, 2004.

garner attention, but of the wrong kind. In October 2002, Microsoft slapped thousands of butterfly stickers and decals promoting its MSN 8 Internet service on sidewalks and bus shelters in New York City. The company was fined by the city administration and ordered to remove the stickers, which proved much more costly and time-consuming than placing them in the first place. Similarly, IBM paid fines in Chicago and San Francisco after its guerrilla teams spray-painted "Peace, Love and Linux" on city sidewalks and streets. The guerrilla attack relied on tagging as many public locations as possible.

A leading New York–based guerrilla marketing agency called Go Gorilla Media states on its Web site that its mission is "to bombard and overwhelm consumers with advertising messages as they go about their daily lives." The company lists twenty-eight guerrilla marketing services it offers, such as placards affixed to trees, projections aimed at building walls, street sampling teams, and sidewalk stencils.

To be sure, this type of guerrilla marketing is indeed street-friendly. Companies and brands that cannot afford to advertise in the more traditional media find themselves with one or two viable options: the street or online. Guerrilla marketing is an ideal methodology for both venues. Guerrilla marketing is also a key methodology to reaching elusive youth, who do not rely on the same traditional media for their product information or brand loyalty. Since they are not coming to us, the guerrilla marketers reason, we must go to them. Attacking guerrilla-style can get you in the door with the kids. Hopefully they'll allow you to stay there . . . if you've knocked on the door with creativity, relevance, and chutzpah.

Yet many guerrilla marketing campaigns, and the brand managers who approve them, forget the other dictum of successful guerrilla marketing, that it must have the support of the populace. The first step to this goal is to refrain from adding to the clutter. Without a clear benefit to the consumer, a guerrilla marketing campaign is nothing but marketing terrorism. The second step to gain support is to guarantee that the consumer is in a place and at a time where she is most receptive to interacting with a brand. And the third step—the one that is virtually guaranteed to get the populace on your side—is to be blatantly, unapologetically, and sincerely *authentic* in the approach and messaging of the guerrilla campaign. Yet many guerrilla marketers miss the last point entirely.

Secret Agents of Capitalism

On December 5, 2004, the *New York Times Magazine* fronted a cover story called "The Corporate Manufacture of Word-of-Mouth." The exposé detailed the machinations of a Boston-based company called BzzAgent, one of hundreds of companies worldwide whose mission is to spread buzz about brands, services, and products. What separates these agencies and entities from traditional marketers is that their ability to stimulate and propagate word-of-mouth is dependent on buzz agents, not professional marketers. These buzz agents are regular folks. They are not paid by corporations or agencies. Some may receive small compensation for taking part in surveys, or receive product as payment, but most are simply volunteers.

The magazine piece positions BzzAgent as one of a number of marketing companies that contend that "the most powerful forum for consumer seduction is not TV ads or billboards, but rather the conversations we have in our everyday lives."[74] The increasingly fragmented media, coupled with unabated clutter, intrusiveness, and the consumer's highly attuned resistance to traditional marketing, have led

74. Rob Walker, *The New York Times Magazine,* December 5, 2004, p. 70.

many companies to view word-of-mouth as the next big thing in marketing. This may take various marketing monikers: viral marketing, buzz marketing, trend seeding, guerrilla marketing, cool-hunting, etc. Whatever the terminology—which marketers famously bicker over—the notion behind word-of-mouth marketing is "in one way or another, to break the fourth wall that used to separate the theater of commerce, persuasion and salesmanship from our actual day-to-day life."[75]

In the simplest of terms, buzz marketing seeks to gather volunteers to try out products and brands, and then sends these people out in the world to talk up their product experiences with other people. Certainly, the power of word-of-mouth has been recognized for centuries, or as one buzz marketer put it, buzz has been around "since the first caveman said to the other 'there are more buffalo over there.'"[76] Word-of-mouth is exceptional in convincing, influencing, and affecting consumer behavior, mostly because we hold our peers to have more credibility than advertisers and marketers.

Recently, however, marketers have put word-of-mouth to use in a much more sophisticated manner, with companies actively creating a structure around the way buzz spreads, to harness and direct it, and to watch closely the sales results once the buzz campaign is "over." Buzz, therefore, is becoming a major weapon in a marketer's arsenal.

BzzAgent currently has more than 75,000 volunteer agents in its network, talking about and spreading buzz for clients such as Lee Jeans, Anheuser-Busch, Ralph Lauren, and DuPont. Another buzz shop, called Tremor, is a highly ambitious and well-funded operation started by Procter & Gamble. It boasts more than 250,000 agents in its network—mostly teenage girls and the "influencers" of their generation. These agents not

75. Ibid.
76. Natalie Alvarez, Big Fat interview, *Maisonneuve Magazine*, November 2001.

only spread buzz about hundreds of P&G's products, but they are also utilized by Tremor to spread word-of-mouth for other noncompeting firms. In fact, the success that P&G has had with Tremor led the packaged goods behemoth to plan a spin-off buzz shop called Tremor Moms.

Secret agents, as many buzz marketers call their street teams, rely on their natural ability to converse with others, and their typically larger network of friends and acquaintances, to talk about new products and brands before the rest of the hoi polloi get to hear about them. Because these "influencers" enjoy the respect of their peers, and because they have so many peers compared to the rest of us, they are ideal buzz spreaders. Once a client has signed on for a word-of-mouth campaign, agencies such as BzzAgent search through their databases to find the best candidates for the program. The candidates are selected by profile and geography, sent coupons or products, and unleashed by the company into the marketplace.

Seemingly, BzzAgent thereafter relies on the natural impetus of word-of-mouth to do the marketing for them. The power of conversation, and the clutter-breaking attributes of peer referrals, are supposed to take over and "tip" the brand or product into mass consciousness and, consequently, healthy sales. According to new marketing guru Seth Godin, this is the future of marketing. In fact, the *Times* points out, he used BzzAgent to market one of his books, *Purple Cow*. He believes that honest peer-to-peer marketing to spread word-of-mouth is the latest—and best—form of media.

"Honest" is a key word for Godin. But exactly how honest is BzzAgent's methodology? Before the company sends out its teams, it provides the agents with a number of talking sheets, compiled and tweaked with input from the client, and other support material on the product being marketed. This support material can include a sample script of a phone call a buzz agent can place to a bookstore, pretending they forgot the name of a particular book. Of course, they are working for the book's publisher and know perfectly well the title of the book they're asking about. The training material could also include pointers on how to place a review of the book on Amazon, or encourage buzz agents to write editorials to local publications in praise of the particular book.

BzzAgent also tells its volunteers that "they are under no obligation to hide their association with the company and its campaigns, [but] the reality is that most of them do hide it most of the time. They don't tell the people they are 'buzzing' . . . for some company in Boston that charges six-figure fees to corporations."[77] This is because to disclose their affiliation would most likely make buzzing ineffective. Volunteers and agents say that "it seems more natural" if people don't believe that products are being pushed. To be upfront would ruin the interaction. How comforting it is to know that marketing has finally reached its culmination: deceiving consumers (who are often friends and relatives of the buzz agent) with a "more natural" marketing pitch.

BzzAgent is based on the power of word-of-mouth that is delivered within a context of conversation or recommendation. For instance, the buzz agents will talk to grocery store managers when buzzing about a client's sausage product, talk up a tissue-wipe product at a Christmas party or wedding, or drop recommendations to their friends and family on a fabulous book they are reading. These interactions are highly personal and usually require quite a bit of verbal communication to convince the potential consumer. The marketing experience that is delivered to the consumer is exceptional because of this interaction. The longer the consumer and buzz agent have known each other, the greater

77. Ibid., p. 130.

the level of trust and receptiveness to the marketing experience. There's just one small problem here: the consumer doesn't know she is being marketed to. The conversation may be personal and meaningful to the consumer, but it is based on a deception. The conversation, therefore, is not authentic. Still, other buzz marketers are even less overt and much more disingenuous in their methods to spread word-of-mouth.

What's a Roach Marketer?

For longer than anyone would like to admit, liquor marketers have been engaged in buzz marketing activities in bars and restaurants around the world. The practice they perfected also uses buzz agents, much like BzzAgent itself, yet they have traditionally been called "leaners" instead of "agents." A New York City–based company called Big Fat perfected the art of leaning, and by rolling out hundreds if not thousands of leaners in New York, San Francisco, San Diego, Chicago, and Boston, the company introduced the often-derided marketing technique called "roach bait marketing."

The notion of leaners is ingeniously simple. At crowded bars throughout the city, very attractive and personable female brand reps would approach guys at the bar, lean in, and tap them on the shoulder. Once she gets the attention of the dumb struck lad, she asks him to order her a drink from the bar, because she can't get the attention of the bartender herself. She mentions the vodka brand by name, and picks a mixer to go with it. She then reiterates that she only drinks the vodka brand, and none other. The guy orders her a drink with the money she gives him (depending on his level of chivalry, he may even pay for the cocktail himself). While the drink is being prepared, the leaner talks about the brand a little more. She gets her drink, thanks him, and walks away.

This interaction is then repeated dozens of times that night, at the same bar or one a bit farther down the street. It can be repeated for a number of brands and products as well. Leaners can lean in and ask for a light to their cigarettes, hyping the brand in the process. They can lean in and ask if their perfume smells good, and proceed to chat it up as a perfect gift for the wife or girlfriend. They can lean in and ask someone his or her opinion about the music being played, thereafter mentioning their newest favorite band or singer.

The notion of leaners expanded into "roach bait marketing" when this type of marketing moved out of the bars and into the everyday lives of consumers. The term is significant in what it is meant to conjure up: a roach hotel where one roach picks up the brand or product information and spreads it among the rest. Many times, unlike leaners, the "roach bait" is done without any personal interaction at all.

For instance, Big Fat paid apartment building doormen in New York City to keep empty boxes and packages bearing the name and logo of an online retailer at their front desks, in the hopes that residents would be subtly influenced by the placement. If other people in the building are using this retailer, they would reason, I should try it out, too. Big Fat, which counts Nestlé, PepsiCo, Brown & Williamson Tobacco, and USA Networks as clients, also conducts "request" programs by sending teams into stores to ask for a brand or product they know the store doesn't carry. Finally, after weeks of pestering by the roachers, owners and store managers are pushed into stocking the requested goods.

Perhaps the most famous roach marketing campaign was launched in 2003, when Sony Ericsson created a $5 million undercover guerrilla campaign to promote their übercool T68i—a cell phone that can take, send, and receive digital pictures. Sony Ericsson used actors and actresses to pose as cheerful tourists and bar-hoppers who are armed with the cellular gadgets. They would engage consumers directly by asking them if they could take a picture with the phone for them, or create interest and word-of-mouth by receiving pictures and laughing about them in trend-setting environments. Once this roach campaign was announced to the press, editorials in the *New York Times, Bloomberg News,* and the *Globe and Mail* hastily beat the drums against "the secret agents of capitalism," with liberal use of Orwellian references.

Yet the success of the campaign, and the buzz that Sony Ericsson's agents caused, led many marketers and agencies to dive headfirst into conducting roach marketing campaigns for their products and clients. My former company, Gearwerx, did as well. We were hired by a major multinational packaged goods company in Canada to hype a new hair spray that eliminated the smell of smoke. The relatively small budget required that we create a simple buzz-activating campaign that introduced smokers to the product. Roach marketing seemed a natural fit, mainly because we found that smokers were naturally chatty with other smokers, forging a common bond unique to the pariah groups of puffers. The roach campaign I created took advantage of the sociability that smokers share.

A well-dressed, pretty woman in her twenties approaches a group of office workers who gather in front of a building to smoke a few cigarettes and gossip. These tobacco cabals are a mainstay in any downtown core, where conversations between strangers are easily sparked with a flick of a Bic. She approaches them casually, lights a cigarette, and joins the smokers' huddle. After starting up brief chatter with the group ("I have a job interview in this building. I'm a little nervous."), she stamps out the cigarette, pulls a vibrant-green bottle out of her purse, and proceeds to spray her hair and clothes with the concoction.

Noticing the inquisitive looks on the faces of her fellow smokers, she explains that she's using a new product for smokers and shows everyone the bottle. This, she says, gets the odor of smoke out of her hair, something that her boyfriend—or potential new boss—wouldn't like. A number of smokers ask her if they can use the spray before going back up to their cubicles. They, too, don't want to smell like smoke when they return to the office. All of them pass the bottle around and spray it on, give it back to the pretty woman, and wish her luck in her interview.

I no longer recommend nor conduct these types of deceptive roach marketing campaigns (because they don't mesh with the XM ethos), but many other agencies and marketers choose to equate guerrilla marketing with the practice of roach marketing. Increasingly, roach marketing is aimed at teens and young adults, who are more than anyone else immune to overt commercial pitches and traditional marketing tactics.

Buzzing Teens

According to Teenage Research Unlimited, U.S. teens spent more than $175 billion in 2003, or on average about $103 each week. Numbers like these have corporate marketers drooling for the opportunity to be part of those hundred bucks spent each week. Marketers also know that major household purchases such as TVs, computers, cars, and vacations are influenced by the kids in the family. It's called the "nag factor." Yet reaching the youth, let alone engaging them, is proving exceptionally difficult. Television viewing is down for the group; so is magazine readership. Online usage, however, is skyrocketing. From chat rooms and instant messaging to file sharing and personal blogging, the average teen is an Internet omnivore. When time spent online playing games is factored into the media habits of teens, it is evident that speaking to teens means finding them online. Furthermore, the language they speak is different from our own, or better yet, they are immune to standard ad-speak or commercial pitches. And to complicate matters further, teens tend only to listen to other teens.

Marketers navigate these foreign landscapes with the help of buzz agents, the teen influencers who are the crucial link to spread word-of-mouth. A buzz entity such as Procter & Gamble's Tremor boasts of identifying one-quarter million influentials and giving them the unique privilege of receiving free product samples, CDs, and movie passes to talk about among their friends. They also use this huge network to infiltrate popular chat rooms and message boards to disseminate buzz about their brands.

The practice of sending secret agents into the matrix of online chat and message boards is not new. Video game marketers and music studios have perfected the art of insinuating messages into the cyberchatter of gamers and file-swappers during the past five years. The gaming community is an incredibly fertile ground to plant and nourish buzz. Mavens or influentials know everything about the most popular games, get the inside scoop about upcoming games hitting the marketplace, and find out the secret codes and "cheats" that are exclusive to the game's developers themselves. Other, less informed and diehard gamers are the perfect "connectors" or "bees" who spread the information to other gamers. The cumulative buzz reaches a tipping point, and the game's developer gets a large chunk of a teen's weekly $103 spending average. The same process applies to seeding buzz about a band or performer. Mavens and influencers find and know of all the newest artists and music fads. Connectors pick up on the exclusively cool information and sprinkle it around the Internet.

The game developers, many of which are run on make-it-or-bust budgets, use this type of seeded chatter to get interest and trial for their latest games. For some time the practice was a grassroots affair, with avid gamers getting a preview or prerelease of the games directly from the developer. To get these gamers to chat up the game, the product had to stand up to the test of the hard-core gamers. More recently, developers began paying online agents to plant rave reviews for their games. The anonymity of message boards made this quite easy. If anyone disagreed with the post on a message board, for instance, another agent would visit the boards and support the original rave review. This online word-of-mouth methodology was soon appropriated by packaged-goods companies, car makers, electronics marketers, and, of course, Hollywood.

Roach marketing has now permanently traversed into cyberspace, but in even more underhanded ways than planted messages. Marketing companies are setting up entire Web sites, blogs, and large message boards that look like noncommercial cyber communities. These destination sites and boards may look like clubs, communities, and even dating sites, but in reality they are sophisticated cyberenvironments for gathering or disseminating product information and buzz. For instance, a site called SoulCool looks like a hip and inviting place for teens and young adults to meet and communicate with each other. Moderators on the site would direct the discussion boards, or set up internal clubs called "cribs" for the site registrants to meet privately. SoulCool can then recruit site users to spread the word about new CDs and movies that are soon being released, not divulging that record companies and movie studios are paying the site to spread the buzz. Often a corporate site can be wholly overt with its commercial entreaties. For instance, Emedia Wire reported that a campaign launched on P&G's Tremor started with an e-mail that read "Tremor and Old Spice need you to create the first-ever Red Zone Girls calendar. That means loads of gorgeous girls for you to check out and vote on." The e-mail was sent to a thirteen-year-old boy.

This type of indiscriminate and inauthentic buzz marketing, primarily aimed at tweens and teens, has led to an outcry from consumer and parent groups. The National Institute on Media and the Family launched an investigation in 2004 to study and expose marketers who are taking advantage of an unsuspecting audience, or sending them inappropriate content from their clients. The institute focused on the marketing firms that created enticing Web sites that clearly target minors and teens, and lured this demographic with offers for free gifts (CDs, T-shirts, stickers, concert tickets, sometimes even money) when they became "secret agents" of the site. The sites would then continue to send products and commercial offers for their agents to spread among their friends. The institute's initial research suggested that many of the online campaigns conducted by buzz marketers violate guidelines set up by the Children's Advertising Review Unit and the National Advertising Review Council. The irony of buzz marketing to teens and kids is evident: marketers think that this market is overly sophisticated when responding to traditional marketing and in using new media, so their marketing efforts must assume deceptive buzz marketing tactics.

For instance, a company called Girls Intelligence Agency (GIA) combines the titles "buzz agents" and "influencers" to call its 40,000 members "agent influencers." The company specializes in marketing movies and beauty products to girls and women age eight to twenty-nine. A key to GIA's undercover marketing efforts is setting up slumber parties for its agent influencers and their friends. The company would send their agents a "party in a box" kit, which may include a number of beauty products or a new movie release DVD. All the elements—popcorn, gifts, branded gifts, theme games—are provided to the agents by GIA. The agents, in turn, invite ten or fifteen of their friends to sleep over at their house and use the branded products. GIA tells prospective clients that it is able to take their products "behind enemy lines—GIA takes you into girls' bedrooms."[78] The company notes that if 6,000 girlfriends are partying on the same night, they can potentially spread word-of-mouth to 300,000 girls.[79] The company positions itself as a "big sis" to their agents, providing them with support and guidance as well as insights into the "next big thing" for their demographic.[80]

Inauthentic Buzz

The slumber-party-in-a-box concept from Girls Intelligence Agency is actually quite a compelling marketing idea. In fact, it's quite experiential. The idea of marketing personally, and giving the consumer a memorable experience, is at the heart of the slumber party marketing campaign. The problem with the way GIA markets is that the company often does not disclose that it is a marketing agency to their agents. Instead, they position the company as a club or community that allows its members—after participating in polls or questionnaires—access to cool new beauty products and new movies. Many of the agents, as well as most of the invited girls, have no clue that they are being marketed to by GIA's paying clients. Furthermore, the invited girls' parents have no idea either. GIA asserts that they get parental permission from their agents to host the parties, but parents of the invited girls do not have any knowledge of the marketing nature of the sleepovers.

The execs at Girls Intelligence Agency would dismiss any complaint of inauthentic marketing, suggesting that they really are not "pushing" any product and that the decision to spread word-of-mouth about their

78. Nell Minow, "Have You Heard?," *Chicago Tribune,* September 21, 2004.
79. Ibid.
80. Ibid.

clients rests solely with their "agent influencers." Again, the notion is that these girls are sophisticated enough consumers to be able to discern and accept or reject a marketing campaign directed at them through their friends. Then why call them secret agents? Other buzz marketers, such as Big Fat's CEO, contend that consumers are savvy enough to parse out the buzz and decide for themselves what buzz to use. The buzz marketers get the brand or product information out there, and then sit back and let the consumer decide.[81] Then why do they only hire "influencers" to spread the hype?

Marketers are not just using the Web to recruit secret agents and plant information on message boards. Many have even tried to build entire Web sites and blogs to look like authentic, do-it-yourself projects that subtly push product to site visitors. For instance, a personal blog was found by fellow bloggers to feature a series of links pointing to ads from Mazda hyping their new M3 model. The blog, called HalloweenM3, was posted on Google's blog-hosting service Blogger.com and was supposedly written by a twenty-two-year-old blogger named Kid Halloween. Fellow bloggers began to get suspicious when his list of favorite movies all included lengthy car chase scenes. The blog's only entries were both linked to Mazda's M3 commercials, the same ads that appear on Mazda's viral marketing agency's Web site. More digging by the blogging community revealed that the site was hosted by Rackspace, an expensive hosting provider that is usually cost-prohibitive for regular bloggers. These clues all pointed to a commercial enterprise, not a personal Web log. Massive online chatter and postings about the fake blog led Mazda to pull it from cyberspace, even though the company declined to comment to journalists on the move.

81. Catherine Donaldson-Evans, Fox News Channel, August 17, 2001.

Pete Blackshaw, cofounder of the Word of Mouth Marketing Association (WOMMA), has held up this example as a perfect illustration of "how bloggers are holding advertisers at much higher levels of accountability. . . . Mazda now needs to deal with the ugly reality of this mishap resurrecting itself every time a consumer—or a media writer or a financial analyst—Googles the term 'Mazda blog.' "[82] The increased interconnectivity that the Internet has instituted among people is making these engaged and aware consumers into "copy cops" and "unabashed truth seekers."[83] Marketers who continue to deceive and dissemble the consumer will, in most cases, be caught. At the very least, inauthentic marketing will raise more than a few eyebrows from a chattering crowd, perhaps even enough to start a negative word-of-mouth reaction.

This risk hasn't impeded marketers from faking authenticity. Fake blogs are popping up all over the Internet, much like cyber agent influencers controlled behind the scenes by marketers and their clients. Video game marketers—the pioneers of online buzz, fake posts, and cyberagents—have taken blog hoaxing to the next level of dissembling their marketing intentions. An "innocent-looking" homemade site called www.ilovebees.com was spread in cyberspace, and then mysteriously appeared to be hacked for no good reason. A blog set up by "Dana"—a niece of the site's owner—emerged soon after ilovebees.com was launched. The blog used a standard Blogger template, and was ad-supported by BlogSpot, Blogger's free blog-hosting service. To the average Internet surfer, the site and the accompanying blog seemed to be truly homemade. For weeks, "Dana" would post clues and mysterious stories about the fate of her uncle, and the site that he set up that was

---

82. Ross Fadner, "Blog Promoting Mazda Removed After Drawing Fire," *Media Post Media Daily News*, November 1, 2004.
83. Ibid.

mysteriously hacked. Apparently, shortly after the hack attack, her uncle disappeared. Chatter about the site among bloggers and surfers began to rise, until a number of cybersleuths discovered that the entire hoax was an elaborate prerelease marketing effort for a Microsoft X-Box game called Halo2, developed by Bungie Studios. The buzz about the hoax was greater than it was for the site and blog. Many felt tricked by the tactics; others, more keen to the sensibilities of "game geeks" and "cybernerds," thought that this was the only way to reach them.

Game developer and marketer Sega has rolled out its own elaborate blog hoax to hype the release of ESPN NFL Football 2K4 game, which was competing against the heavily favored Madden Football 2004 from Electronic Arts (EA). The unbranded and homemade blog revolved around a fictional video game tester named Beta-7, who began to suffer from blackouts and uncontrollable fits of violence after playing the new Sega game. To document and publicize these strange out-breaks, he started writing a blog on www.beta-7.com. Video posts showed strangers tackling pedestrians on the street. Other bloggers began contributing their own stories of blackouts and violent fits after playing the game. Confidential memos obtained from Sega were "leaked" on the blog, showing corporate concern over their consumers' health problems and instigating a cover-up campaign to keep the adverse side effects hidden from the public. Finally, after four months of blogging, the site was "shut down" by Sega's heavy-handed team of lawyers, and replaced with a Sega-sanctioned antiseptic site called Gamerchuck.

Of course, it is now clear that Beta-7 was a fake blog written and manipulated by a boundary-pushing ad agency. In effect, the entire campaign was a guerrilla marketing campaign without disclosure. It was conceived by Portland, Oregon–based Wieden & Kennedy to compete with the marketing muscle of EA's Madden franchise, and to cut through the blogging chatter to reach the hard-core gamers. The ad hoc, do-it-yourself nature of the blog was spectacularly calculated by a major agency, which even hired the producers of *The Blair Witch Project*—the do-it-yourself movie hoax phenomenon—to create the video clips and personal testimonies of Beta-7 and his cohorts.

A dedicated team from Wieden & Kennedy "lived and breathed" this campaign, running it off the cuff and improvising new story lines for four months before the launch of the game. The deception was multifaceted. As reported in *Advertising Age* magazine, the creative leads at Wieden & Kennedy sent out nine copies of the game to real-life gamers in unmarked envelopes, then quickly sent them a corporate letter from Sega demanding the return of the games. The agency's creatives bought fake classified newspaper ads seeking other game testers who were experiencing the game's side effects. They even posted messages on the blog itself claiming it was a hoax.[84] To this day, even as the world has been made aware of the hoax, postings on the blog declare that Beta-7 himself insists that the idea that the whole thing was a marketing hoax is actually a cover-up by Sega.

The editors at *Advertising Age* called the guerrilla marketing attack "one of the most daring and creative campaigns," and "fascinating improvised, interactive theater."[85] True guerrilla marketers call it deceptive, disingenuous, and inauthentic. The agency creatives and Sega execs would counter that dissembling tactics are necessary tools of the marketing trade when trying to reach the hard-core gamer or Web-savvy teen. True guerrilla marketers would say that they are not working hard

---

84. Jonah Bloom, "Inside Wieden & Kennedy's Great Sega Marketing Hoax," *Advertising Age,* January 19, 2004.
85. Ibid.

enough to reach gamers in a straightforward manner. If the idea is good enough, and the experience is authentic enough, there is no reason or benefit in hiding a marketing intention.

The music industry has been no less active in jump-starting buzz with deceptive and inauthentic tactics. Generating buzz for musicians perhaps started with Frank Sinatra, whose early-career manager hired throngs of cheering girls to stand outside his less-than-sold-out concerts. Music execs quickly followed up with payola—in which radio DJs were paid to spin particular records—to guarantee word-of-mouth and exposure. These two standby marketing tactics have transformed into online chat group buzzing and paid secret agent influencers. Music labels, flush with multimillion-dollar ad budgets, rely on hundreds of small boutique agencies and online communities to market their artists for them. In exchange for some free CDs, stickers, and T-shirts, hundreds of thousands of teens and young adults are spreading buzz about artists who are paying clients of the communities the teens belong to.

One such marketing community, called i-Squad, positions itself as "the first program on the net to reward music fans with points for helping their favorite artists. Our members make a big difference! The more active you are, the more chances you have of winning contests and getting better rewards from the online store by trading in your points! It's free to join and easy to take part."[86] Another music and entertainment buzz site, called BuzzAlong, says it's the "inside connection to information on upcoming albums, movies and video games. It also gives you access to exclusive contests to win world premier movie passes, concert tickets, cool gadgets, CDs, and T-shirts. Simply fill in the information to get connected."[87]

86. From the Web site: www.i-squad.com.
87. From the Web site: www.buzzalong.com.

This type of "fan club" marketing agency found itself in the middle of controversy at the tail end of 2004, when it was discovered that a number of "agents" lied when calling radio stations to request a pro-military ballad called "The Bumper of My SUV" by country singer Chely Wright. More than a dozen fan club members were encouraged by their manager to send letters to radio stations pretending they were the wives and sisters of men in the armed services. They would call in live on the air, pretending to be ex-servicemen. The fan club also infiltrated armed forces message boards and chat rooms to spread the buzz for the song. The campaign was exposed when the song was listed by *Billboard* magazine as the second-fastest-selling single in the country even though Wright was not signed to any major label, a rarity in the music business, which relies on the promotional and sales muscle of the big labels. The increased interest in such fantastic grassroots promotional success was the campaign's downfall. Eventually one of the buzz agents confessed to a Memphis newspaper about the deception.

Ethical Dead Ends

It is no surprise then that recent poll figures show that marketers and advertisers are seen as used-car salesmen and miracle-cure hucksters by jaded consumers. According to the Gallup Organization's poll from December 2004, only 10 percent of polled consumers rated ad execs' ethics as "very high" or "high," just ahead of car salesmen who scored 9 percent. By comparison, lawyers were next, with 18 percent. Only 51 percent of the respondents rated ad professionals' ethics as "average," and 35 percent rated them as "low" or "very low." The poll suggests that the perception of ethical conduct has been sliding steadily for ad execs and their ilk. By the way, nurses topped the list with 79 percent of the "very high" vote, followed by grade school teachers (73 percent) and pharmacists (72 percent).[88]

Unless marketers embody the simple notion of authenticity in their marketing strategies and tactics, the Gallup polls will continue to show the populace growing increasingly mistrustful of all things marketing. Disapproval numbers will continue to rise, brand trust will keep eroding, and the consumer will become even more calcified. In fact, it is the calcification of the consumer to traditional mass marketing that is making word-of-mouth an integral part of not just guerrilla marketing but also of the entire marketing mix for a brand, product, or service. Buzz works, and often the chase for its fruits takes form in less than honest tactics.

BzzAgent's own research offers clues to the effectiveness of buzz. A case study for Wharton School Publishing—a new venture from the Wharton School of Business at the University of Pennsylvania—posted on their site described a control test in which BzzAgent spread almost a thousand of its agents over five urban markets. No other marketing—media, guerrilla, promotional, etc.—was conducted in the areas. Twenty weeks later, the company compared these five areas against five control markets and found that the markets in which the agents operated outperformed the control markets by 66 percent in sales. The company also reported a four-week moving average of sales showing test markets trending up and control markets going down.

A case study for buzz marketing like this would convince many mainstream marketers to shift budgets into word-of-mouth programs. But it shouldn't convince them to shift their ethical boundaries as well. These boundaries are blurred when there is no obvious commercial framework to the campaigns, whether it is physical roaching using buzz agents or

88. Mercedes M. Cardona, "Ad Pros Still Get Low Scores for Honesty, Ethics," *Advertising Age*, December 7, 2004.

if the campaign is conducted online with planted posts and fake sites and blogs. When we are watching television, we are all prepared for the advertisements, product placements, and celebrity endorsements that come with it. There is context to the commercial messages being directed at us. But when there is no distinction—when random conversation or cool Web sites are actually marketing pitches—then marketing inauthenticity turns into consumer victimization. This is a key point to consider when devising an experiential marketing program: it should be conducted when and where the consumer chooses or is most receptive to it. By denying the consumer this choice and by taking advantage of her receptiveness to it through fake sites and deceptive word-of-mouth, marketers run the risk of further alienating consumers from creative marketing.

On the surface, buzz and roach marketing have indispensable experiential elements. Word-of-mouth is certainly a one-on-one interaction. Many consumers find it a benefit to know of new products or sites first, and often the imparted information is beneficial also. Buzz marketing is also heavily dependent on new technologies, or a new application for existing ones. The use of blogs for marketing effectiveness, for instance, is a perfect example. And clearly, word-of-mouth is principled on grassroots activation. These are all hallmarks of successful experiential marketing. Yet without authenticity, the experience is muddied by ethical constraints, and the consumer's adverse reaction to a blurred ethical boundary is palpable.

The backlash has already begun. Prompted by consumer advocacy groups, government watchdogs in both Canada and the United States have begun investigating less than authentic marketing practices and gauging their legality. The questions governmental agencies are considering are not ethical; they are legal. The Federal Trade Commission and the Federal Communications Commission are looking into forcing TV networks to disclose the integration of brands or products into programming, and how much they were paid to do so. Furthermore, the disclosure may need to be made onscreen at the beginning or end of the programming. The precedent for advertising disclosure rules was reinforced in 2002, when the FTC forced search engines to make a clear distinction between paid and unpaid content in search results listings. The FTC also stridently enforces that infomercials and advertorials are clearly identified on TV and in magazines, respectively.

Yet federal intervention will not be the demise of deceptive and inauthentic marketing. The marketplace will quash the practice, because marketing that blurs the line between the real world and its commercial counterpart will lose the support of the people. How many times will the typical consumer be duped with a hoax blog before he turns on the company that is duping him? And how long will we continue to listen to planted word-of-mouth and manufactured buzz before we stop believing what we hear? "For some [consumers], the ethical question amounts to just a vague twinge of discomfort when they realize a friend's excitement over a new product is part of an orchestrated corporate effort to create buzz on the street," writes Wharton School of Business professor Lisa Bolton. "For others, it raises the specter of a paranoid future where corporate marketers have invaded every last niche of society, degrading all social interaction to a marketing transaction, where no one can be certain of anyone else's true opinions or intentions."[89]

Research shows that negative word-of-mouth is seven times more powerful than positive word-of-mouth. That means that inauthentic buzz

89. Lisa Bolton, "What's the Buzz about Buzz Marketing?," *Wharton School of Business Marketing Magazine*, January 12, 2005.

marketing is its own worst enemy. If consumers are increasingly con-fronted with unethically derived buzz, the negative word-of-mouth will easily outweigh the positive. Furthermore, the paradox of buzz mar-keting—authentic or not—is such that the more it's done, the less effective it becomes. This paradox is exponentially compounded when some mar-keters choose to engage in buzz marketing through deceptive and inau-thentic means. "When everyone starts to do buzz marketing, it will just add to the clutter," Professor Bolton continues. "Then it will be about whoever has the most unique or effective campaign, whether it's a buzz campaign or not. It will be about what works. The rest is just noise."[90]

Subviral Marketing

In early 2004, sneaker maker Puma got a huge boost in buzz. Hipsters, fashionistas, and Internet junkies set the message boards ablaze and servers humming by distributing and downloading the greatest print ad Puma had ever conceived. The purveyors of übercool eagerly began to pump up Puma's street cred by referencing the image as a ground-breaking and brilliant leap in display ad creativity. It was provocative, daring, unambiguously sexual—even dirty. Certainly dirty.

Without inadvertently floating into the pornographic, I'll try to explain the ad obliquely: a woman in Puma sneakers is shown kneeling on the ground and, um, servicing a guy in Puma sneakers. The picture is cut off at the woman's shoulders, for a smattering of ambiguity. Oh, yeah, there's a Puma bag in there somewhere, corner logo placement and an unmentionable coup de grâce, too, but I won't go into it. Soon after the release of the images, Internet chatter on blogs and word-of-mouth

90. Ibid.

buzz in most urban circles of pop culture dilettantism were awash in Puma pandemonium.

Because the ad pushed the boundaries of mainstream thinking and broke social taboos—certainly exhibiting an ethos that is warmly embraced by the youth-dominated counter-culture and underground scenes—it was an instant success. Not surprisingly, the "alternative" crowd already marched in Puma sneakers. The resonance and relevance of the image was obvious.

But there was a problem: Puma never commissioned the ad. In fact, as soon as buzz reached critical mass, they declared the ads a fake and blitzed out cease-and-desist orders to various bloggers and sites, dangling legal action above anyone posting the "defamatory image." The heavy-handed corporate tactics started another round of blog buzz just as quickly as the ads themselves. This time, however, the buzz was less than favorable.

But what if you subscribe to the notion that even bad press is good press? Many cyberpundits, such as gawker.com, memefirst.com, and adrag.com, began to insinuate that Puma had sneaked in a buzz marketing double-dip through a remarkable online strategy: surreptitiously releasing the ad itself, then vehemently denying it had done so. Puma's counsel said in a statement: "Please be advised that such an offensive image was created without our knowledge or consent." Welcome to the wacky world of "subviral marketing."

Subviral marketing hinges on subversive parodies of well-known brands that are then distributed as either picture or video e-mail—usually with a "fwd:" tag in your in-box—and is based on the theory that satirizing a brand effectively triggers its mnemonic recognition in the consumer's subconscious. Subviral content has to look amateurish, feel subversive, usually display risqué content, and be totally deniable as corporate intrusion. Since subviral marketing won't really work if the companies fess up to releasing the parodies, the best subviral campaigns are indistinguishable from genuinely amateur Internet parodies.

According to London's *Guardian* newspaper, subviral marketing is the latest trend increasingly being employed by brand behemoths such as Budweiser, Levi's, and MasterCard. I should admit that 20 percent of my daily e-mail output involves forwarding off Internet detritus to peers across the world. Of course, I need to first filter out all the mundane, moronic, and puerile gaga that inexorably finds its way into the in-box—about 99.99 percent of all bit packets coursing through the pipelines. But a good and engaging "fwd:" will get my attention, and subsequently the attention of my peers, perhaps enough to spark a potential tipping point.

Subviral marketing hopes to capitalize on that creative spark, and whereas a buzzworthy amateur parody comes across once in a blue moon, a brand parody developed in top creative shops around the world has immediate impact in cyberspace. And therein lies the temptation for major mass marketers to embrace self-mocking machinations.

Since the Puma photo hit the scene, dozens of Internet brand parodies have been put under the microscope by cyberpundits. There's the Nokia short video that shows a ceiling fan flinging a cat across the room. There's a Levi's spoof called "Rub Yourself," which reveals an onanistic teenager doing exactly what the title purports. There's the infamous MasterCard "Priceless" parody about a drunken teen couple and the guy's less than successful attempts for a happy ending on the girl's front porch. And who can forget Budweiser's "Wassup" parodies that inundated Western society's outlook a few years ago? These are now suspected of being prototypical subviral campaigns that tipped over into mass phenomena, with wide debate as to whether the clips are amateur subversive genius or ad agency brilliance.

Ultimately the debate is inconsequential because it's ephemeral, as most things on the Internet are. But from a marketer's perspective, lessons learned from subviral marketing are not inconsequential in the least. As a report by New York–based marketing and branding firm Harvest Communications attests, "whether they are negative or positive, brand parodies offer companies invaluable consumer insight that is not forced out of a focus group, but homegrown and authentic. They offer us clues about what resonates with customers, what concerns them and [are] possible early indicators of public opinion."

Certainly Puma got a sneak peek into the heads of their target customers. For two weeks after the images were posted, thousands of message board posts relayed the rants, raves, and opinions of the so-called mavens, connectors, and influencers of pop culture. Today marketers can create interest and buzz using creative executions rather than buzz agents alone. Major brands and corporations are mandating that their marketing and advertising suppliers get creative with their ideas, not with the ways to willfully deceive the consumer. The types of sites are characterized by a sort of creativity and chutzpah that is a bit too racy and risky for a mainstream brand to embrace fully throughout their entire marketing mix. Yet by isolating the boundary-pushing creative to a microsite, marketers are able to experiment with what works and monitor what doesn't.

Sometimes, to further distance the brand from the over-the-top creative, marketers release their work on the Internet without attribution or pretending that the creative was created by amateur fans of the brand. The buzz that is created, however, is predicated on the deniability of the creative execution itself. But there is something inherently wrong with the notion that the only way to break through the clutter with dynamic creative is to deny creating it in the first place.

Buzzworthy Buzz

Experiential marketers depend on the fact that the experience of each individual human being with the marketing campaign will be positive and relevant enough to organically spread buzz. Buzz marketing is an invaluable experiential marketing tool, but one that can work only if authentic and upfront with its intentions. It is up to experiential marketers to ensure that all future marketing doesn't add to the noise. Still, many traditional marketers are satisfied with creating word-of-mouth by any means necessary. This strategy is ill-advised and short sighted. A recent study from Dublin-based Research and Markets showed that in Europe, 58 percent of consumers do not trust corporations and therefore rely on the "relative credibility, honesty and impartiality of word-of-mouth."[91] If artificial buzz becomes the norm with marketers, then brand trust and the consumer's faith in word-of-mouth endorsements will virtually disappear.

Why would marketers want to pursue inauthentic marketing strategies? The typical answer involves something about the increasing difficulties reaching the consumer through traditional marketing and advertising. The almost total disavowal of mass media marketing by the younger generations, and the interconnectivity that these generations leverage through new mobile technologies, is also cited as a main reason for stealth buzz activities and employment of buzz agents. Although the reality of an ever-sophisticated and immune consumer is certainly upon us, resorting to inauthentic marketing tactics is a disconnected rationale from the desires of that consumer. To say that a fake blog or Web site is the only way to reach her is entirely erroneous. And to spark

91. "Viral and Word-of-Mouth Marketing Study," Research and Markets, October 15, 2004.

word-of-mouth through paid buzz agents and deceived participants is just plain lazy. Legitimate buzz can be sparked rather easily if you are willing to be authentic and experiential with the marketing campaign.

Take, for instance, the idea of a fake blog. One of the most talked-about and successful blog campaigns of 2004 was Nike's Art of Speed. The shoe giant commissioned fifteen hipster filmmakers to interpret their ideas of speed through short films. Nike then approached the very popular postmodern gossip site *gawker.com*—part of well-known blog developer Denton Publishing—to produce the Art of Speed Web log. Although some blog purists objected to the commercialization of the blog medium, most of them commended the excellent integration of content and personal publishing that Nike pulled off by leveraging www.gawker.com's authenticity and ethos. The effort paid off. A corporate behemoth such as Nike had won over cynical bloggers and online pundits with a marketing campaign that didn't camouflage its intentions.

Miami hotshot agency Crispin Porter & Bogusky has broken through the clutter with dynamic creative and Internet seeding without resorting to deception or dissembled messaging. In April 2004 their groundbreaking work for client Burger King was able to connect with a media-savvy and extremely chatty youthful audience through innovative online marketing that started a viral (buzz spreading like a virus from one consumer to another) stampede. It was called www.subservientchicken.com. The site—advertising the new Burger King Chicken Tender Crisp sandwich and playing off of Burger King's "Have It Your Way" tagline—featured a man dressed in a chicken suit standing in the middle of his living room. Visitors to the site were able to type in commands to the chicken, and the chicken would perform them. The site generated more than 46 million hits in one week.

The site's design is a play off of more "mature" Webcam sites dedicated to late-night Webcam "action." Users type in commands, and the chicken does them. The site spawned more than a dozen web sites dedicated to documenting all the commands the chicken will perform. If someone typed in an inappropriate command, the chicken would wag a finger at the user. Fan sites began to reverse-engineer the site to figure out what naughty actions the chicken could make. Less obsessed fans of the site would visit to type in a handful of commands, chuckle at the simple coolness of the campaign, and pass it along to their friends. The chicken got 6 million to 8 million daily visitors. Average visits lasted seven and nine minutes.[92] Three thirty-second TV commercials displayed the address for the site and ran on MTV, Comedy Central, Spike TV, and BET. The commercials feature the same chicken in an amateur-cam setting and a number of twentysomethings giving the chicken its orders.

The chicken quickly garnered major buzz among the hipsters and young media omnivores. Even though the integrated subservient chicken campaign was both a mass media and Internet play, and done for a mainstream ad shop for a multinational fast food chain, the campaign was remembered mainly for the site and the word-of-mouth it generated. Although there was a bit of initial head-scratching for the existence of the chicken, the young audience quickly embraced the cool absurdity of it, and the technology that enabled a Webcam guy in a chicken suit to act out personal commands for millions of people. Crispin Porter & Bogusky never hid their advertising intentions. The Burger King logo appeared at the bottom of the site, and the television commercial was clearly an ad for a chicken sandwich. Yet the buzz for

92. Janis Mara, "Burger King Hen Whets Chicken Yen," *Clickz News* (formerly *Internet Advertising Report*), April 16, 2004.

the subservient chicken was phenomenal enough to extend the campaign for two new chicken sandwiches.

More recently, Crispin Porter & Bogusky unleashed another buzz-generating site, www.comeclean.com, where visitors are encouraged to type in their confessions to wash away their sins, and can read other visitors' sinful confessions. The typed-in confessions then appear above a sink, where they can be washed away with soap that can be bought with a click of the mouse. The site was created for Method, a San Francisco-based soap marketer.

Reputation Networks

Creative executions like this and others are the latest trend in marketing that harnesses word-of-mouth without being deceptive or dodgy. They are a testament to those that say buzz marketing is not reliant on buzz agents alone. The best buzz is sparked by good creative and fresh messaging, not creative scripts delivered by paid messengers. Stodgy mainstream brands such as Microsoft, Best Buy, Alaskan Airlines, and Intel are using fabulously creative microsites to reach an elusive marketplace. They are able to leverage their mainstream marketing budgets into driving a cynical audience to a creative execution that quickly wins them over with humor, mystery, parody, and technology. This makes the site memorable and the brand engaging. And the intended audience is surprised and entertained enough to start the viral word-of-mouth pass-along. If the site reaches the tipping point and "tips" over, a creative microsite such as Subservient Chicken can run circles around traditional advertising and marketing—at a fraction of the cost.

These types of sites are excellent online examples of experiential marketing and will soon become a mainstay in brand building and advertising. By making a site visit as experiential as possible with personalized interactions, deep engagement, memorable creativity, innovation, and authenticity, a brand can quickly establish an element of audience attachment and trust that is missing in traditional marketing and advertising. By being authentic—certainly irreverent but authentic—the brand regains trust in the eyes of the consumer. If this trust can be translated online with the tools and technology to spread buzz outside of physical word-of-mouth, then brand reputation can acquire greater momentum than word-of-mouth spread by buzz agents.

The bottom line is that "as sophisticated as marketing became, it has never overcome the ability of people to smell the BS behind all the marketing perfume."[93] *The Cluetrain Manifesto* posits that the marketplace is one giant conversation, and "the only advertising that was ever truly effective was word-of-mouth, which is nothing more than conversation. . . . Further, these voices are telling one another the truth based on their real experiences, unlike the corporate messages that aim at presenting what we can generously call a best-case scenario."[94] In this context, word-of-mouth marketing performed by the likes of BzzAgent and Girls Intelligence Agency is tapping into the next phase of marketing, one that is no longer dependent on mass messages and media empires. But is it authentic?

The chapters in this book are all based on the premise that experiential marketing is the best methodology to tap into the buzz that is indispensable to brands and companies trying to break through the clutter. Yet word-of-mouth—quality and valuable buzz—cannot be established

93. Rick Levine, Christopher Locke, Doc Searls, and David Weinberg, *The Cluetrain Manifesto* (Cambridge, MA: Perseus Books Group, 2001), p. 80.
94. Ibid., p. 83.

without trust or positive reputation. That is why the Word of Mouth Marketing Association (WOMMA) published a code of ethics for marketers deploying word-of-mouth campaigns. The upstart buzz advocacy group—which counts Procter & Gamble's Tremor, BzzAgent, BuzzMetrics, and Intelliseek as governing board members—hopes a self-promulgated manifesto will keep criticism about inauthentic marketing out of the word-of-mouth sphere.

At the time of this writing, the "WOMMA Code" was released as a draft to a wide spectrum of marketing and business professionals, to add comments and amendments. So far it looks something like this: "1. Consumer protection and respect are paramount—we respect and promote practices that abide by an understanding that the consumer—not the marketer—is fundamentally in charge, in control, and dictates the terms of the consumer-marketer relationship. 2. We practice openness about the relationships among consumers, advocates, and marketers. We encourage word-of-mouth advocates to disclose their relationship with marketers in their communications with other consumers. We don't tell them specifically what to say, but we do instruct them to be open and honest about any relationship with a marketer and about any products or incentives they may have received. Manner of disclosure can be flexible, based on the context of the communication. Explicit disclosure is not required for an obviously fictional character, but would be required for an artificial identity or corporate representative that could be mistaken for an average consumer. 3. We respect the rights of any online or offline communications venue (such as a Web site, blog, discussion forum, traditional media, live setting, etc.) to create and enforce its rules as it sees fit. 4. We manage relationships with minors responsibly. 5. We protect privacy and permission."

To the cynic, a bunch of buzz marketers publishing a code of ethics on buzz marketing isn't going to stop inauthentic marketing from occurring in everyday conversation online or on the street. To other, more pragmatic types, the WOMMA Code is a proactive attempt at stymieing any legislative efforts to curb online chat marketing, especially that aimed at children and teens. To the realist, it is important to note that WOMMA has not yet figured out how to enforce its own "code" or whether they will force a giant like P&G—one of its governing board members, no less—to stick to it. But it is a good start at stopping inauthentic marketing, nevertheless.

But a WOMMA Code really isn't needed anyway. It will certainly curb the abuses and liberties taken by unscrupulous marketers, but it won't be the demise of inauthentic marketing. Reputation systems will do that for us. Controlling brand reputation is no longer in the hands of brand managers. It's in the hands of networked consumers who are part of vast, interconnected social networks that can spread buzz about an inauthentic marketing campaign faster than the campaign itself. The Internet has already opened up the conversation for these networks through chat rooms, instant messaging, and message boards, which carry millions of published and searchable brand recommendations, warnings, and discussions. Weblogging will tip this type of recommendation-sharing into an epidemic.[95]

To new media guru Howard Rheingold, reputation is "even more important in commerce that it is in conversation. Without some kind of trust metric, e-commerce would never have become possible."[96] Just think of eBay as an example. Even though the company clears billions in merchandise sales through millions of vendors and buyers, it offers no

95. Howard Rheingold, *Smart Mobs: The Next Social Revolution* (Cambridge, MA: Perseus Books Group, 2002), p. 116.
96. Ibid., p. 123.

warranty for its auctions. It is a site that puts buyers and sellers together
for a small listings fee, manages the auction process, and provides a reputation management system for its users. Incredibly, 99.9 percent of all
transactions were successfully completed. Millions of strangers feel
secure enough on eBay to come together and do some business without
fear of being ripped off or defrauded. Retail businesses have higher rates
of theft than eBay, primarily because the reputation system automatically weeds out and excludes the troublemakers. Buyers and sellers on
eBay rate each other on a scale of +1, 0, or -1, and comment on the site's
message boards about each other. All feedback comments have to be
connected to a transaction. In other words, only the seller and the winning bidder can leave comment. Over time, reliable sellers get a good
reputation and the less scrupulous ones never make a sale.

Retailers are paying close attention to reputation networks, and marketers should do the same. Today's consumers and customers are
flocking to their peers in social networks for recommendations on what
to buy. Although there are still a relatively limited amount of sites that
allow consumers to buy something online through a referral from a
friend or relative, social networking is seen as the "next big thing" for
the Internet in years to come. In e-commerce terms, a site call Yub is
using social networking to sell products. Yub is designed so that when a
visitor clicks on and purchases a product linked from a Yub profiled
member's content page, the member and the purchaser split a reward,
such as a coupon valued at 2 to 5 percent of the friend's purchase. Yub
is also providing its technology platform to other retailers, allowing
them to piggyback off it to launch their own e-commerce social networks. Pretty soon thousands of retailers will allow their own visitors to
do the buying and selling for them. People will be able to search for
people as well as products according to specific interests and needs.

People's reputations—not brands, products, or companies—will compose the marketplace of the future. In this marketplace the only choice for marketers is to reduce the hype and increase the honesty.

Chapter 4

Experiential marketing is based on engaging people in memorable ways.

Tell me and I'll forget.
Show me and I may remember.
Involve me and I'll understand.

—Confucius, Chinese philosopher, 551–479 B.C.

This proverb may have been meant for something other than being appropriated by experiential marketers. Perhaps Confucius meant this quote for mathematics, or maybe it was civics that he was speaking of. Maybe the involvement he was referring to was in agriculture or engineering. Perhaps Confucius was talking about, well, Confucianism. But whatever the quote may have meant to his followers thousands of years ago, today it has graced the covers and inside pages of myriad PowerPoint presentations shot up on the boardroom screens by hundreds, if not thousands, of experiential marketers in North America and Europe. This quote has been repeated over and over by marketers who are trying to convince an ad-obsessed marketplace that there is something better. This is the quote that cuts to the heart of experiential marketing and that positions this chapter's tenets clearly against the general ethos of mass marketing.

Advertising and traditional marketing are all about telling consumers something. It's a one-way—a monologue—a cynical dictum from the top, down through the pipes to the masses. Experiential marketing truly rejects this paradigm. Instead, the practitioners of experiential marketing hold dear the last two Confucian lines of the koan. They seek to bring the brand and product from behind the electric screen, or off of the printed page, and show it directly to the consumer. Then they seek to involve her, to engage her, and to embrace her. This, as Confucius ultimately says, is how the consumer will truly remember and uncompromisingly understand the brand or product.

Who would ever know that it was Confucius—and not the likes of Phil Knight at Nike or Starbucks' Howard Schultz—who was the first experiential marketer? Confucius knew that the value of telling an individual something could not begin to compare with the value of showing the thing he is talking about to his friend. Furthermore, the value of showing it is far less than the value of giving the thing to his friend and letting him understand it for himself. If this thinking is taken into the marketing realm—and the "thing" is a product or, more abstractly, a brand—it mirrors and inspires the thinking of experiential marketers. The immediate real-world analogy to this thinking is the way that cars are sold to practically everyone in the world. Billions of newspaper, magazine, billboard, classified, radio, poster, and TV ads are created to tell us about a car. A one-on-one personal interaction with a salesman in the showroom, and a hands-on test drive, show us the car beyond the two-dimensional visual cues of print and TV advertising. But how often do consumers get involved with the car or the carmaker's brand?

Of course, to traditional marketers the involvement comes from the salesman's pitch and a scheduled test drive around the block. For those marketers who believe in staging an experience to achieve true involvement, this is not enough. Just think of all the balloons dropping in the background of a TV pitch for another "crazy, blowout, clearing the lot, everything must go" car sale. The lack of response to this tactic has led most carmakers to offer cash incentives and myriad forms of discounts to get consumers to buy their cars. This is simply the exact opposite of what experiential marketing seeks to accomplish.

The experience should be the value driver, not a cash incentive or an oversize coupon. The showroom experience and the test drive are not entirely experiential because involvement has not been transformed into *engagement*. Consumers expect the pushy salesman and they demand the test drive. There is nothing surprising or memorable about being involved in this way. It is a service performed by all car marketers.

The Confucian approach has been sublimely echoed and expanded by Joseph Pine and James Gilmore in their seminal work *The Experience Economy*, published twenty-five hundred years after the great master uttered his three-liner. The first half of their book deals with taking the *involvement* evoked by Confucius and transforming it into *engagement* by staging brand and product experiences. Their insights and sentiments are easily applied to the car industry example. "In a Service Economy, the lack of differentiation in customers' minds causes goods to face the constant price pressure indelibly associated with commodities. As a result, customers more and more purchase goods solely on a price and availability." Hence all those showroom rebates, TV hooplah, 0 percent financing, and "you pay what we pay" price promotions.

It is clear that companies must stage experiences for their offerings, which is as tangible as any service, product, or commodity. But it is not enough to simply wrap an experience around a traditional offering to sell them better, like a car dealership trumpeting its latest blowout sale. As Pine and Gilmore contend, to realize the full benefit of staging experiences, businesses must "deliberately design engaging experiences that command a fee. . . . This transition from selling services to selling experiences will be no easier for established companies to undertake and weather than the last great economic shift from the industrial to the service economy."

The car industry, not surprisingly, is embracing the shift earlier than most other business segments. They are transitioning their marketing initiatives into designed experiences "that are compelling, engaging, memorable—and rich" to lead the way into the emerging experience economy. General Motors' Saturn brand, for instance, has positioned itself as the car company that eschews pushy salespeople and instead focuses on the hassle-free experience of the consumer. Their latest advertising platform is based on humanism and emotional attachment to the Saturn brand, and their TV ads reflect the hands-off approach to selling cars. Volkswagen has picked up on this sentiment with its latest salvo of ads. And Scion, a specialty brand from Toyota, has positioned itself as almost an "antibrand" to the way cars are sold, relying on the notion of customizable cars as opposed to a take-it-or-leave-it approach in the showroom. Since each individual consumer is unique, the Scion people expect to deliver him a car that is just as unique as he is.

A New Test Drive Experience

Of course, these ploys and brand positions are meant to differentiate car manufacturers from their competition. But it is telling that the differentiation is not coming in the form of price deals, rebates, or the latest celebrity-endorsed shill. These efforts are aimed at making the car-buying experience better, and therefore positioning the brand as consumer-focused and relevant compared to traditional car salesmanship. Still, car marketers find that a repositioning is not enough because it does not fully engage the consumer. Sure, the new-brand promise of "have it your way" car buying is a valuable way to sell more cars. But consumers are demanding even more. In response, car behemoth General Motors introduced the "twenty-four-hour test drive' in early 2003, and in doing so, introduced an entirely new way of engaging consumers, and keeping them engaged after the test drive is over.

Between April 2003 and July 2004, more than 766,000 consumers were able to get into a GM vehicle, take it off the lot, and spend the next twenty-four hours putting it through its paces. Since the offer allowed the potential buyer to drive the car for as many as a hundred miles, the possibilities of getting engaged with the car are wide open. Imagine the differences from a showroom test drive. A consumer can get into his or her ride and pump up the stereo. She can drive to all her friends' houses, pick them up, take them for a spin into town, and get their opinions. She can go to the grocery store to see how many shopping bags fit into the trunk. The family can all pile into the car and see how the kids like it. They can witness the fuel efficiency for themselves, instead of trusting the window sticker promises. After a hundred miles, how much does it cost to fill up the tank? And how does it feel to wake up and see the car in the driveway in the morning? These experiences are key engagement tools meant to take the car-buying process into the consumers' world, instead of expecting them to relate to and appreciate the traditional showroom experience. After more than 750,000 twenty-four-hour test drives, the company sold 270,000 cars.[97]

The success of this program prompted the likes of Subaru, Audi, Cadillac, and Volvo to offer twenty-four-hour test drives to their

97. Kristi Arellano, "Try Before You Buy," *Denver Post,* January 9, 2005.

potential customers as well. The idea spread further to other high-priced goods, such as washing machines and ovens. The "try it before you buy it" concept—an experiential marketing strategy based on engaging the potential consumer with the product, instead of selling it to her—has been wholly embraced by Maytag in their "test drive" stores throughout North America. Working with their independent retailers, Maytag is committed to setting up test-drive areas in their stores, where consumers can get a hands-on experience with their products. For example, before buying a Jenn-Air convection oven, a consumer can bring in a twenty-five-pound turkey to see if it can fit and how well it gets cooked. Consumers can bring in a load of laundry and try out the washing machine and dryer. Many consumers bring in their favorite comforter or other large items that they are attached to in order to see for themselves that the machines will be able to handle them. The test-drive stores even keep rolls of cookie dough or dozens of pairs of jeans on hand, in case consumers forget to bring something to try out the machines and ovens. Maytag has opened forty-one stores with the new format and plans fifty more in 2005.[98]

Much like the twenty-four-hour test drive, these "try before you buy" initiatives have been developed to show a potential customer how the product's fits into his or her life. Instead of the typical bells and whistles of come-on salesmanship, this experiential approach allows consumers to be engaged in the product's attributes on a personal level. This is not simply an interactive showroom, where one can push buttons or turn knobs. Best Buy, a company known for allowing consumers to fiddle with their products in the stores, is building mock rooms in their retail spaces furnished like any typical den or living room but outfitted with

---

98. Michael Barbaro, "In-Store Testing: A Recipe That Sells," *Washington Post,* July 8, 2004.

the latest electronics offerings. The retailer invites consumers to hang out, kick off their shoes, and watch the big game on wide-screen plasma screens and surround-sound speakers.

This type of marketing isn't a quick sales tactic. A typical shopper spends an average of two hours at Whirlpool Corporation's twelve-hundred-thousand-square-foot studio store. The company says that 90 percent of shoppers buy a Whirlpool appliance after experiencing it in the "test drive" store.[99] At Maytag stores, the ones set up with "test drive" rooms see sales twice as large as at the regular stores. More interestingly, consumes buy more than one appliance after seeing how the range, refrigerator, and dishwasher work and fit together. In a marketplace where 75 to 80 percent of consumers leave a store without making a purchase because of an inability to find products or to differentiate among them, engaging consumers with a "test drive" is the latest experience that gets them to buy.[100]

The Ultimate Test Drive

If appliancemakers are taking cues from the car dealerships' test drives, they must be contemplating even greater consumer engagements, as car marketers are now taking test drives to the next level. Automakers have begun pouring big money into elaborate events that give hundreds or thousands of prospective customers a chance to go for a spin. But this is no ordinary drive around the block. Car marketers are using event marketing, either staging their own or piggybacking on existing events, to provide potential car buyers a one-of-a-kind experience they will never forget.

99. Ibid.
100. Retail Industry Leaders' Association.

For example, in 2004 Ford had set up a temporary test track in the parking lot of Dodger Stadium in Los Angeles to let more than two thousand consumers take a fast-paced lap in a new Ford 500 sedan and Mustang coupe, while local hard rock bands played live to provide the sound track to the thrill. General Motors set up four test courses at El Toro air base in California and invited ten thousand potential customers to drive virtually the entire car lineup that GM offers. Cadillac connected with hundreds of thousands of 2004 Super Bowl attendees in Jacksonville by stationing more than four hundred of their most popular and head-turning models around town and in front of trendy restaurants, offering dinner test drives to high-end consumers. Giving an even bigger thrill is DaimlerChrysler AG's Chrysler unit, which will get hundreds of potential customers to buckle up with professional drivers and take a hundred-mile-per-hour spin around the track at the Daytona 500 in a Dodge Viper or Charger. For the Chicago Auto Show in 2005, Chrysler spent about $3 million to truck in tons of dirt and gravel to build a half-mile test track, including an off-road course, to demonstrate the climbing capabilities of its Jeep cars. It figures that about seventy-five thousand consumers will take a spin in the dirt.[101]

The reason for staging these types of events is quite obvious: the experience. The thrill of the drive, and the enhanced experience of trying out the features of a vehicle at an optimal place to do so, is an incomparable sales tactic. Furthermore, these events allow carmakers to connect with a specific consumer base, such as affluent consumers who wish to compare a Cadillac STS to a BMW, or ethnic consumers such as the Hispanic market, which Ford targeted with the Dodger Stadium event.

Mercedes-Benz USA's "Love Mercedes Tour" sends the entire car

101. Neal E. Boudette, "Auto Makers Give a New Spin to Test Drives," *The Day*, February 5, 2005.

lineup to twelve cities across the country, allowing consumers an extravagant driving experience on a number of modified courses, while simultaneously raising money for college scholarships in each market. Mercedes has been conducting experiential driving events like these for fifteen years, simply because the company is able to "build relationship and establish the connection with the brand in a way that's relevant, nonintrusive, and, let's not forget, fun," leading most consumers attending these events to be "significantly more likely to buy a Mercedes once they've had the opportunity to get behind the wheel."[102] These events are so successful and compelling that *other brands* are signing on as sponsors. In 2004 the Love Mercedes Tour featured corporate "partners" such as Benjamin Moore Paints, Evian Spring Water, Saks Fifth Avenue, Canon Power Shot, MSN Direct, and Wilson Sporting Goods alongside Mercedes' recognizable logo.

To create such an experience takes considerable investment. In fact, experiential driving events are more expensive than traditional advertising in terms of impressions and cost per thousand (CPM).[103] But they are impressive in scope, immersion, engagement, and memorable brand affinity. For instance, GM requires about a million square feet of open asphalt for its Auto Show in Motion driving event. There are only about thirty-eight places in the whole country where this is feasible. This is a logistical nightmare. There are rental issues, insurance issues, maintenance issues, and scheduling issues. There are a thousand and one more headaches than calling up an ad agency and ordering a slew of new ads. But that is why staging experiences is more a discipline than an art.

And it's worth it. It gets consumers to buy. After querying consumers at a Boston event, Cadillac found that only a third of them had an

102. Ibid.
103. Paul Ferriss, "Off Road with Purpose," *Marketing Magazine*, August 23, 2004.

"excellent" perception of the brand before they got into one of its cars. After the event was done, more than 80 percent of those same consumers thought Cadillac was an "excellent" brand. After thirty-six thousand visitors to the New York Auto Show took a Jeep on the off-road course, about 8 percent of them bought a Jeep within six months. That means that close to three thousand people bought a car because of the experience.[104] You can't reach those levels of consumer response with direct mail, e-mail, or TV advertising. Clearly, the experience can enhance a brand. Better still, the experience sells product.

If the experience is truly engaging, you can charge for it heartily. The Canadian subsidiary of Mercedes Benz puts on one-day courses at an Ontario racetrack with Formula One–themed driving event for $12,000 per participant. Mercedes-Benz also puts on a Driving School event that gets consumers into eighteen different Mercedes-Benz models for $1,000 a day. BMW Canada's Driver Training gets participants into the 330 series for $480 a day. The car marketer also has introduced target-specific events called the Young Persons Driver Training for sixteen- and seventeen-year old drivers, as well as a Ladies Only Driving Training course . . . all for a fee, of course. A weekend-long Winter Driver Course, complete with a three-night stay at a four-star hotel in Quebec, costs $3,800, which incorporates BMW's 7 Series luxury sedan and the X5 SUV. "Ultimately, a business is defined by that for which it collects revenue," Pine and Gilmore attest, "and it collects revenue only for that which it decides to charge." Clearly, an engaging experience is worth the decision to charge admission.

104. Suzanne Vranica, "Super Bowl XXXIX: Obstacle Course vs. "Potty Palooza'," *Wall Street Journal*, January 24, 2005.

The Main Event

Forward-thinking brand marketers are at the forefront of staging experiential events to engage each individual consumer, and provide a valuable one-on-one opportunity to connect with the core consumer. These
events are made for the core consumer. In fact, according to BMW, about
30 percent of consumers who attend the Driver Training events are
current BMW owners.[105] These people are brand evangelists. They are a
potent source of viral buzz pass-along and word-of-mouth. If they have
a phenomenal experience, they will let their peers know about it. "People
want a lifestyle experience, an activity in which they can participate and
walk away with a positive feeling based on that participation. They want
that experience to be interesting, memorable, and unique to their particular psychographic—which is a reflection of the activities, interests
and opinions of a specific population."[106] It is no longer enough to hold
an event that is designed for the masses. Experiential event marketing
cannot be all things to all people.

In a blur of commercialism and spirituality, GM sponsored an evangelical concert tour to buckle up the Bible Belt in 2004. The "Chevrolet
Presents: Come Together and Worship" tour featured a multimedia worship service, distribution of free evangelical pamphlets, and a concert by
holy rockers Third Day. The average venue size for the tour was fourteen
thousand seats. That's no tent revival; it's a major tour. So is Chevy a God-
approved truck? Are the Four Horsemen really Cavaliers? On the surface,
a major corporation sponsoring religion is unsettling to many people.
But why? Major corporations have for years sponsored contentious gay
pride initiatives and campaigns, enough so that some nonprofit gay rights

105. Paul Ferriss, "Off Road With Purpose," *Marketing Magazine*, August 23, 2004.
106. Sylvia Allen, "The Future of Event Marketing," *Event Solutions,* January 18, 2005.

organizations have come to bemoan the saturation of corporate presence in a rights movement. What makes the religious movement verboten to advertisers? It's just good niche marketing by using experiential event marketing to connect with a core consumer base.

Event marketing is loosely defined as a series of planned events that gets the consumer to interact hands-on with a product or service. It also can be seen as a form of brand promotion or brand communication tactic that ties the brand to a meaningful activity. It involves taking a company's story, product, or brand out of its more traditional advertising and marketing venues to "engage consumers or key stakeholders in a unique, out-of-the-box way that's credible and relevant."[107] In Canada, beer marketer Guinness has taken its brand story and premise to launch a series of events through its Guinness Party of Canada platform, culminating in a rally at Parliament Hill to lobby lawmakers to make St. Patrick's Day a national holiday. The event, along with invitation-only beer-themed events for Guinness Party members, has raised sales for the brand by a dramatic 20 percent.[108]

The propensity to spread brand value, perception, trial, and purchase through experience has contributed greatly to the rise of event marketing to engage the consumer in ways that traditional marketing has been failing to do. According to an annual survey by the George P. Johnson Company, 82 percent of responding marketing agencies planned to use event marketing as part of their overall marketing mix in 2004, a 6 percent increase from the year before. Event marketing is a fast-growing tactic, and an indispensable part of the experiential marketing mix, because events offer an incredible opportunity for one-on-one interactions and because the consumer is most receptive to the

107. Sarah Dobson, "The Main Event," *Marketing Magazine*, September 13, 2004.
108. Ibid.

brand when it is surrounded by a great experience. Live events, many of which include entertainment and hands-on product interactions, can range from huge concerts such as Vans Warped Tour or sports extravaganzas such as NASCAR races and the Super Bowl, to smaller events at street festivals and malls, which also can garner the best interactions.

Event marketing also can include highly targeted mobile tours or guerrilla street teams, which travel to specific locations to engage specific consumers. In fact, the definition of event marketing is somewhat broad. It can include terms such as *intercept marketing, field marketing, mobile marketing, guerrilla marketing, grassroots marketing, proximity marketing,* and *live marketing*. It can include sponsorships, street sampling, product launches, media events, and promotions. But the undercurrent to all these terms and phrases is simple: it is marketing where and when the core consumer is most receptive to learning about and experiencing a product or brand. And it is a time to engage the consumer. Anytime she can get closer to a product or service outside of the traditional mass media, and interact with the product and service in a credible and relevant way, you have a campaign that's clearly under the event marketing umbrella. In other words, event marketing is experiential.

Promo magazine reported that U.S. marketers spent a total of $132.4 *billion* on event marketing in 2002, a 15 percent jump from the prior year. In 2003, that figure rose another 15 percent, and 2004 was expected to grow by 20 percent. The recognizable need by marketers to reach and be relevant to a jaded and highly sophisticated consumer is certainly fueling these numbers. Event marketing is an easy-to-understand manifestation of the rise of experiential marketing, because live face-to-face interactions with consumers are at the heart of the practice, which leads to meaningful consumer engagement with the brand. Coupled with the notion of "bringing a brand to life" or activating it though nontraditional methods, the rise of event marketing is bound to continue as an experiential discipline.

Nike's agency in Italy recently produced an event tour that mimicked its TV commercials for a new soccer shoe. Called the Scorpion Knock-Out Tour, the events featured an exact replica of the TV commercial, setting the tour to the plot of the ads by creating a three-on-three soccer tournament held inside the belly of an abandoned ship. Consumers were already exposed to the high-energy, quick-cut style of the ads, so they understood the event as soon as they engaged in it. The core consumers—diehard soccer fanatics—did more than just step into a branded environment; they were immersed in the ad itself. Westin re-created the ad platform for its Heavenly Bed campaign by turning Wall Street into dozens of hotel rooms, with models taking a nap in the new beds. For Sheraton's introduction of the Sweet Sleeper beds, Westin took over Central Park to stage the world's biggest pillow fight with six hundred employees and guests. By rolling out events that mirror the ads, Westin and Nike were able to provide a brand experience that resonated much more deeply with the consumer, and the brand message was better understood in their hearts and minds while more engaging on the ground.

Engaging and Memorable

Event marketing is no longer a simple one-off tactic. Instead of being an afterthought aimed at supporting a traditional advertising campaign, thrown together after the brand messaging has already been created, event marketing is now considered a crucial part of campaign strategy by those in marketing boardrooms as they try to establish emotional connection and personal interaction between brand and consumer. A seminal study commissioned at the end of 2003 by event marketing powerhouse Jack Morton Worldwide (which developed and executed the Athens Olympics opening ceremony) surprised many marketers with figures and stats that showed just how important event marketing is to the overall marketing mix for a brand or product. The survey, unceremoniously titled "Experiential Marketing Survey," opened a lot of eyes in the marketing world when it released its key findings in January 2004, which were supported with a follow-up study in mid-2005.[109]

- Experiential marketing increases return on other marketing investments. Almost nine out of ten say participating in experiential marketing would make them more receptive to advertising.

- Seventy percent of consumers say participating in experiential marketing would increase purchase considerations.

- Eight in ten consumers who have participated in an experiential marketing campaign told their friends about it.

- Nine in ten say that the most important thing they want from marketers is "to give information about the brand/product."

- "Seeing/trying" through an experience is the best way to get that information.

- Entertainment and face-to-face dialogue are critical; 61 percent would prefer to try a product as part of an experience integrating entertainment; an on-site representative is the number one factor that makes an experience interesting.

- The new wave of consumers—teens and young adults—is 40

109. Laura Shuler, Jack Morton Experiential Marketing Survey, January 2004.

percent more likely to buy a product or adopt a brand after experiencing it at an interactive event.

· Face-to-face dialogue is a key component in developing an experience. So is some form of interactivity or entertainment.

· An on-site brand ambassador is the number-one factor that makes an experience interesting and relevant. "In addressing the question of what characteristics make a marketing experience more effective and appealing, consumers most value the opportunity for immediacy, dialogue, entertainment and interaction."[110]

· Experiential event marketing is "effective across many product categories; food/beverages, cars, computers/software and cell phones are top categories for experiential marketing across gender and age."[111]

· Overall, 61 percent of consumers prefer participating in an experience where they can try a product "in conjunction with some form of entertainment, compared with only 34 percent who prefer a straight product sampling."[112]

The survey has some interesting and quite valuable insights into the characteristics of effective experiential event marketing. First, the top experiential event marketing destinations for men and women are shopping malls, local fairs, and other public events, such as concerts and sports matches. Second, consumers are willing to spend up to an average of fourteen minutes participating in an experiential marketing

110. Ibid.
111. Ibid.
112. Ibid.

event. Fourteen minutes! Compare that to how quickly we tune out a thirty-second commercial. Consumers will spend the least amount of time—six to seven minutes—at so-called destination events such sports matches and concerts, where there's strong competition for attention. Third, consumers relate better to smaller groups of people to provide their experience, whereas the younger generations of consumers are much more open to large-scale events. Fourth, the weekend seems to be the most accepted time to participate in a marketing experience. Women like the daytime; men like the evenings more.

Out of this study on live event marketing, a few very prominent features of experiential marketing become evident. There is the emphasis on a one-on-one interaction. There is also the expressed desire of interaction and some sort of entertaining engagement, with the effect of bringing a brand to life or allowing for hands-on trial of a product. There is the imperative of targeting and connecting with influentials to drive buzz and/or purchase. Clearly, it is a form of marketing that is dependent on consumers deciding and preferring when and where they like to be marketed to. And finally, there is the underlying notion that experiential marketing is poised to become the marketing of the future.

Among eighteen- to twenty-three-year-olds, 31 percent said that experiential marketing tactics such as live events are their preferred method of communication and 40 percent said events are most likely to make them purchase a brand or product quickly without the influence of mass media. To marketers, this attitude should be both a blessing and a curse. Experiential marketing at events, for instance, can finally be that panacea of marketing to combat mass marketing apathy. It also can be, if executed badly, the demise of a brand or product. But if executed with an experiential mind-set that incorporates the imperatives of experiential marketing, events offer marketers an ideal interaction where consumers can touch, play, test, and begin to attach themselves to brands and products.

In October 2003, IMI International queried more than seventeen hundred consumers through telephone interviews and online interactions and found that in the twelve months preceding the survey, 77 percent of the participants bought a product after "experiencing it," "sampling it," or "trying it."[113] According to IMI International, the participants chose and selected experiences and events "as the marketing method that most often prompts them to make purchase decisions."[114] Almost identical results from polls in Canada and Australia were presented by IMI as proof of this affinity in other marketplaces.

The study also showed interesting findings about when, where, and how consumers want to experience brands through event marketing. For instance, the study found that a brand sponsoring regional events such as local team games achieved far greater payback in terms of favorable consumer opinion than it would if it sponsored a national event. In line with the Jack Morton study, local events, in-store programs, and malls were the ideal locations to stage an event marketing campaign. Guys enjoy "test drives" of more complex products such as computers, electronics, and cars. Women prefer sampling events with clothing, household, and personal care products. These sampling events are effective when conducted in conjunction with experiential elements such as dynamic presentations, entertainment, and hands-on interaction.

Interestingly, the IMI International survey also uncovered a consumer desire to interact one-on-one with field reps at these events. From this desire, consumers preferred smaller events as opposed to large "cattle

---

113. Kathleen M. Joyce, "Scene and Heard," *Promo Magazine*, January 1, 2004.
114. Ibid.

call"-type mob scenes—although the younger generation of respondents were much more open to large events such as concerts or sports events. Smaller events such as grassroots gatherings, in-store entertainment and mall tours refrain from "cycling people through" to allow a more personal interaction between brand and consumer, and the brand's ambassadors must be personable and knowledgeable enough to make the event experience relevant, resonant, and compelling to the consumer. According to the survey, "consumers develop greater affinity for the brand when they can speak with representatives and ask questions."[115]

The Samsung Experience in New York City is a clear example of event-based experiential marketing being used as a strategic driver for the brand. The South Korean electronics maker and marketer was long seen as a second-tier player, with a majority of its $15 billion in U.S. sales stemming from supplying hardware to Hewlett-Packard and other resellers. To consumers, it was known as a price-driven brand. Traditional marketing was doing nothing to change that perception, nor did it allow consumers a chance to learn about the new, and increasingly complex, electronics products entering the marketplace. TV and print ads were not tying the Samsung brand and technology to a consumer's experiences of everyday life. So in late September 2004, Samsung Electronics America unveiled the Samsung Experience, an "interactive funhouse of virtual reality experiences, product displays, video clips and other techie things, all featuring Samsung cell phones, flat-panel television, laptops and other products."[116]

The location of the Samsung Experience gives away the company's desire to attract the affluent consumer; it is on the third floor of the

115. Ibid.
116. Claudia Deutsch, "Samsung Ramps Up Advertising," *The New York Times,* September 20, 2004.

Time Warner Center, an extravagant vertical mall on Columbus Circle in Manhattan, where some of the most expensive restaurants and office spaces in the city overlook Central Park and the Trump Tower. The company chose this extremely expensive location because "New York, and the [Time Warner] Center, is a window to the entire United States market." So far the Samsung Experience has proven to be quite a successful form of window dressing.

A huge electronic banner welcomes and invites all mall patrons at the street-level lobby. Before entering the experience on the third floor, visitors stop at an orientation table, where a touch-screen presents a detailed map of New York City. By touching on a particular building or area, consumers trigger a number of place-specific videos showing how a Samsung device adds to the richness of life. Each video clip then presents a related screen explaining the featured products. Once inside the gallery, guests are wowed by rotating panels that surround them with a virtual speakeasy, "in which waitresses carry trays of Samsung phones instead of drinks. A stylized living room has a Samsung home theater, a playroom has video games, an office has computers and phones. People can snap pictures with Samsung cameras and e-mail them to friends, or download special rings onto Samsung phones. The outside doors and inside walls feature moving graphics of flowers proliferating. It shows off motion technology, but it's also a breather, a soothing element of nature in a really high-tech environment."[117]

Samsung also holds product-related tutorials in the gallery. The Samsung Experience is offered to its retail partners to hold meetings and view products in the space. The experience is staffed with well-trained brand ambassadors to explain how each product fits within the

117. Ibid.

consumer's lifestyle and technology needs. The company has also built a cyberspace mock-up of the physical space in New York to connect consumers around the world with those in the gallery. The online destination is able to tell visitors which rooms are experiencing heavy traffic, and which products the consumers are playing with at that exact moment. And anytime someone logs onto the Web site, a light begins blinking for him or her in the gallery. Samsung also hopes to entice tourists to New York to participate in the experience by offering to loan hard-disk video cameras. With a simple credit card swipe to secure the loaner, visitors can borrow a camera for a few days to record their experiences in New York City, then return to the store, where special kiosks can burn the videos onto a DVD to take home.

One thing that the Samsung Experience won't do is actually sell any of the products. Although this experience is an optimal way of bringing the brand to life—a living, breathing commercial—it is designed to be about selling the dream of using the products, not literally selling the products themselves. Sony, however, has a sales component to their experiential stores. Sony's Style stores in New York and San Francisco are designed to both showcase and sell products, with a showroom on the first floor and an ultrahip lounge in the basement. Its latest gallery installation, called the Qualia, focuses on very high-end components such as a $3,000 digital camera or similarly priced headphones and players. Interestingly, Sony has hired a staff of luxury goods experts—not techies, gadget geeks, or models—to provide personal demonstrations of the digital suite of products. One staffer that spoke with a reporter covering the opening night of the Qualia experience had an MBA from a prestigious Paris university and was as well versed in brand strategy as he was in product gadgetry.

It will not be long before experiences such as these are made available at major events such as the Super Bowl or the Olympics. Furthermore, the success of these experiential destinations will drive them outward throughout the country, with high-end malls and boutiques providing a great venue for the experience. Another electronics marketer has already taken the show on the road in South America. Philips Electronics launched its Philips Electronics Circus in twelve cities south of the border—literally, a three-ring circus complete with ringmaster, knife thrower, magicians, acrobats, clowns, midgets, and wild animals. Some of these performers are living, breathing people in costume, while others are digital video images playing on Philips equipment. The three-ring circus has a seating capacity of six hundred guests, and the three- to four-hour show incorporates live action in the rings with projections shot up on screens and displayed on plasma and LCD televisions. The circus travels to high-traffic events such as the soccer, rugby, and field hockey championships to get consumers to physically experience the products and be awed by the technology integrated into the experience. By providing the archetypal entertainment of a circus, and adding a hands-on component to experience the products, Philips was able to make the tour an experiential marketing showpiece in Latin America.

True Engagements Are Memories of a Lifetime

The circus, tinged with the special nostalgic glow of long-remembered childhood marvels, reminds us that an effective experiential event has to do more than get our attention in the manner of the loudest street hustler. Pine and Gilmore point out that "because so many exemplars of staged experiences come from what the popular press loosely calls the entertainment industry, it's easy to conclude that . . . to stage experiences simply means adding entertainment to existing offerings. That would be a gross understatement. Remember that staging experiences is not about entertaining customers, it's about *engaging* them."[118]

What does this mean? Here's an example from my former company's recent campaign for Coty Canada's Adidas for Men line. Before the term "metrosexual" exploded on the popular consciousness of North American males, the major skin care company—leveraging this famous sports brand—released a new line of facial products for men. Knowing that a regular guy would not know what an exfoliant is, even if it kicked him in the head, we decided that education and hands-on trial were the keys to a successful launch. Where girlfriends, wives, and mass marketing had failed, a guerrilla attack was charged with changing perception and inhibitions.

Teams of guerrillas in pickup trucks were deployed into the male jungle—sports events, ski hills, concerts, nightclubs, parks, and beaches—to get guys to stop and get a facial right on the spot. Sound impossible? These teams had the not-so-secret weapon for reaching guys on the move: hot girls. A mobile and interactive skin-care salon staffed by highly qualified beautiful female facialists would solicit guys to receive a free facial that incorporated the company's entire line of products. Guys were more than ready to get into the chair, and many were lining up twice for the experience. Most importantly, while receiving the facial, they learned more about proper skin care and all of the available products. The barrier was broken; "metrosexuality" had arrived in Canada.

Of course, this is a minor example of how a one-on-one experience, conducted at a time and a place where the target market is most receptive to the branded experience, can change perception and consumer behavior almost instantaneously. The facialists were perfect brand

118. Joseph Pine and James Gilmore, *The Experience Economy*, p. 29.

ambassadors to engage a typical guy, give him an experience he would never forget, and at the same time impart essential brand messaging within a relatively long (five to ten minutes) brand interaction. Compare that to the level of engagement accomplished through a thirty-second commercial. There's no contest.

But true consumer engagement runs deeper than pretty girls giving guys street facials. Catherine Stone, former chief experience officer at the Coca-Cola Company and now owner of Engage Consulting in Atlanta, sees consumer engagement as a far-reaching proposition. "The dictionary defines engagement as to get *and* hold attention, and that to me is the key to experiential marketing and what differentiates it from so much of the other marketing that is going on today. Most marketing is about getting attention: 'See me! Buy my stuff!' It doesn't take into much account the life and concerns of the consumer, other than the basic demographic information needed to know whether one has money and whether one might be inclined to buy." She continues: "Holding a person's attention requires so much more. It means really getting to know them, being willing to stay in the relationship and invest in it for the long haul, and being willing to make the relationship mutually beneficial. In my vision of experiential marketing, we create long-term strategies for developing relationships through a series of planned, impactful experiences over time."

Here's an example of what she means: For a while, when I came back for home visits and took my father's Jeep out to run errands, drivers would honk, flash their lights or wave at me at intersections and on roads every time I was behind the wheel of his TJ. I had no idea what was going on. Was I speeding? Were my headlights broken? Was something on fire outside of the car? I couldn't understand the reason for all this attention until I realized that it was not just other drivers who were honking and waving at me. They were all Jeep owners. Just by getting behind the wheel of a Jeep, I was instantly transported into a society of off-roaders, a cabal of diehard brand evangelists who recognized each other's membership status with a flicker of the headlights or a wave of the hand outside the window. Instead of secret handshakes, Jeep owners know their fellow members by the amount of mud on their bumpers. The moment I clued into this communication, and decided to join it by returning the honks, waves, and flickers, I was transported into a consumer world I had not known existed. The cabal had a common bond and a secret language. By digging a little bit deeper, I found that they had their own rituals as well.

The pilgrimage for the Jeep brand—akin to the performance of the hajj in Islamic terms—is the annual Camp Jeep. More than fifty years ago, early Jeep owners started an off-the-cuff weekend-long driving trek across California's Sierra Nevada by way of the Rubicon. For the first weekend trip, more than 155 people showed up. They looked around in amazement, shook hands, laughed, and called the gathering a Jeep Jamboree. Since then, Jeep owners and off-road enthusiasts have been holding their own jamborees across the world. The owners show up, share some stories, and hit some trails. In the United States, more than thirty different jamborees were held in 2004. "Hundreds of people from different places and spaces, hundreds of different jobs, hundreds of different personalities, all united by one common denominator—their Jeeps."[119]

Ten years ago, Jeep's senior manager of brand events, Lou Bitonti, had an epiphany after attending a bunch of jamborees across the country. He famously wrote it down on a bar napkin: Camp Jeep. It will be a huge jamboree, accessible only to Jeep owners, and it will be an unforgettable

119. "Trail Rated: Camp Jeep's 10th Anniversary," *Event Marketer,* July 2004.

experience. Since the first Camp Jeep debut at Eagle Park, Colorado, in 1995, this property, which was birthed by brand enthusiasts and scribbled on a bar napkin by a Jeep exec, has become "the preeminent annual owner-loyalty program, a sold-out three-day event used strategically and tactically to not only reward customers, but to retain them. . . . It's the ultimate piece of the event marketing continuum. Awareness events spark interest. Prospect events try to push a sale. And owner events reward those consumers for crossing over from prospect to customer."[120]

The experience that customers are rewarded with at Camp Jeep is indeed extraordinary. Although the location of the camp changes each year, the layout and ethos of the place remains the same. If the ads on TV create a Jeep world on a small screen, Camp Jeep allows them to enter it. Each summer, thousands of Jeep owners and their personal guests pay $275 to $335 for three days of exclusive concerts, classes, and extremely memorable experiences. The company lets their customers play in a make-believe world of Jeep City, complete with boulder runs, rock shows, cookouts, and camping. This experience isn't to get them to buy another Jeep; the experience is made for them to never want to own anything but a Jeep.

DaimlerChrysler pulls out all the stops when it comes to creating the Jeep experience. No expenses are spared to put on the event, although almost half of the costs to put on Camp Jeep are offset by revenues from admission charges and monies from other companies wishing sponsorship exposure. Activities at Camp Jeep are divided among eight themed villages:

· **Jeep 101 Village.** A series of custom off-road courses to learn Jeep skills is set up as a centerpiece to the experience. There is

120. Ibid.

also Survival Willy's Island, where new Jeep models are show-cased. There is the 4x4 Playground, where drivers take a forty-five-minute obstacle course. The 4x4 Trail Rides offer fifteen off-road trails of various degrees of difficulty, and the Rubicon Challenge Courses mirror the extreme trails of the early Jeep Jamboree days. There's even a Jeep 101 course for remote-controlled Jeep cars.

· **Engineering Village.** Groups of Jeep owners, divided by the models they own, get a seventy-five-minute session with Daimler-Chrysler engineers to learn about their cars from the inside out. More importantly, the owners get a chance to personally suggest improvements to their models for the future, as engineers and automotive suppliers listen and take notes. The idea is to estab-lish a candid and meaningful conversation—a dialogue between consumer and marketer—to go over Jeep technology and consumer-driven improvements.

· **Camp Kids Village.** Kids can create Jeep bumper stickers, back-pack tags, and bracelets. They also can create Jeep music videos and giant Jeep murals.

· **Music Village.** A rock and roll exhibit surrounds a full-blown concert stage sponsored by Sirius Satellite Radio, where three major artists perform throughout the weekend. Owners also can sign up for a DJ spinning class.

· **World of Jeep Village.** Four individual tents present the past, present, and future of the Jeep brand called the Jeep Museum. An Off-Road Basics area gets Jeep reps talking about the latest prod-ucts and accessories. A Keep Your Jeep Looking New area covers the basic maintenance requirements for a Jeep, while the Camp Financial area allows Jeep owners and guests to learn about the latest Jeep credit cards, finance packages, and special offers.

· **Sports and Adventure Village.** An Adventure Tower provides a military-style obstacle course, and a High Climbing Tower lets guests fly on a zip line. The Camp Scuba Tank teaches them scuba diving. Guests can learn how to fly-cast and fly-tie a fishing rod. They also can participate in animal tracking lessons, paint ball tournaments, yoga classes, water tubing excursions, GPS-powered scavenger hunts . . . even salsa dance lessons. True outdoors enthusiasts can take photography lessons and hikes, and the kids can build a birdhouse or take animal calls lessons. This village has it all.

· **Thrills and Spills Village.** This "extreme sports" pavilion features top BMX and off-road bike riders, a skate park, and freestyle motor cross stunts. It is sponsored by SoBe drinks.

· **Expressions Village.** Owners and their guests can get massages and facials at the Spa Oasis, and participate in wineglass painting and outdoor grilling classes. There are woodcarving tutorials, watercolor classes, and other painting activities.

Activities are not exclusive to Jeep customers; DaimlerChrysler has leveraged the camp for its own internal activities and interactions with key stakeholders. Dealerships have held annual meetings at Camp Jeep. Jeep trains its instructors—certified sales people who canvass Jeep's North American dealerships to evangelize the brand—at the camp as well. Each year, DaimlerChrysler can position the Camp to serve different strategic objectives. One year the camp would become a platform for a new vehicle launch. The next year it may revolve around dealership education. Camp Jeep also acts as a great way to see what works with the core consumers and what doesn't. The popular events at the villages are a great testing ground to develop other experiential events—like Jeep 101—that are used for awareness building and prospect marketing at car shows and grassroots events.

Most of all, Camp Jeep transforms Jeep owners and their guests into bona fide brand evangelists. Every year, for example, the *coup de grâce* to the three-day experience is the Jeep Jubilee, a communal picnic dinner and concert by a Grammy-quality artist. The jubilee is brought to a close with a video retrospective of Camp Jeep and the company that invented it, followed immediately by a fantastic fireworks display. One Camp Jeep exec is quoted as saying that "each year that it ends, we look around across the crowd and we see tears."[121]

It is fair to say that Camp Jeep is currently the pinnacle of experiential event marketing. It is as transformative as a Christian revival and as ritualistic as a religious pilgrimage. There are production and entertainment components that rival Hollywood sets and Disney activities. For three days, consumers interact one on one with brand ambassadors, doing so at their own whim and fancy. They make friends and spread buzz. They make lifelong memories. They acquire years' worth of water-cooler conversations with non-Jeep owners, describing the experience in their own words and with their own naturally authentic enthusiasm for years to come. And the Jeep brand is the underpinning of the entire experience.

Emanuel Rosen, in his book *Anatomy of Buzz*, drives an often-mentioned point: the key to successful buzz, and the way it travels through the marketplace, is marketing to as many network hubs as

121. Ibid.

possible. "Thinking of markets and categories can be useful," he writes. "So can thinking of your relationship with every individual customer. But when you think of buzz, think of customers as part of a network. Your objective is to maximize the number of positive comments about your product that flow among nodes in this network . . . without stimulation, word-of-mouth can spread at a very slow rate—often too slowly for success in today's highly competitive markets. Intense . . . effort may be required to push the word and to leapfrog directly to the most productive hubs or into untapped clusters."

Camp Jeep moves around the country. And Camp Jeep is open to all Jeep owners and their guests. The suburban Cherokee family gets to play, converse, and carry on with the diehard Wrangler off-roader and extreme sports enthusiast. Liberty-driving yuppies can hang out with Rubicon-owning Gen Y'ers. And when they all return home the morning after the fireworks finale, they all have individual stories to tell their friends, coworkers, and families. With an intense effort from Daimler-Chrysler such as Camp Jeep, the brand hits both productive hubs and untapped clusters. The result is Jeep owners greatly influencing and contributing to Jeep purchases. Camp Jeep not only spreads word-of-mouth about the brand experience, it seals the deal as well.

With experiential marketing like this, you don't need to rely on traditional marketing and mass advertising alone. According to the January 24, 2005, edition of the *Wall Street Journal*, DaimlerChrysler declined to spend $2.4 million for a thirty-second commercial on Super Bowl XXXIX and decided to spend its advertising dollars on a live event at the Chicago Auto Show. The theme to the event was (you guessed it!) Jeep 101, which featured a 157,000-square-foot indoor driving range complete with thousands of cubic yards of dirt, soil, boulders, concrete, fallen timber, ravines, hill climbs, and other off-road driving experiences. The decision to eschew a Super Bowl ad was prescient. Ad recall rates for the 2005 extravaganza were the lowest in years, while tens of thousands of prospective car buyers spent an average of *twenty-two minutes* at the Jeep 101 area. The trade-off doesn't seem fair: thirty seconds on TV for $2.4 million, or twenty-two minutes for about the same price. The experience with the brand is incomparable. More importantly, after rolling out a 60,000-square-foot Jeep 101 area at the New York Auto Show, local dealership sales spiked 8 percent, compared to the company's average 1 percent post–auto show boost.[122]

Engagement and Evangelism

Motorola also didn't buy any TV advertising during Super Bowl XXXIX. The communications marketer instead set up an elaborate football-themed obstacle course across the river from the stadium. It also employed dozens of brand ambassadors to walk the streets of Jacksonville and offer Super Bowl–goers a hands-on "test drive" of the latest Bluetooth gadgetry. Since the environment during Super Bowl weekend is festive and passionate, the experiential marketing was engaging as well: GM took over a city block for a celebrity go-cart race, and Cadillac donated more than four hundred vehicles to shuttle Super Bowl guests between hotels and restaurants.

For all those fans who converged on Jacksonville, the positive brand connections they experienced from these types of engaging marketing may have numbered in the hundreds of thousands. If a percentage of these fans came back home and told about their brand experiences to their friends over a beer or at a barbecue, the number of brand impres-

---

122. Suzanne Vranica, "Super Bowl XXXIX: Obstacle Course vs. "Potty Palooza'," *Wall Street Journal*, January 24, 2005.

sions would be in the millions. When compared to the low ad recall rates of a commercial seen by ninety million Super Bowl TV viewers—those who actually didn't get off the couch during commercial breaks—the idea of impression versus impressive becomes clear. An impressive experience beats out one based on impressions. The impressive experience is also many times more memorable. In fact, the "sweet spot for any compelling experience . . . is similarly a mnemonic place, a tool aiding in the creation of memories, distinct form the normally uneventful world of goods and services."[123] By staging experiences, forward-thinking companies are transitioning their consumers into a different marketplace centered around creating memories, and therefore a world populated by brand evangelists who have discovered, understood, and internalized a brand into their lives.

This does not necessarily mean that brand evangelists are a company's repeat customers. Just because someone has 53,000 miles on Air Canada does not make him a brand evangelist for the brand. Frequent-flier rewards do not necessarily translate a repeat customer into a brand evangelist. In fact, I frequently fly Air Canada and never relate a great experience to my friends, because I have never experienced one with Air Canada. I don't have a frequent-flier account with Jet Blue, but I often tell of the great experience I had flying with the company, especially after the ground crew waved us off from the gate during a snowstorm in Burlington.

Brand evangelists have had such positive brand interactions and such memorable brand experiences that they passionately recommend the brand, product, or service to their friends and family. They are the sort who remember the brand and purchase it when looking for gifts to give

123. Joseph Pine and James Gilmore, *The Experience Economy*, p. 43.

to others. Brand evangelists believe themselves to be part of a greater whole. They are the type who wave to other evangelists in the street, like all those believers who waved at me from their Jeeps.

An experience can be like an epiphany. It takes engagement to reach it. This means allowing the consumer a relevant and memorable marketing experience that is optimally placed in the consumer's world. For DaimlerChrysler, it is Camp Jeep and Jeep 101. The company has uncovered the essence of the brand experience that consumers really talk about—off-road adventure, camaraderie, and environmentalism. They create an intensely personal dialogue with their core consumers before, during, and after the experience, and become intimately connected with the key influencers throughout different social networks to drive buzz among the masses. The memories associated with the experience must transform the consumer, and translate into a deeper understanding of the brand's place in their lives. Importantly, a memorable marketing experience keeps a consumer as an evangelist, not simply a loyal customer. Most traditional advertising does not foster brand evangelists. But for experiential marketers, ensuring the proper consumer experience is a paramount condition for converting consumers into brand evangelists.

It is no surprise that the root of "evangelism" is based on "bringer of the glad tidings." Experiential marketing is indeed a new promise to the consumer, a different way of measuring marketing success. Media proliferation and audience fragmentation have made word-of-mouth more important than ever for marketers, especially when confronted with an increasingly competitive marketplace where acquiring a new customer is five times more expensive than holding and engaging an existing one. Brand evangelists, therefore, are one of the most effective ways to bring the good brand news.

Importantly, brand evangelists bring the news from the marketplace back to the brand by contacting the company freely to offer comments, criticisms, and suggestions for improvement. Those companies that actively listen—those that seek to further engage with their consumers—are thriving. The next chapter will show how engaging the consumer can easily translate into empowering her or him to begin cocreating the brand with the company. And it will present another forward-thinking car company that has harnessed experiential marketing to launch an entire lineup of cars without a single advertisement. It'll be a fun ride.

Chapter 5	**Experiential marketing** will empower the individual consumer and unleash the power of grassroots evangelism.

I n late 2003, Toyota birthed a new brand—and three models under it—without any mass advertising. No TV ads showing the cars zipping through mountains. No print testimonials from professional surfers or race car drivers. No radio ads touting the lowest finance rates and money-back deals. Nothing was done to let the average consumer know that a new car brand had entered the market. Despite the lack of mass media marketing, Toyota was able to sell 99,259 cars from the new brand that year.

The brand that Toyota rolled out is called Scion, and is positioned squarely at the young car purchaser. The brand was created "to target the leading edge of Gen Y, in other words the earliest adopters, or the people who are likely to influence others within their generation" according to Brian Bolain, national sales promotions manager for Scion, and therefore necessitated a nontraditional approach to reach them.[124] Toyota decided to reach their ideal consumers from the bottom-up grassroots level, instead of blitzing them from the top-down mass media pipeline.

124. On-line/e-mail interview with Brian Bolain, April 2005.

"Success of interesting or provocative nonautomotive brands suggests that mainstream advertising, or widespread use of mass media, is not essential to gain the attention of this market," Bolain explains. "Additionally, grassroots activity is what provides a brand with its 'flavor.' Of course, mass media is still essential at some point to generate awareness, particularly for a new brand. But it's not the source that consumers will use when they get closer to their purchase decision."

Toyota execs desperately needed to connect with the younger buyers. The average age of Toyota buyers is about forty-five, compared with about thirty-seven for Honda, thirty-five for Volkswagen, and thirty-two for Mitsubishi. Toyota had well-founded concerns about attracting the next generation of new-car buyers—the Generation X and Y of consumers—and counting them as customers when they reach their thirties and forties. Reaching this consumer base is imperative for the car industry. It is estimated that by 2010, Gen Y will make one in four car purchases, and by 2020 they'll represent 40 percent of the market.[125] Hence the idea of the Scion brand, a funky and stylized car that provides a number of customizable features, easy-to-understand pricing, and a no-pressure sales environment in the showroom. But the marketing of the brand is what really stood out. With a brand firmly aimed at the youth market, the marketing for the Scion could not afford to use mass marketing to get their attention. The brand had to go where the consumer was, at times and places where he was most receptive to the marketing, and in ways that allowed maximum word-of-mouth to generate interest. The marketing had to be played out at the grassroots level, talking to each individual consumer one at a time.

The initial grassroots marketing efforts for the Scion brand—which

125. Ibid.

includes the xA, the xB, and the tC models—were developed to attract a twenty-two-year-old male buyer with a "command of style," according to Bolain. "We believe that this type of individual can help us create a buzz, [and] validate these vehicles for a broader segment of the market." Now that Scion had discovered their target brand evangelists, the brand was introduced to them under the radar at youth lifestyle events and venues such as nightclubs, DJ nights, urban film festivals, college campuses, and trendy magazine launch parties. There was no sales pitch involved. One car, usually the xA or xB, would simply be parked outside of the events. If the kids expressed interest in the car, they were taken for a quick test drive around the block. That's all.

"We must enable our marketing efforts to seamlessly integrate with consumers, and allow them to pay attention to us when it suits them, but ignore us if the timing is not right," Bolain is quick to add. "For example, with our national Consumer Test Drive promotion, which we do each year, we go directly to neighborhoods where our target is likely to congregate, at an interesting restaurant or store. We then give passersby the chance to drive a Scion in a no-pressure environment, and if they choose to participate, we give them a small gift certificate to the establishment we're at that day, along with Scion merchandise. But it's always the consumers' choice, and it's very easy for them. If we were to follow the traditional model of invitational test drive events, attendance would likely be low, as these consumers are extremely time-poor."

By being exclusively at the grassroots level, Scion was able to create word-of-mouth buzz among the most influential urban Gen Y trend leaders through nontraditional lifestyle events and communications based primarily on music, art, film, fashion, and the automotive aftermarket. The last grassroots target—the auto aftermarket crowd commonly referred as "tuners"—was especially integral to reaching the key influencers who spread buzz. "Tuners" are kids who drive tricked-out street cars, usually loaded with performance-enhancing accessories and cosmetic add-ons. Tuners are *The Fast and the Furious* fanatics, street racers, and car buffs who constitute a tightly knit community in which word-of-mouth is the key way for learning about new products and brands. Because the Scion brand was positioned as a car company that offered hundreds of customizable features and effects, targeting this grassroots segment was instrumental to the cars' success. After seeing the new models, the tuners quickly got the word out among their friends.

Going grassroots also allowed the Scion brand managers to attack specific geographical areas instead of rolling out the launch with a nationwide campaign. The brand chose to launch the cars in a three-phase strategy to maximize both marketing and operational efficiencies. "The buzz that was generated when the cars were only available in cer-tain parts of the country—first California only, then adding the East Coast and Southeast/Southwest, then finally national availability—was invaluable," Bolain explains. "And the time in between each wave of rollout enabled us to perfect each of the operational changes we put in place to support Scion's unique business model."

Each phase of the rollout also featured different methods for reaching the consumer. For instance, the vice president of the Scion division noted that "the number-one way the customer in California found Scion was by seeing the vehicle on the street. In-person discovery and the Internet are the keys to the purchase process." The rollout on the East Coast saw the Scion parked outside of lifestyle venues and events. The national rollout incorporated a full-blown car tour, event marketing, and some mass media exposure. In effect, the marketing for Scion "is a laboratory in which we can take chances that we might not wish to take with larger-volume products," says Bolain. "It enables us to use a layered strategy that starts with grassroots efforts and extends to limited mass media, and learn what resonates with our target."

Scion is continuing to market at the grassroots level, although after two years of underground marketing it will devote about a third of its marketing budget on mass media in the future. The majority of the estimated $50 million marketing budget is still devoted to "tastemaker events" at leading-edge music, fashion, and tuner-focused intercept locations. Importantly, Scion is trying to give back to the community by supporting up-and-coming DJs, artists, and other tastemakers instead of blowing their budget on high-profile celebrity endorsements. It is also successfully leveraging the Internet by using live chat to attract the Gen Y audience. Marketing to the youth, according to Bolain, "is a dynamic process that requires constant attention. This audience is more impressed by the amount of effort we make as marketers than the amount of money we spend."

Awareness numbers, as much as sales figures, confirm Brian's last statement. "Awareness [for the Scion brand] when last tested was more than 55 percent nationally, and more than 75 percent in California among consumers younger than thirty-five. This compares to 18 percent less than two years ago, so the awareness growth has been quick. And 'heard about it from a friend' is as likely a means of learning about Scion as traditional media in our survey. This confirms to us the importance of grassroots and word-of-mouth efforts." In fact, about a quarter of consumers in California found out about the Scion just by seeing it on the street or at an event. The second-highest awareness factor was the friend referral. Magazine editorial coverage—not to be confused with magazine ads—came in third. To date, Scion's buyer profile suggests that Scion has hit its target. The median age for Scion buyers is thirty-five, and 57 percent are male. Most importantly, 76 percent of Scion buyers are new to the Toyota family of brands. And that's exactly what Toyota wanted to achieve with Scion.

Brand Evangelists

Clearly, the Scion brand has discovered a new way to market to the future consumer, and the company continues to discover grassroots marketing initiatives that it can learn from and build on. However, the underlying premise for its grassroots approach remains the same: target the brand evangelists and let them spread the word themselves. The previous chapter described the root of evangelism as "bringer of glad tidings." For marketers and brand executives, brand evangelists can seem like a solid group of people who are loyal to their product or service. "We have over a million brand evangelists," they may say, and point to their database of frequent fliers, store card holders, or bulk buyers. But these lists are just names on paper or hard drive. Brand evangelists are different. They are truly the bringers of glad tidings. They are the progenitors to the new consumer, and by extension, they are the harbingers of marketing in the oh-so-near future.

Pretty soon in the marketplace, every brand, product, and service will have its own brand evangelists. It must. It would not be in business otherwise. The rise of brand evangelists is nothing short of a quiet revolution. Brand evangelists will force companies to restructure, retrain, and rethink not just their marketing strategies and tactics, but their entire operations and systems as well. From an experiential point of view, brand evangelists will define the brand experience. From an experiential marketing point of view, they will also demand engagement, cooperation, and cocreation from the companies trying to reach them. This will not be done with traditional marketing. It cannot be accomplished through more eyeball impressions, or newfound distribution channels. To reach them with mass marketing would be, as the global chief of marketing at McDonald's declared at an Association of National Advertisers meeting, "a mass mistake."[126]

The intrusion on the consumer's life that mass marketing and advertising impose is intolerable to the new consumer. The reliance on brand marketing to drive business is no longer viable either. Brand evangelists may love the brand, but not because of the ads on TV. They love the brand because it provides them with an experience no other brand can deliver. That experience will be translated by word-of-mouth to peers and family on their own terms. The experience will be sought out and influenced by media and information that is on-demand, easy to access, and firmly in the consumer's hands. The individual will be at the forefront of business, and the marketing must seek him or her out individually. And as with the rise of the individual brand evangelists, there will be the rise of the brand detractors. Power swings both ways. Marketing will therefore not only be an act of experientially connecting with the individual consumer to ensure brand evangelism, it also will be an act of mitigating the rise of brand detractors through authentic and empowering experiences.

Of course, this is nothing new to established businesses. Everyone knows that the more your customers recommend your service, brand, or product, the more likely sales will increase. We've all heard stories of that "crazy" customer who recommends the business to everyone she meets. A brand evangelist can launch a company into success better than most venture finance. So why do companies desperately try to speak to everyone while conversing with no one? The answer is simple: get money now. The business climate—that of Wall Street firms and the marketing

126. Scott Donaton, "Adjusting to the Reality of a Consumer-Controlled Market," *Advertising Age,* October 18, 2004.

conglomerates that serve them—is results-driven, often in increments of weeks instead of years. In a tightly squeezed economy where thousands of competing products are virtually indistinguishable, and when corporate boards and itchy shareholders demand instant jumps in revenue, the only way to stay in the game is to scream the loudest and spend the most. This means mass advertising. This means Super Bowl commercials and the back cover of *Maxim* magazine. This means repetition and a mailbox full of machine-written mail. This means driving in the brand message like a steam train through the back yard, whether the consumer likes it or not.

Of course, with everyone getting louder, no one is ever heard. For years, the screaming and spending have been escalating, and response rates for mass marketing and advertising have been declining. Undaunted by the hard stats, ad execs started measuring amorphous things such as "brand awareness" and "brand equity" as positive signposts for breaking through the clutter. It took the übermarketer of all marketers—the global marketing chief for McDonald's—to bring up the obvious: mass marketing has become a mass mistake. Or perhaps more kindly, mass marketing has run out of steam.

Thus we turn back to the bringers of glad tidings, the brand evangelists. Just think off all the commercials and ads that we see every day—close to four thousand of them—and then ask yourself these questions: How did I find out about that restaurant I went to last week? How did I find out about the cool new hotel on my last vacation? What really made me buy or lease my car? Who did I talk to about buying that Mac or PC? Why do I bank where I bank? How did I choose to buy the CD in my player? Most likely, one of the answers would somehow include a friend, family member, or work peer. Equally likely, a TV commercial didn't do the trick. A personal conversation did.

And this is the good news that evangelists bring. They offer not only the glad tidings of a brand or product promise, they also bring forth a new way of marketing those brands and products. Individuals market products, not commercials. And these individuals are part of a social fabric that cannot be defined by segmented groups or defined demographics. That is why they cannot be reached by the top-down, command-and-control structures of mass media and mass advertising. People do not live in labeled silos. No one is exclusive to a "target audience." Individuals do not engage each other and converse with each other as an audience. They do so together, away from the watchful eyes and prying research of media buyers, agency planners, and Nielsen statisticians. These conversations are conducted where mass media have no control. Instead, they are prevalent at the grassroots level of the marketplace. Here, consumers call the shots.

Understanding the inherent power of the individual consumer is integral to rolling out an experiential marketing campaign. Equally important is understanding how that individual rests within a broader framework of interconnected conversations and brand engagements; in other words, how to reach her or him at the grassroots level. Knowing these two fundamental tenets of experiential marketing allows marketers and their brands to begin to harness the power of the individual, who may be the brand's latest and greatest evangelist. It also means opening up the brand to these evangelists, to make it transparent and accommodating to them, and allowing them to truly call the shots in a brand's (or company's) development, growth, and strategy plans.

So this is the quiet revolution. In the sea of ad clutter, competing messages, and increasingly cynical attempts to reach more eyeballs, a new consumer yearning is beginning to emerge. It is the yearning by people to reconnect with each other. Not only has the shotgun approach of mass marketing alienated us to the point of ineffectiveness, but also the latest tactics to segment us are not proving any more successful. There is still no dialogue. Our inherent desire to connect with one another is stronger than our need to buy more things.

The Demo Is Gone

The quiet revolution of the empowered consumer may have been made manifest in an equally quiet turning point in the marketing world. There were no news reports to announce it, not much commentary to mark it, and no one—consumer or marketer—was really affected by it. Still, to experiential marketers and those who champion the individual consumer, a quiet press release about a corporate acquisition got the bells to start tolling.

In early November 2004, a leading publisher of trade magazines covering the world of marketing and business announced that it had acquired the monthly *American Demographics* magazine from Primedia, a competitor in the world of trade business rags. The acquiring publisher was none other than Crain Communications, the publisher of marketing and advertising bible *Advertising Age* and other important marketing-related titles. The acquisition may have gone completely unnoticed except for one perplexing announcement from Crain: right after the acquisition was complete, *American Demographics* would be immediately scuttled. Crain bought the magazine to kill it. The age of demographics was officially over.

For close to twenty-five years, *American Demographics* had covered the study of demographic trends and strategy, disseminating their demo mantra to hundreds of thousands of marketers and agency execs who needed a way to get their products and messages to various groups of consumers. The publisher of *Advertising Age* assassinated the trade magazine that gave ammo to advertisers eager to learn about the consumer clusters they were advertising to. Without demographics, they had no idea who they were speaking with. With demographics, they would know that it was a woman, age twenty-five to thirty-four, with a household income of more than $50,000 and living in an upscale zip code. For close to a quarter of a century, the study of demographics ruled marketing. And now the demo was officially dead.

The use and acquisition of marketplace information for strategic marketing have always been influenced by the forms of media commonly used at each specific point in time. At first, studies of consumer behavior were developed in the 1890s after the appearance of weekly magazines that were financed by advertising. This was the beginning of the so-called *commodification of audiences*. But these studies of the consumer market that began during the industrialization period didn't create much interest in consumers or their behavior. These early studies were mainly focused on the institutional dynamics of markets and distribution systems. Research on consumer behavior, attitudes, and motivations began to develop in the field of advertising psychology, with experimental research on the effectiveness of this new medium of persuasion. Magazine publishers, who were burdened with high production costs and thus relied heavily on advertising revenue, were the first to market its readership as an "audience of consumers." The notion of demographics was born.

At first all of this was done without any scientific backing. Among the things used for such studies were letters to the editor, or photographs of subscribers' homes in magazines such as *Ladies' World*, where editors were able to understand the social class of their readership. In the immediate postwar era, the first real stress on understanding consumers was brought about by big publishers who set up their own research departments, also spawning a number of research consultancies that focused on surveying readers for demographical data.

In the 1930s, mass-circulation magazines as well as radio networks such as CBS began to maintain readers' panels, which in some cases consisted of more than a thousand people and represented different ages, occupations, and income levels. These readers and listeners were used primarily to answer surveys on their consumption patterns and lifestyle preferences. Topics included meal planning, food preparation, and laundry fashions, among others. CBS checked in even more detail with its "pantry checks," when for several weeks interviewers visited homes of housewives on the panels to really understand consumption habits. This allowed for truly valuable demographic purchasing studies. At this time, publishers still assumed that the cultural space of a magazine represented the practices and attitudes of its readers. Radio simultaneously promoted the creation of ratings research. This standardized typology (the ABCD system) differentiated households according to income, and clearly emphasized income differences much more strongly than lifestyle choice.

Despite the use of demographic parameters, there was no real notion of the population's motivations and attitudes. In 1942 the Nielsen ratings index gave backup to such speculation. For example, the small share of the radio audience within the "A" group explained not only economic factors but also that these people had a wide range of social interests that limited their listening time. As for the "C" group, their high ratings were attributed to their lower education, which made listening to radio the chosen method of receiving information.

To this day, the ABCD typology is still used, but it has been challenged ever since the end of World War II. It is argued that it doesn't provide real data on consumer practice. In 1949, W. Lloyd Warner from the Chicago research company SRI maintained that advertising agencies and their clients often waste money because of their ignorance of the actual makeup of class cultures. American consumption habits were completely transformed after that war. The standard of living rose sharply as suburbanization, new objects, television, domestic appliances, and new institutions such as the shopping mall altered the overall culture. Consumer researchers such as Warner were profoundly influenced by these changes, and argued that geographically rooted, communitarian taste and consumption habits mattered less than before. Consumer behavior was less affected by class-specific taste cultures.

Television changed the media environment dramatically, surpassing the press as the main source of information by the 1960s. The heady days of postwar boom made marketing a no-brainer. Companies needed to get their products in front of eager consumers. It didn't matter who they were reaching, as long as they were reaching them. TV was perfect. The program sponsorship model—"The Tide Comedy Hour," for instance—was abandoned for the "scatter plan" format of TV advertising, where advertising time was sold in the now traditional thirty- or sixty-second spot format across a number of channels and broadcast times. There was too much money flowing around to limit advertising to sponsorship alone. There was too much competition among brands to allow a monopoly on airtime. The spot format opened up advertising to competing brands with deep pockets, and as long as consumers were still buying, advertisers would continue spending on advertising. The mass media landscape was therefore inundated with ads. Business became more competitive. The clutter increased. And the consumer was less likely to buy something just because she saw an ad on TV. This generated the real need for audience segmentation and more detailed research.

The market research sector boomed. By 1963 the industry was ten times as large as it was three decades earlier. The social scientist became a common figure in marketing circles. This resulted in more detailed and deeper descriptions of consumer behavior and doubts about the strengths of the ABCD system. The shot that changed the marketing world forever came in the early 1960s, when the ABC network inked a deal with Nielsen to combine its ad delivery measurement with the network's research department.

Demographics thus became a detailed study of segmentation. ABC's viewers were put into various slots based on variables determined by the demographic experts. People were pigeonholed into neat little clusters based on their age, sex, income, and other criteria. The justification for spending millions on snippets of TV time, and the rationale for future spending increases, were now based on demographics. Media research companies such as Nielsen would measure how many households saw a commercial, and demographics would determine what kind of consumer was most likely to live there. ABC would therefore be able to sell its clients not only an audience measured by numbers, but also a "target" audience measured by age, income, gender, and geography.

Of course, common sense would indicate that no one is ever characterized by these variables alone. Even if confronted with a demographic doppelgänger—same age, same gender, same income lever and same zip code—I am certain that he is not me. He may be like me, but he does not necessarily buy the same things, watch the same shows, read the same magazines, and view the world as I do. But common sense does not prevail when the margins are being squeezed, competition is breathing down your neck, the board is putting on the screws, and sales are slipping. In this context, when a broadcaster assures that your message will be heard by your target audience, and the advertising agency promises that the message it created will break through, then it's pretty easy to believe them. Consequently, a company's brand management departments would develop their profiles of the consumers they were looking to reach. These variables were then turned over to media planners who figured out which media would be most effective at reaching them. The ad agency would craft the appropriate media-based message. The list of appropriate media would then be handed over to the buying departments to negotiate the best prices for airtime and scheduling.

The problem that never fully surfaced, intentionally or not, was that the messages were not being received based on the prescribed metrics and profiles. There was a disconnect between those who the demographical research suggested would be watching the commercials and those who were actually watching them. This disconnect was further exacerbated by the proliferation of media choices and the resulting fragmentation of the audience. Demographics weren't really "targeting" anyone. Instead of coming to this obvious conclusion, marketers and their research threw more bits of information into the consumer profiling soup. "While it became eminently clear the demo was a crappy surrogate for consumer targeting, nobody did anything about it; they just talked and danced around. They came up with ways of factoring, or modifying demographic analysis that would bring it more in keeping with the way they analyzed consumers."[127]

The resulting proliferation of databases, surveys, and methodologies in the 1960s through the late 1990s marked the high point of *American Demographics*. Every new variable and measurement tactic was discussed and dissected in the magazine. The science of demographics became awash in new techniques, theories, and studies to target and effectively

127. "Real Media Riffs," Media Post, November 19, 2004.

reach the elusive consumer. It didn't matter that the study of demographics wasn't really working, as long as new tools were coming out to keep the obvious obscured.

Paralleling the heyday of demographic study, some marketers began to look at the notion of studying the psychological factors of consumers instead of their demographic statistics. They began to discard the notion of demographics as the best segmentation technique. The first break came with motivation research (MR), a commercial adaptation of Freudian psychology that suggested that the real sources of consumer decisions lay in the hidden depths of their unconscious. Through in-depth interviews with consumers, MR attempted to understand hidden motives behind consumer decisions and transform them into marketing campaigns. It was the consumer's personality that explained his or her brand choices.

The practice of psychographical measurement thus grew out of the dynamics of MR. Psychographic variables included consumer attitudes, opinions, and interests. Simultaneously, advances in technology allowed marketers to employ hundreds of variables to understand interests, attitudes, and choices to build massive cross-referenced databases. Thus the demographic variables used by the ABCD system were replaced by hundreds if not thousands of psychographic variables. The databases got as cluttered as the media channels and messages.

Going farther than just consumer demographics, marketers and their research partners are now measuring all sorts of lifestyle choices and consumption patterns to determine their "targets." But adding more amorphous variables into the database does not translate into a better understanding of the consumer, nor does it allow marketers to better pinpoint their messages to the right audience. For instance, a now famous study conducted by planning guru Erwin Ephron found that the difference between demos and the actual targets for products in the pharmaceutical category can be as much as 25 percent.[128]

Obviously, the science of demographics—and the psychographic cohort—are waning in popularity. Perhaps that's why *American Demographic* ceased to exist. In its zenith, the use of demographics to connect with consumers was seen as a panacea to mass advertisers using mass media. Statistical analysis based on demographics, and later psychographics, were able to convince advertisers to spend hundreds of billions of dollars on mass media such as broadcast and cable TV, radio, print, and outdoor media. Today the demo research doesn't support reality. By shutting down the magazine, Crain Communications may have symbolically been auguring in a new mind-set for marketers who need to view and understand their consumers, and how advertisers are connecting with their audiences in a new way. Demographics are not enough. We must engage on a deeper level. Unfortunately, this realization is past due. The revolution by the individual consumer has already begun.

The Quiet Revolution

All advertisers really want from their media buying and research is a guarantee that consumers would look at their advertising. The thousands of media choices, and the staggering amount of advertising that accompany them, are making that guarantee dubious at best. When looking at the new generation of consumers, the task of reaching them through mass media is virtually impossible. In fact, some companies, such as Brand-Port, are pushing a pay-for-view model. The online company cajoles its

128. Ibid.

four hundred thousand members to watch thirty- and sixty-second ads, and then pays them based on how many ads they viewed. If TV, print, and radio ads cannot increase brand share, the company reasons, then its model helps at least to increase share of mind. If you're getting paid to watch the ads, you'll probably remember them, too.

Still, the ad industry is obsessed with the measurement of millions of its ads. Demographics may be a flawed concept, but that doesn't mean that marketers are dropping it. In fact, increasingly more complex mechanisms are being developed to measure ads. The much-touted Project Apollo—a partnership between Arbitron and Nielsen Media and backed by Procter & Gamble—is said to enable TV and radio media to be measured on the basis of the actual consumers they reach, not simply the demographic surrogates for the product purchasers. Nielsen is also set to start measuring how many people are watching the commercials, instead of just the amount of eyeballs that watch the program. Complex organizations such as the Radio Advertising Bureau's Media Effectiveness Lab and the Advertising Research Foundation/Interactive Advertising Bureau's Cross Media Labs have been set up to bridge the aforementioned disconnect between advertising's reach and effectiveness.

Yet these tweaked and tuned-up forms of demographic study still miss the obvious point: individual consumers are not parts of consumer clusters, they are individual consumers. Strike that; they are not consumers, they are instead "prosumers." Although the ranks of prosumers may be small now, they will be quickly the determining factor for marketing. Pretty soon marketers won't be trying to reach prosumers with advertising, but instead forming their campaigns and messages based on their recommendations, input, and creativity. Moreover, the prosumers will create the advertising themselves. As the number of blogs, video cameras, and easy-to-use editing systems continue to enter the market, the prosumer revolution will truly take hold. The prosumer will be in control of advertising not solely in the ways they access and interact with media. They will control the advertising by producing it themselves.

Marketers such as Ben McConnell and Jackie Huba are championing the brand evangelists and prosumers of the future, the people they call citizen marketers. "As tools, technology, bandwidth, and skills for citizen marketers expand, so, too, will the variety of products and services showcased. Already today, some citizen marketing is as good as, if not better than, the marketing produced by companies and their agencies."[129] Whatever the terminology—brand evangelists, prosumers, or citizen marketers—the notion is the same: sooner than later, individuals will have control over brands, products, and the companies that produce them. So why continue speaking to them as clusters, silos, or segments? It just doesn't make sense anymore.

"Most companies are deathly afraid of allowing consumers to play with their brands and change them," says Engage Consulting founder Katherine Stone. "That's why corporate brand teams have brand architectures, brand positioning statements, brand essences, etc., all written out in excruciating detail and studied to the fullest so that the brands can be nailed down as if this were an exact science. Consumers must take it or leave it. I much prefer brands that allow me to express myself and leave some impression of my own on the brand. I like the example of eBay—it has become the brand that it is because of the impact that sellers and bidders have made on it. The brand has very basic guardrails, and the rest is left up to the people. It's a very democratic way (and by that I mean little d, not big D) of dealing with brands."

This "small d" democratization process has been nurtured for years by successful online businesses. Message boards and online chat have

129. Ben McConnell and Jackie Huba blog: www.customerevangelists.typepad.com.

been leveraged to connect and reconnect with consumers, and isolate the brand evangelists as future allies in getting more consumers to try the brand, product, or service. Most companies, however, have continued to use the Internet to build brand, move product, increase sales, and get more eyeballs. In effect, they've used the Internet as they would use TV or other mass-based media. They won't let go of the reins. The idea that consumers can themselves make commercials and disseminate them with the same if not better efficiency as mass media scares them to death. Companies "that assume online markets are the same markets that used to watch their ads on television are kidding themselves," say the authors of *The Cluetrain Manifesto*. More importantly for this discussion, they clearly don't believe that "markets consist of human beings, not demographic sectors," and therefore "companies that don't realize their markets are now networked person-to-person, getting smarter as a result and deeply joined in conversations are missing their best opportunity."[130] They are not connecting with the prosumer.

But who exactly is the prosumer whom they fail to connect with, and who is bringing the glad tidings of a better marketing world? I've read many definitions, and the following come close to explaining her or him. A prosumer can be an amateur in a particular field, but is knowledgeable enough to require equipment that has some professional features ("professional" + "consumer"). This includes pretty much includes all Generation Y consumers, who know more about their iPods, X-Boxes, and turntables than we older folks can imagine. A prosumer can help to design or customize the products he or she purchases ("producer" + "consumer"). P&G's Tremor project tries to incorporate these

---

130. Rick Levine, Christopher Locke, Doc Searls, and David Weinberg, *The Cluetrain Manifesto* (Cambridge, MA: Perseus Books Group, 2001), p. xxiii.

types of influencers into their product innovation, design, and packaging endeavors. A prosumer may create goods for her own use and also possibly to sell ("producing" + "consumer"). Importantly, a prosumer is the type of person who takes steps to correct difficulties with consumer companies or markets and to anticipate future problems ("proactive" + "consumer"). These prosumers are proactive in spreading both good *and* bad buzz about a brand. And finally, a prosumer can no longer be conned. Marketing to the prosumer must be an act of authenticity.

The Internet, undoubtedly, is changing the industrialized economy into the experiential one. The most basic change has been a shift in the role of the consumer—from isolated to connected, from unaware to informed, from passive to active—to become a prosumer instead. With access to unprecedented amounts of information, prosumers can make more informed brand decisions. For companies still stuck in the industrialized mentality of restricting the flow of information to consumers, this shift is radical and is challenging their traditional way of doing business. Prosumers can access information on businesses, products, technologies, performance, prices, and consumer actions and reactions from around the world. Prosumers are also deeply networked. Why shouldn't they be? Human beings have a natural desire to coalesce around common interests, needs, and experiences, and the explosion of the Internet and advances in messaging and telephony only drive this desire deeper. Consequently, "thematic consumer communities, in which individuals share ideas and feelings without regard for geographic or social barriers, are revolutionizing emerging markets and transforming established ones. . . . More crucial, consumer networks allow proxy experimentation—that is, learning from the experiences of others. The diversity of informed consumers around the world creates a wide base of skills, sophistication and interests that any individual can tap into. . . . As people learn, they can better discriminate when making choices; and, as they network, they embolden each other to act and speak out."[131] Herein lies the growth of the prosumer base; the more networked consumers become, the more emboldened they are to engage with the companies that are trying to reach them. And the more they become engaged, the more they will challenge the marketing status quo.

In the midst of this shift in business paradigms, companies can no longer employ the command-and-control structure of ramming products and product messaging down the throats of prosumers around the world, nor can traditional demographics pinpoint who the prosumer really is. He is too mutable, mobile, and fluid in his media habits and lifestyle preferences. Perhaps that is why traditional marketers are petrified by the rise of the prosumer. The prosumer lies outside the traditional reach of mass media, advertising agencies, and marketers. He is therefore an anomaly to traditional marketers. And ignorance breeds unwarranted fear. The paradox is that as marketers develop increasingly sophisticated demographic methodologies to try to speak to their consumers, they are denying their most valuable assets—the company's prosumers—the ability to speak back.

The Prosumer and Cocreation

In their book *The Future of Competition,* C. K. Prahalad and Venkat Ramaswamy present a new economic model that warns companies against ignoring the rising power of the prosumer. When trying to create value, the authors argue, companies need to routinely collaborate with consumers to create personalized value through cocreation. In the

---

131. C. K. Prahalad and Venkat Ramaswamy, "Co-opting Customer Competence," Harvard Business Review Working Knowledge Series, February 8, 2000.

world of cocreation, every individual who interacts with the company is a prosumer, without the artificial distinctions among enterprises and households. Cocreation, the authors maintain, "is not the transfer or outsourcing of activities to customers or a marginal customization of products and services. It isn't scripting or staging of customer events around the company's offerings. Those kinds of company-customer interactions no longer satisfy most consumers today. It's the cocreation experience (not the offering) that is the basis of value for each individual."[132] In other words, cocreation is the process of allowing the individual prosumer to determine the design of the products and services in the future, the marketing messages that accompany them, and the sales channels where they are available. The experience of cocreation is more important to drive value than the result of the process itself. Engaging the prosumer in the cocreation process is paramount, and the "use of interaction as a basis for cocreation is at the crux of the emerging reality" of marketers worldwide.[133] Companies can no longer assume that they can create value without the active participation of the prosumers. They cannot hold true anymore that their brands and services are the exclusive value driver. The individual holds that power.

Admittedly, the company-focused attitude to value creation runs deep. It has been the basis for marketplace competition for more than a century. So it is no surprise that the consumer-focused idea of cocreation has not taken off in business circles. Most marketers consider cocreation to mean a form of outsourcing small activities to customers, or cosmetic customizations of products and services. True cocreation is more profound than these small changes in an existing company-focused attitude toward the prosumer. "It involves the cocreation of

132. Ibid.
133. Ibid.

value through personalized interactions that are meaningful and sensitive to a specific consumer. The market begins to resemble a forum organized around individuals and their cocreation experiences rather than around passive pockets of demand for the firm's offerings."[134] Is it any wonder that in a future marketplace such as this, the notion of demographic science is almost completely obsolete?

The translation of cocreation into the marketing world is already upon us. It started with consumer-focused online forums and services such as *Planetfeedback.com, Thecomplaintstation.com,* and *Epinions.com,* to name a few out of hundreds of similar sites around the world. Millions of consumers can now actively exchange views, complaints, opinions, and comments about companies and their brands, products, and services on blogs, community sites, forums, boards, viral e-mails, and text messages. Consumers are beginning to feel their muscles, reasoning that if they are buying a company's goods and services, they are therefore key stakeholders of the company whose individual voices need to be heard when marketing to them. The prosumers are even more vocal, determining that their deep engagement with the company allows them more power to influence the marketing. More importantly, all are typically creative and increasingly have access to professional hardware, software, and online distribution channels to actually *show* companies their individual opinions, rants, and recommendations.

These prosumers are the active players in what McConnell and Huba call the rise of citizen marketing, which is "produced without the benefit of expense accounts, big budgets or pajama-clad creative directors. Citizen marketing is more believable and impactful than the stuff being produced for mass media today. Their creative work is based on their

134. Ibid.

intimate knowledge of the product, thereby making it authentic."[135] The tenets of experiential marketing are closely aligned with the ethos of citizen marketing. It should not be a surprise, therefore, to see a close correlation between the increased ability of the prosumer to become a citizen marketer and the rise of experiential marketing to satisfy the prosumer's engagement needs with a brand or company.

One would think that all marketers, not just experiential marketers alone, would embrace these citizen marketers as indispensable to their marketing strategies. Instead, they consider citizen marketing as a threat to traditional marketing hierarchies, and as a practice that can only help to muddy the marketing messages that are determined at the top with their agency partners. Only a handful of forward-thinking companies—those that understand the experiential expectations of the new consumer—are opening their arms to their efforts. They are in effect imitating the open-source attitude of software development, and are integrating citizen marketers into their overall marketing management by giving them the tools and permission to join in on the cocreation of the marketing message.

Marketing Cocreation

In 2003, more than 120,000 people from around the world registered to join Boeing's World Design Team, an Internet-based global forum that gets pilots, aviation enthusiasts, and airline prosumers such as frequent fliers and business travelers to actively participate in the development of the company's new plane design. The purpose of the World Design Team is to get these prosumers to provide the company with crucial feedback on their designs while they are being developed, not after the plane hits the

135. From the McConnell and Huba Web site: www.creatingcustomerevangelists.com.

market. Activities on the site included a number of message boards, conversations with the Boeing design team, in-depth discussions on what members like and don't like about air travel, and recommendations on what features they would love to include in the plane of their dreams. The site iPodLounge.com (a site not created by Apple) receives more than 5 million hits each day as iPod enthusiasts hit the boards to talk about their iPod usage patterns and to demonstrate to Apple what the next generation of iPods should include and look like. Many of these prosumers post pictures and descriptions of their modified devices, plainly showing the Apple development team and their marketing colleagues exactly what they have in mind. Shoe designer John Fluevog has a section on his site titled "Open Source Footwear," on which diehard Fluevog wearers can submit designs for future shoes. The winning design actually gets put into production.

Many off-the-counter video games are being modified by extremely tech-savvy (and probably very geeky) youth gamers with added textures, characters, levels, story lines, and items. These new games, usually developed and tweaked from first-person shooters such as Quake, Doom, and Half-Life, are called "mods." Mods are produced outside of the game developer's studios by the game-buying consumer, who then develops either an enhanced version of the original game or an entirely new game in itself. One extremely successful mod is called Counter-Strike, which started out as the shelf game Half-Life about four years ago. Counter Strike is downloaded to the computer and runs over the legal version of Half-Life. It now sells more copies than the original game itself: more than a million gamers host it on their servers each day.[136]

Products are not the only things that prosumers create or customize. They are making their presence felt throughout entire business operations,

136. Trend Watching Web site: www.trendwatching.com.

including the marketing and advertising departments. And some forward-thinking companies are actively encouraging them to do so. Converse, a iconic ninty-six-year-old brand based in North Andover, Massachusetts, totally opened up its marketing to the prosumers who loved the brand and saw immediate results. The company began soliciting fans of Converse to create their own commercials about the brand and post them on the Converse Gallery Web site, accessible from the company's main site. The goal was to engage tastemakers such as independent filmmakers, artists, fashion designers, and musicians to cocreate the advertising that Converse was going to roll out nationally, and to give consumers the chance to translate their love of the brand in the form of a twenty-five-second spot commercial. Since the Converse brand has been lately appropriated by creative and alternative-lifestyle consumers who don't respond to traditional marketing and don't like to be sold to, the Converse Gallery was aimed at giving them a sense of ownership of the brand and allowing them a forum to express it.

The campaign was not a contest. It was not meant to find someone who made the best commercial. Rather, it was "something that made a statement above and beyond traditional advertising."[137] That statement is the actual experience of cocreation, and the authenticity of the Converse brand to allow their prosumers—composed of thirteen- to thirty-five-year-olds—to showcase their originality, creativity, and self-expression. And by actually using the submitted clips for TV and online advertisements, Converse is making the ultimate statement: we believe in you, we trust you, and we're behind you in all your endeavors.

More than seven hundred films from fifteen countries have been submitted to the Converse Gallery. Converse simply adds a standard

---

137. Marc Graser, "Consumer-Created Video Ads Boost Converse Sales," *Advertising Age,* February 7, 2005.

six-second tagline and image of a Converse model to the end of the best clips. The first wave of ads was introduced online at conversegallery.com in August 2004, and twelve of those spots were then put into rotation on target-specific networks such as MTV, Comedy Central, Cartoon Network, ESPN, and other cable stations. A second wave of thirteen prosumer-created spots was released in November 2004, and a follow-up cocreation campaign was launched for print ads and outdoor billboards in five major U.S. markets as well.

Converse's online shoe sales doubled in just one month after Converse Gallery was launched, with many of those sales occurring right after someone watched a prosumer-created ad. Traffic to converse.com has jumped 66 percent compared with the previous twelve-month period, with more than a million people going to the site and 400,000 people visiting conversegallery.com directly. December traffic increased almost 200 percent compared to the year-ago month. But these impressive increases are not the real measure of value. The real measure for Converse is the cocreation experience itself, and the enhanced brand value that is firmly entrenched in the prosumer's mind. Remember, "it's the cocreation experience (not the offering) that is the basis of value for each individual."

Some companies are already discovering this value in experience. Brands such as Coors Light and Mercedes-Benz have also invited customers to cocreate advertising campaigns. Mazda has partnered with publishing giant Condé Nast to run a contest for consumer to submit photos of their interpretation of the "zoom-zoom" slogan, which will be used as advertising in Condé Nast's publications.[138]

Other companies are less open to the idea of cocreation, or even the

---

138. *Adrants,* www.adrants.com.

notion that prosumers can create their own amateur ads. In a famous David-versus-Goliath moment, Time Warner sued a fifteen-year-old fan of Harry Potter in 2001 for using the name of her favorite character as a URL address on her Harry Potter fan site. Hundreds of brands get parodied online, and with their success come the inevitable lawsuits from the brands' proprietors to cease and desist the dissemination. A controversial consumer-created mock ad for Volkswagen, created by two aspiring ad agency types early in 2005, showed a would-be suicide bomber getting into a Volkswagen Polo. Although he blows himself up inside, the car is depicted as being so tough it can absorb the blast without harming the pedestrians around it. The ad was widely circulated around the Web—by delighted fans and appalled critics alike—as Volkswagen initiated law proceedings against the creators. And, of course, the heavy-handed approach of the recording industry against file-sharing has propelled suing your own consumers into an art form.

But how can you sue a guy such as George Masters, a thirty-six-year-old schoolteacher from California? He got famous pretty fast for an ad he created in his basement as a homage to his Apple iPod. Working a couple of hours at a time for about five months, Masters created a sixty-second feel-good animated ad that features flying iPods, beating hearts, and trippy psychedelic graphics swirling to the sounds of "Tiny Machine," an obscure song by 1980s pop band the Darling Buds. He posted his work to get feedback from friends and Internet chat buddies. Within days the commercial was viewed thirty-seven thousand times. It was an off-message and it had nothing to do with Apple's existing advertising creative work. But people loved it. Even agency execs praised it as a "pure" advertisement, a "straight-up," consumer-produced spot.[139]

---

139. Leander Kahney, "Home-Brew iPod Ad Opens Eyes," *Wired News,* December 13, 2004.

Apple, not surprisingly, condoned the ad and chose not to send in the legal wolves.

Apple also refrained from legally going after the Neistat brothers, Casey and Van. The two New York City residents were disgruntled at the short life of the iPod battery, which lasts only eighteen months; cannot be replaced by the user; and, at the time, cost $250 to be replaced by the company. The brothers started a site called *ipodsdirtysecret.com* in protest. The first thing they posted on the site was a recorded conversation with an Apple customer service rep, who basically said that the best thing to do was buy another iPod. At the time, New York City was inundated with colorful silhouette posters hyping the iPod. So they videotaped themselves stenciling "iPod's irreplaceable battery lasts only eighteen months" on thousands of the posters throughout the city. They edited down the clip to four minutes, which cost them $40 to make, and posted that on their Web site as well. Within weeks the site was on the lips of hundreds of thousands of hipsters and iPod users nationwide. Soon after the buzz reached the tipping point, with more than 2 million hipsters viewing the clip, Apple announced that it was extending the battery life and implementing a cheaper battery-replacement offer.

The cocreation movement is exposing a clash between the emerging network culture of grassroots action and the industrial mass culture that has been the dominant force in our society for several decades. It is a clash between networked individuals and mass media demographics. It is a battle between a greater role for consumers to determine the marketing they want, versus the one-way marketing muscle of traditional mass media. Some companies, such as Apple and Converse, are seeing the possibilities of leveraging brand evangelists, grassroots activities, and cocreation into a competitive advantage. They are the first to realize that tapping into and mining the intellectual capital of their devoted customers—their prosumers—will produce relevant and authentic content and ideas. This is then easily extended to provide the prosumers access to almost everything the company does. Why not? An Ogilvy Loyalty Index found that the prosumer is worth six times the value of a "typical" consumer. Connecting with each individual prosumer on the grassroots level is the way to reach them.

Perhaps that's why Johnson & Johnsons's Tylenol brand is spending nearly $2.5 million each year to fund events and lifestyle venues for "fringe" subcultures populated by eighteen- to thirty-four-year-olds such as skateboarding competitions, DJ battles, underground film festivals, breakdancing contests, and snowboarding events. What's unique to the campaign—called Ouch—is that at no time does the brand suggest that these consumers actually buy Tylenol. The company doesn't splash its name across the events, nor does it sample any product there. Instead, Tylenol gives money to the event organizers and key influencers—the prosumers—to help them stage the events. The company calls these prosumers their "pain partners."

Not only does Tylenol's Ouch campaign support these events financially—with an expressed directive to their pain partners that there should be no pushing of the product—they also enhance the experience with cool freebies distributed at the events. For instance, at a New York film festival, the company distributed a white box emblazoned with an event-specific slogan: "Great pain leads to great art." In the box, young consumers would find a mini Etch A Sketch, an aromatherapy candle, a CD of soothing music, and a sketchbook; all carried the "Ouch!" moniker, but no Tylenol branding. This hands-off approach to pushing product is perfect when trying to reach the alternative crowd and the prosumers who compose it. There is reason to this madness. Company research indicates that if a brand such as Tylenol can "recruit" the eighteen- to twenty-eight-year-old consumer, he or she will be a lifetime user.

The experience with the brand is more important than the branding. According to C. K. Prahalad, "the power of consumer communities comes from their independence from the company. In the pharmaceutical industry, for instance, word-of-mouth about actual consumer experiences with a drug, and not its claimed benefits, is increasingly affecting patient demands. Thus, consumer networking inverts the traditional top-down pattern of marketing communications."[140]

The success of the Ouch campaign—conducted for J&J by New York City–based Faith Popcorn—has let the company connect with the pain prosumer through a number of different grassroots extensions. It has partnered with überhot comic writer and illustrator Ron Rege Jr. to come up with a series of Ouch comics, which carry absolutely no Tylenol branding inside. The comic guru also designed a limited-edition series of figurines—the Twins and their nemesis the Agitator—that are based on the Ouch comics and produced by Critterbox, one of the most well-respected and revered manufacturers of high-end art toys. The demand for the couple of thousand of these figurines caused a mob scene at the handful of local comic book stores that carried them.

Recognizing that the comic book scene is a heavily grassroots-influenced marketplace, the Ouch campaign also sponsors artists and writers such as Buddy Nichols, Rick Charnoski, Stephen "ESPO" Powers, Jordan Crane, Tobin Yelland, Jocko Weyland, Mark Lewman, Rich Jacobs, and Neck Face. That's covering a lot of ground, even before you throw athletes such as Tony Trujillo, Joel Tudor, Janna Meyen, Asia One, and Crutchmaster into the mix. But this approach

140. C. K. Prahalad and Venkat Ramaswamy, "How to Put Your Customers to Work," *CIO*, April 14, 2004.

has paid off handsomely, with Ouch being embraced by prosumers across the country. By branding from the bottom up, instead of the traditional top-down pattern of marketing, Tylenol has been warmly embraced by the core youth prosumer, so much so that the brand even made it into the song lyrics of underground favorite Ben Kweller without any payment or prompting from the company (how refreshing!). The song, which is sold on Apple's music store and exchanged freely as an MP3 file, is called "Tylenol."

Chapter 6 | **Experiential marketing** will deliver relevant communication to consumers only where and when they are most responsive to them.

S ince 1982, the world has known that ET likes Reese's Pieces. When the cute extraterrestrial took the peanut butter candy from a young Drew Barrymore in Steven Spielberg's blockbuster film, he marked the modern beginning of "product placement." After sales of the candy jumped by a reported 66 percent immediately after the movie's release, marketers' eyes were opened wide. Since they are on a constant and desperate quest to get their brands in front of consumers, competing against other similar and dissimilar brands like moths at a flame, product placement was quickly embraced as an elemental part of both marketing and movie financing. Since then, product placements and brand-specific content have been infiltrating the media with astounding speed.

In effect, marketers and advertisers are looking at the past for clues on how to market in the future. When television was in its infancy, entertainment was branded entertainment: *Texaco Star Theater, Kraft Television Theater,* and *Pontiac Presents Playwrights 56* were TV trailblazers in using content to sell product. It was a beautiful marriage until someone invented the thirty-second spot in 1958. After that, TV became an ad, ad, ad world.

Today, content wrapped as advertising—and advertising wrapped as content—are making a massive comeback. The growing partnership between Hollywood and Madison Avenue has dramatically changed the way products are marketed, and is bound to expand for years to come.

Product placement and branded entertainment are a no-brainer for mainstream brands, and Hollywood is more than happy to take them in with open arms, so much so that brands are giving directors and screenwriters a run for their money. A beer brand such as Heineken was once happy just to be included in the script or scene of a particular movie. Today the Dutch suds marketer would ensure that Heineken was involved in all aspects of comarketing and cross-promotions for the movie, including print ads, radio spots, TV appearances, and PR. Pushing boundaries even farther, brand managers demand access to the scriptwriting process and final editing of films and programs. Of course, this type of brand control comes with a steep price tag. Miramax Studios, for example, was asking $35 million for the rights to be the Green Hornet's car in an upcoming movie based on the superhero.

Fees like this have movie studios and television networks leaping with joy at the opportunity to integrate brands into their programming. In has been reported that after watching Steven Spielberg's *Minority Report*—which prominently featured Lexus, Gap, Reebok, Guinness, and American Express in the script of the movie—the copresident and co-COO of Viacom, Leslie Moonves, quickly realized that "if Spielberg can do it" then "we can, too." He then led Viacom, which owns CBS, Paramount Television, MTV, BET, UPN, and Showtime, on a network charge for advertainment and product placement deals. The fervor with which marketers and content producers are courting each other led *Advertising Age* editor in chief Scott Donaton to quip to the *New York Times* on September 6, 2004, that the "gold rush" reminded him of the Internet ten years ago.

The rush's sole purpose is to get brands ingeniously or disingenuously integrated into network programming, such as the Mars Bar in *The Apprentice,* or Campbell's Soups in *American Dreams.* Hasbro's game Operation was creatively written into the script of *Scrubs,* a show about young doctors in a hospital. American Express, however, was less creative when it sponsored *The Restaurant,* a reality show based on, ahem, running a restaurant. In one scene, the star chef is filmed telling his maître d' to "call American Express. They have this Open for Business program that will take care of everything you need."

Clearly, marketers are not altogether great scriptwriters, but they are giving flailing network television a resuscitative revenue stream. Because of falling ratings, a much fragmented audience, and an explosion of media alternatives such as specialty channels and the Internet, media producers are more than eager to recoup steadily decreasing revenues. Ad-skipping technology such as TiVo and personal video recorders, plus an increasingly sophisticated consumer who refuses to respond to a buckshot marketing approach, have traditional marketers worried as well. Consequently, product placement is a sweet coupling of convenience, like an arranged marriage to Claudia Schiffer.

In fact, marketers are so enamored with product placement that they have gone so far as to cut production studios out completely to develop their own programming. A media buying company called MindShare, owned by the WPP Group, coproduced a TV show with ABC titled *The Days* and split ownership and commercial rights with the broadcaster. MindShare—whose corporate slogan is "Head-Space Invaders"—then sold its portion of commercial time to its longtime clients such as Unilever, Kraft, and Kellogg. Why go looking for appropriate content for your clients when you can just custom-make it for them?

Even a commercial can become content. Miller Brewing Company is developing a TV show based on its five-year-old ad campaign for Miller

High Life, which is a surprise hit with twentysomething hipsters that helped stop the brand's sliding sales record. Pepsi has developed its own programming with *Pepsi Smash* on the WB Network, a teen-friendly one-hour music show. Product placement can even lead to new products. After sending out competing teams to come up with a new toy idea on Donald Trump's *The Apprentice,* Mattel surprisingly put into production a toy thought up by the contestants in one episode. The Morph Machines line hit shelves in February 2005, with each SKU retailing for about $30. Packaging is cobranded with both the Mattel and *The Apprentice* logos.

At the tail end of 2004, Nielsen Monitor-Plus declared that product placement was one of the fastest-growing TV-related marketing forms. While Nielsen's new product placement tracking service does not provide explicit dollar values, the company said that the top ten brands more than doubled the number of product plugs, compared with the first nine months of 2003. The top ten brands generated 8,145 "occurrences" on network television during the first three quarters of 2004, led by Coca-Cola Classic (2,245 exposures) and Pepsi (1,109). The top ten programs that featured product placements accounted for 18,454 brand occurrences, led by shows such as *American Idol, The Apprentice, Pepsi Smash,* and *Big Brother 5.*[141]

Product Placement: A Flawed Panacea?

Traditional and mass media marketers may look to these numbers and pat themselves on the back. Once again, they've leapfrogged the consumers' resistance to ad intrusion with a dynamic form of commercialism and down-low forms of commercials. But many forward-thinking

141. Joe Mandese, "Product Placement Emerges as Fastest-Growing Part of '04 Ad Market," *Media Post,* December 10, 2004.

marketers are worrying that the panacea offered by product placement to advertisers and studios is just not there. Worse still, product placement may be "a flawed and unworkable concept that has been huckstered almost to death." In a passionate and terse editorial on his Web site and in his newsletter, media industry heavyweight Jack Meyers announced the partnership between Hollywood and Madison Avenue to be dead and buried, mostly because "product placement is in reality only an additional form of commercial inventory, adding another level of commercialism to an already over-cluttered television marketplace. . . . [W]ithout research to determine return-on-investment, product placements are simply a new form of messaging with questionable value, but one that many marketers misguidedly believe they must embrace to respond to expanded penetration of digital video recorders and video-on-demand." Once again, marketers have missed the point and gone after tired eyeballs instead of engaging consumers with memorable experiences.

But the effectiveness of product placements is dependent solely on the novelty of its use, and sooner or later the novelty will certainly wear off. Once the thrill is gone, says Meyers, "there is as much chance that product placement will create negative brand equity as positive spin." Meyers says that product placement has worked in only a limited number of programs, such as *Survivor, The Apprentice, Trading Spaces,* and *The Restaurant,* but has little effect or relevance in scripted programming or sitcoms. Furthermore, product placement is a bad idea for advertisers because "advertising is designed to create environments in which marketers can present their messages on their own terms. In product placement, program executives define the message, not advertisers and their agencies." In other words, the future of product placement and advertisement rests on the ability to allow marketers, not studios, to determine where and how their products and brands are embedded or hyped. Doesn't this sound like a call for more experiential campaigns rather than a soup can close-up in your favorite sitcom? Besides, "TV viewers are becoming more savvy and aware of product placement techniques" anyway.

In fact, an eMarketer and *Media Post* survey in late 2004 found that 80 percent of media planners think consumers notice TV product placements, yet 46 percent of consumer say the placements leave no impression on them. In addition, the study found that 11 percent of consumers are left with a negative impression of the placed product. It's obvious that when a majority of consumers notice a marketing campaign but are left with no impression (the good kind) from it, and more than one in ten may be totally turned off by it, there is something inherently missing in the experience of that campaign.

Simply throwing brands into the script should already be a passé practice. The new consumer will quickly realize and reject branding out of context, product placement without relevancy, or a marketing message without experience. Consequently, "many thoughtful producers of scripted programming are already becoming wary of even minimally intrusive product inclusion for fear of alienating viewers," Meyers writes. Most viewers of reality programming don't mind product placement, however, because it's a programming milieu where the introduction of a brand or product is believable and therefore adds to the viewing experience. Marketing is therefore effective then only if consumers "decide" when and where to accept products and brands in their programming, and only if it adds to the experience.

Marketers' decreasing aptitude to reach and influence the marketplace has led them to alternative forms of marketing, allowing for advertising and marketing messages to be subtly and often subconsciously embedded into all sorts of content. Since a thirty-second spot is no longer effective, they reason, perhaps a two-hour commercial disguised as a movie will do the trick. Or if a magazine ad fails to raise the all-powerful sales metrics, maybe placing product mentions into the editorial will move the needle. In all instances, this ad creep is influenced by marketers' inability to effectively get messages through to the consumer.

Their job will only get harder, for they are facing a growing slice of the consumer base who don't (or can't) eagerly translate traditional marketing into purchases—the students and the low-income youth underground who are frequently un(der)employed and media-cynical. Kids and teens are increasingly converting to brand atheism. Their uncanny ability to smell a marketing pitch is a dire threat to marketers who rely on business-as-usual marketing and common branding. Consequently, the latest trend for marketers is to place brands into content that kids actively seek out and interact with. While the twelve- to twenty-four-year-old market makes up only 18 percent of the U.S. market, for instance, it constitutes 37 percent of the filmgoing public.[142] Proponents of product placement see these figures and compare them to the dwindling minutes that teens spend watching TV or reading magazines. Naturally, the knee-jerk reaction to place brands in movies is quick to follow.

Branding the Game

When it comes to reaching the elusive youth, product placements in movies and television are beginning to pale in comparison to the amount of branded content found in video games. Kids, teens, and young adults play *a lot* of video games. According to the Interactive Digital Software Association, revenue from video games and the entertainment software industry overtook Hollywood sales all the way back in

142. Allyssa Quart, *Branded: The Buying and Selling of Teenagers* (New York: Basic Books, 2003), p. 82.

2002. First-day sales of the popular game Halo 2 hit an unprecedented $112 million in 2004. This beat first-day ticket sales of the blockbuster *Titanic*—the biggest opening in Hollywood history—by more than $10 million. Video gaming is the fastest-growing form of entertainment, and a third of gamers are women. The average gamer is twenty-nine years old, and young audiences consistently rank the Internet and video games above TV on the importance scale.

A Ziff Davis study from 2004 called *Digital Gaming in America* showed that 54.5 million U.S. households played console-based games on the likes of Sony's PlayStation 2, Microsoft's Xbox, and Nintendo's Game Cube. An additional 52.3 million households were playing games on their PCs and Macs. There are 60 million handheld games in the U.S. market, and growing numbers of game-enabled cell phones are hitting shelves every month. In response, marketers spent $414.1 million for advertising in video games in the first eleven months of 2003, according to TNS/Competitive Media Reporting.

Perhaps more significantly for traditional marketers, a TNS/Competitive Media Reporting study showed that 26 percent of the respondents said that their TV viewing had decreased in 2003, and that 20 percent of them said that they expected their viewing to decrease even more in the upcoming year. The main reason for this decline, not surprisingly, was increased video gaming. In total, the interactive entertainment category—as the video games industry is now being labeled—was a $9.4 billion market in 2003. Sales are expected to mushroom to $29 billion by 2005, according to Cambridge, Massachusetts–based Forrester Research, Inc.

Naturally, marketers keen on converting teens and brand atheists to their brands are stampeding into the gaming industry. Product placement costs in movies can run in the millions, whereas video games can cost as much as $100,000 for licensing fees. The growing gaming marketplace, and the cost efficiencies for placing ads in games, have resulted in an astounding amount of brand infiltration. Since it's relatively cheap to get a brand in a game, marketers have gone overboard with product placements, and are cluttering the virtual world for teens and young adults as much as they are cluttering the real one.

For instance, the ubiquity of teen brand Quicksilver seen in a PlayStation video game called Tony Hawk's Pro Skater 3 is impossible to ignore. Here you see Tony Hawk doing a skateboard trick underneath a virtual Quicksilver billboard. As the player controls Hawk's kick-flips, 360s, and reverts, the Quicksilver logo is easily noticed on Hawk's T-shirt. As he is skating through skate parks and parking lots in Tokyo, New York, or San Francisco, the Quicksilver logo is never far away, nestled among other branded billboards for Jeep or Nokia, which paid to be included in Tony Hawk's skating world. In fact, more than thirty companies paid to have their logos embedded in the game. And before players even hit the virtual pavements to shred asphalt on their boards, they need to outfit themselves and their "decks" at the game's virtual store, where they choose among various brands of shoes such as Vans or Action footwear, dozens of boards from the likes of Baker or Birdhouse, and baggy shorts or pants from Circa or All Starz. Before one can even begin to play the Tony Hawk's Pro Skater 3, a virtual sale has to be made.

When one considers that a teenager (and adult) will play Pro Skater 3 hundreds if not thousands of times throughout the year, the amount of brand impressions accumulates into the millions. By playing the game over and over, teens are branded with product mentions and brand placements at much higher rates than they would by watching a television program or going to see a movie. Consequently, Nielsen Interactive Entertainment announced a plan in late 2004 to develop audience measurement tools to monitor the effectiveness of console-based video and PC-based game advertising, with standard media metrics of reach and frequency as well as how long the gamer viewed the ad and what time of day the ad was seen. When a survey points out that teens spend an average of 12.2 hours per week online, but only 7.6 hours per week watching TV, the need for marketers to measure their brands' impressions in gaming will get Nielsen to do the math for them. For mainstream marketers, impression is king.

It's no wonder then that product placement in video games continues to explode unabated. In her book *Branded*, Allyssa Quart runs down a partial list of product placements in gaming: "In the game 'Darkened Skye,' Skye of Lynlora fights the evil Lord Neecroft and his minions with rainbow-colored candy Skittles. In 'Croc-2,' the eponymous loveable out-cast crocodile . . . must buy LifeSaver Gummi Savers if he wishes to make special jumps. . . . Meanwhile, the bananas in 'Super Monkey Ball' are tagged with Dole Food Company stickers. The lighters in 'Die Hard: Nakatomi Plaza' are Zippos and the cell phones are Motorola two-way radios. The cabs in 'Crazy Taxi' go to Kentucky Fried Chicken and the surfers in 'Surf Riders' wear G-Shock watches and use Mr. Zog's Sex Wax. The star of the sci-fi combat game 'Wipeout XL' shares the screen with an ad for the brew Red Bull, although the drink has about as much to do with sci-fi warfare as a teenybopper crooner Aaron Carter."

These examples may seem like cutting-edge marketing, but in fact were culled from games that were released in 2002. That was a seminal year for product placement in video games, when gaming leader Electronic Arts inked a $2 million deal to embed McDonald's and Intel products into The Sims Online, a hugely popular virtual life game. Since then, the virtual worlds of gaming are close to overtaking the real world in the amount of advertising and brand intrusions in them. Oddly enough, video games may be acting as crystal balls to our own cultural future, where everything is branded and the clutter of ad messaging is all-pervasive. And since mostly kids and teens play the games, it would not be outrageous to suggest that they're being conditioned by brand marketers to docilely accept the branded world of the future. As Quart asserts, "Games, like so many other products, aim to harness teens' desire for an ideal—a 'true' world—and give them a branded one instead."[143]

Context Is When and Where

Video game marketers respond by saying that ads in games are permissible because they add a semblance of reality to the game itself. For instance, the main character in Tom Clancy's Pandora Tomorrow uses a Sony Ericsson mobile phone in the game, which is typically accepted by those who play it as a reality prop to the narrative. But these instances are rare and sporadic. Many marketers pay to get into the games not to add to it, but to reach a specific demographic with as many impressions as possible.

Depending on where in-game branding is placed, companies can reach each individual gamer with thousands of impressions. Because of marketers' deep-rooted monomania for reaching eyeballs, their desire for counting impressions simply overrides their need to establish context. But gamers don't want prominently placed products in games unless it's solely real-world modeling that allow them to be included. In other words, the gamer needs to decide and dictate where and when a brand appears in the gaming experience.

PJ MacGregor, vice president of Play—a Starcom MediaVest Group

143. Ibid., p. 109.

unit devoted to branded advertising in gaming—believes that because the typical gamer is young, aware, and marketing-resistant, advertisers need to establish a "value exchange" between the consumer and the game environment, and marketing messages cannot disrupt this exchange. "Advertisers have to be more mindful of this than in other advertising spaces . . . most game environments don't lend themselves to advertising. God help us if we ever see McDonald's cheeseburgers in 'Final Fantasy' [a fantasy quest game]." In other words, if three years ago it was cool for a player to collect Skittles for points, this simply won't fly with the gamer today.

Still, marketers continue to corrupt the experience with impression-driven marketing. A snowboarding game called SSX 3 from EA is heavily sponsored by Honda and DNL, 7UP's caffeinated water brand. Clearly, the only thing a car company and a soft drink have to do with extreme snowboarding is the shared target demographics who play the game. By adding nothing of value to the game, and by appearing out of context to the experience, brands interrupt and debilitate the gaming experience.

At the end of 2004, video-game maker Activision and Nielsen Entertainment released the results of a major new study on the effectiveness of in-game advertising. The study was conducted with approximately five hundred active male gamers, age thirteen to thirty-four, who play video games at least once a week for at least fifteen minutes per session. All had very limited or no experience playing any of the three video games used in the experiment. Unsurprisingly, the study concluded that the more effective an ad is integrated into a video game, the greater the gamer's ability to recall that ad. In fact, an astounding "87 percent of research participants remembered seeing a high-integrated brand much more frequently than other, less integrated brands. This indicates that when a brand appears throughout the game, and gamers must interact with it, that it has a strong positive impact on brand integration and recall."[144] Three in ten participants said that advertising in video games was more memorable than traditional television advertising. In addition, "more than one-third of participants agreed that in-game ads were more effective if they assist a game player in reaching a particular objective. This finding is consistent with the higher awareness, recall, and purchase interest generated by high-interactive brands."[145]

Unfortunately, seamless and relevant integration is the exception to the rule for product placements in gaming. More often, brands appear for no good reason at all, and that's what gets gamers steaming mad. Worse still for marketers, gamers are a chatty and Internet-savvy group of individuals. On thousands of message boards and game review sites, millions of gaming enthusiasts trade horror stories and diatribes against intrusive advertising. Conversely, gamers love contextual brand integration. The Sims dynasty of virtual reality multiplayer games from EA, for instance, features dozens of brand placements but consistently ranks in the top for console and PC gaming sales. On *There.com*, a massive multiplayer online game (MMOG), gamers try on Levi's jeans and Nike shoes before venturing into the virtual community. Their collective voices demand something specific from marketers: that marketing will be conducted solely where and when the gamer chooses, not where and when marketers want to integrate their brands.

Most marketers can't understand this directive. They've been exceedingly conditioned by mass media. As Christopher Locke writes in *The Cluetrain Manifesto*, they tend to look at us as passive consumers who will accept a top-down broadcast model "wherein glitzy content is developed at great cost in remote studios and jammed down a one-way pipe into

144. Activision corporate information press release, October 15, 2004.
145. Ibid.

millions of living rooms . . . their offerings have all the classic earmarks of the mass market come-on: lowest-common-denominator programming developed to package and deliver market segments to mass merchandisers." In fact, late 2004 saw the announcement made by Internet network provider Massive, Inc., and InGame Partners for a new Internet-based system to plug server-based ads into games played online or through console-based games hooked up to the Internet. The new ad delivery system also will be able to deliver ads to screens of captive gamers when their games are being loaded up. Massive's network serves video game companies Vivendi Universal Games, UbiSoft, and Legacy Interactive. These massive game providers are opening up their channels for ads to be delivered online, very much like traditional advertising on television. The gamer will have no control over the ads or where and when they appear in the game, except to unplug from the Internet and play games on his or her console instead, which is uncorrupted by the ad intrusions.

The command-and-control mind-set will be the demise of traditional marketing. Advertising and branding are no longer a game of impressions and demographics. The failure of marketers to understand this is clearly in evidence when misguided product placements and branding efforts ruin the experience for a sophisticated gamer. In the virtual world of fantasy and adventure, nothing is more important for a person playing the game than the *experience* of being in another world. Throwing distraction and contradiction into the experience is exactly how not to market in the twenty-first century.

Context Is the Experience

By saying that marketers need to take and enhance the consumer's experience with a brand or product into account as the foremost marketing tactic may seem to be axiomatic, but it's not. The growing misuse of product placement and brand integration in all of media—not just video games—only demonstrates this more clearly. By recklessly relying on impressions in video games, marketers run a dire risk of forsaking the experience. In doing so, they are not responding to gamers' demands to control and enjoy their experience. Marketers are not doing a good job controlling where in the game they place their brands, when and how often they appear, and how they are integrated into the experience.

Millions of gamers can be considered the first experiential audience for marketing, and one of the first audiences that experiential marketers are tapping into. Moreover, because gamers are predominantly young, they are the sophisticated audience of the future. To reach them and speak to them convincingly for years to come, marketers need to understand their experiential needs. In other words, to market to them in the future, it is important to take lessons from successful gaming marketing where brands and products are introduced into the experience with context at the behest and control of the consumer.

The automotive industry has perhaps benefited most from looking to the experiential needs of gamers and incorporating them into their marketing efforts, using advergaming to connect with consumers, and experiential marketing based on video games to drive the future of the business. The *Detroit News* reported in early 2004 that "gamers are changing the face of vehicle showrooms, automotive design studios, auto shows and commercials. They even are beginning to influence what ends up in American dealerships." In less than a decade, an entire industry has turned its collective ear to the gamers and realized that cars are experiential goods, and their marketing had to be experiential to reconnect with a disillusioned consumer base. They looked to the experience of gaming for clues, and began to provide game developers their cars to deliver a highly successful form of marketing.

Sony's incredible racing franchise for the PlayStation consoles called Gran Turismo is a good example of highly successful and consumer-approved brand integration in gaming. When Gran Turismo first hit the market in 1998, the game featured fifty production vehicles for players to drive in the game. When Gran Turismo 4 appeared in 2004, the game featured more than five hundred production cars, including historic vehicles such as the Ford Model T, "that are accurate down to the names of the paint chips." The experience has been greatly enhanced for the gamer through more cars and more car information. More importantly, the game augured in the future of gaming, because Gran Turismo 4 can be played online as well as on the console. The goal, according to Sony, is to create an automotive community of players, where people not only play the game but also chat about cars, compete head-to-head, and take virtual test drives in a noncompetitive virtual reality.

By incorporating cars into a game through highly contextual placement, and then giving the game as many consumer empowerment tools, Sony's Gran Turismo franchise for PlayStation has had immediate impact on car sales. The *Detroit News* quoted Ian Beavis, head of marketing for Mitsubishi Motors Corporation in North America, as saying that "gamers are part of our company folklore. When the original version of Gran Turismo came out, they put pressure on us to bring the Lancer Evo to America. We finally brought it in and today we sell five hundred of those a month to a very young audience. And they are all gamers." Mitsubishi didn't need complex database analysis to tell them something. They simply listened to their grassroots customer.

But gamers are not the only market that Sony listens to. The company's game developers have been reported to meet with the designers and engineers from Ford at the automaker's Dearborn Proving Ground. They rode in the 2005 Ford GT sports car, took thousands of photos, and recorded horn and engine sounds before setting up a PlayStation to play video games with the Ford engineers. Sony also regularly sets up displays at the dealerships to tout the new technologies built into succeeding versions Gran Turismo, as well as a custom driving-simulator complete with flat screens, a race chair, steering wheel, and brake. Perhaps Sony thinks that it won't be long before a simulator is installed in every dealer showroom, loaded up with Gran Turismo. What is certain is that to provide the best experience for driving gamers, as well as establishing the most contextual and real virtual driving environment, Sony understands that the involvement of the auto industry—engineers, dealers, and marketers—is instrumental to the success of its driving games.

Connecting with their consumers through driving games such as Gran Turismo and Project Gotham Racing 2, and relying on smart and interactive product placements in these games, have led automakers to incorporate the gaming experience into many of their marketing efforts. Automaker Volvo went as far as creating thirty- and sixty-second television commercials for its V40 sedan by using footage solely from Microsoft's Rallisport Challenge 2 game for the X-Box console last year. That's right: the entire commercial was a scene from a video game!

The Advergame

The most recent and proliferating re-creation of the gaming experience in marketing is the introduction of "advergaming" media. Quite simply, advergaming media makes a game out of marketing. Instead of placing a brand or product in a video game, advergaming makes the brand or product the central protagonist in the game itself. The entire game is built around the brand experience. Again, the emphasis is on establishing a better marketing experience, with lessons learned from the demands of the gamer. The advergame follows the same basic principle of gaming: the better the game experience, the more people will play. The better the advergame experience, the more people will be engaged.

A simple difference between a video game and an advergame is, basically, the price. Advergames are relatively cheap to produce. A top-line game such as Gran Turismo—a so-called AAA game—will cost more than $2 million to develop and even more to market. Developers say advergames cost $50,000 to $500,000 to make. To put it in another perspective, development costs for advergames are as little as 99 cents for each time a product appears onscreen, compared to about $15 every time a viewer sees it in a TV ad.

In an *Advertising Age* article, Keith Ferrazzi, CEO of Los Angeles–based advergame builder YaYa, described the difference between product placement in games and the notion of advergaming: "Product placement is where brands are represented with a banner or billboard and the product is sitting there, static. Advergaming is creating a commercial, an advertiser's message." For instance, an early advergame developed for Mars Incorporated encouraged players to line up similar colors of M&M candies. Kraft's advergame site called *candystand.com* is already among the most visited game sites on the Internet. Kraft collects voluntary information from players in exchange for giving them dozens of games, using logos from LifeSavers and other candies in games such as billiards, Ping-Pong, and poker.

Spending on advergames is conservatively estimated to grow to reach $260 million in 2008, up from $79 million in 2003 according to the Yankee Group. Cambridge, Massachusetts–based Forrester Research takes a more robust view on advergaming's growth, estimating that it will be a $1 billion-a-year industry by the end of 2005. Equally important is the audience that advergaming attracts. The number of gamers ages thirteen or over in the United States will hit 126 million in 2008, up from 108 million in 2004. It's safe to assume that for this particular group of like-minded individuals, the advergame will be a major marketing medium. Because advergames are not intrusive, like pop-ups or spam, or sneaky and subliminal, like product placements, they will be welcomed by an already protective audience. An advergame is much more engaging than a banner ad, and perhaps more so than a TV commercial, because an advergame is played voluntarily. An advergame is not a pop-up, either, but found and entered on the player's personal choosing. Furthermore, the advance of technology and ever higher connection speeds to the Internet will take the advergaming experience to equal if not superior footing to console-based games. With higher levels of interactivity and graphics, advergames will in themselves become a gaming *experience*. In other words, advergaming is poised to be an ideal virtual manifestation of experiential marketing.

The use of advergaming, and the activation of the audience it can attract, are leading cutting-edge marketers to surround the gaming experience with on-the-ground marketing. For instance, an advergame from Miller Brewing called Virtual Racing League acts as a cornerstone to a wider marketing push to attract racing fans. Players who enter codes from NASCAR races broadcast on television, or from specially marked beer sold in stores, have a better chance of winning. Miller has recognized that the experience of playing an advergame can be leveraged to support and even lead their promotional and retail marketing efforts.

Perhaps one of the best examples of this kind of leverage is the efforts of DaimlerChrysler AG's Chrysler unit, which makes Jeep, Dodge, and Chrysler cars and trucks. In 2002 the automaker decreased their overall marketing budget, but allocated a paltry sum to an advergaming campaign for its little-known Jeep Wrangler Rubicon 4x4. It was the Chrysler's first foray into using the Internet exclusively to launch a product. In February 2002, gamers were able to visit *jeep.com* and register to play the Jeep 4x4 Trail of Life game, featuring a number of Wrangler models that the gamer would drive through the legendary Jeep 101 course. The Jeep 101 virtual course included real-world driving tips as the player completed the course, at which point the game unlocked the Wrangler Rubicon model for the player to drive on the first of three virtual contest competition trails. The superior handling, torque, and power of the Rubicon would be virtually experienced immediately by the player. Then the ten highest scores on the game would allow the top players to compete head-to-head at the annual Camp Jeep festival in Branson, Missouri. The top scorer of the game also would win the new 2003 Jeep Wrangler Rubicon.

By July 2002 there were a reported 312,000 unique visitors to the game's Web site and 78,000 unique visitors to the Rubicon product information Web site. According to Jeff Bell, vice president of Chrysler and Jeep, DaimlerChrysler Corporation, "250,000 consumers downloaded the game and handed over their names and addresses."[146] More astonishingly, Bell estimates that "about 500 of the first 1,500 people who purchased the Jeep Rubicon had piloted a virtual Jeep prior to walking into the dealership." The sheer experience of virtual off-road driving had sold hundreds, if not thousands, of one of the most expensive Jeep models on the market. More importantly, Chrysler learned that instead of pursuing a mass marketing approach that's pushed at the consumer, it would be infinitely more effective to use an experience-based campaign that pulls the consumer in.

146. Tim Manners, "40-Hour Ads," *Reveries Magazine,* July 28, 2004.

In 2004 Chrysler released an entire suite of online branded video games to support nine product launches. Jeep 4x4 Adventure, Chrysler West Coast Rally, and Dodge Racing HEMI Edition all featured cutting-edge technology that provided a best-in-class experience for gamers, who are both entertained and educated by DaimlerChrysler. In 2004, game development and distribution represented the largest portions of the total marketing budget for the company than at any time before, mostly because PC gamers are twenty-five to forty-five years old, with a sixty-to-forty male-to-female split. That is exactly the sweet spot consumer that is Chrysler's target.

The company quickly realized the potential of an experience such as playing a video game to sell cars and began to improve the experience for the gamer. Instead of hosting the game on its own Web site, which was the typical way to distribute an advergame, Chrysler decided to go where the gamers are. The company established partnerships with MSN, AOL, Yahoo, and other Internet gaming communities. In 2002, conversely, the company's strategy was to drive consumers to Chrysler's site to play the games. By going to where the consumer was most willing to play online games, and by doing it on their terms instead of standard corporate practice, Chrysler saw immediate results with advergaming in 2004.

In 2004, a Dodge-branded advergame called Race the Pros increased awareness for all Dodge brands by 27.6 percent among consumers who played the game. After the game was promoted during Fox broadcasts and online at MSN and Fox Sports, purchase intent for a Dodge brand jumped 19.6 percent. The DaimlerChrysler brand also got some recognition, with a 24.7 percent boost to the parent. According to Bell, these positive results have turned the company away from product placement in video games—the company had bought into the Tony Hawk franchise earlier—and placed it firmly in the advergaming milieu.[147] For instance, the marketing budget for ads in video games at Chrysler was zero in 2000. In 2004 it represented more than 10 percent of the group's total marketing budget. In the same time period, the company has significantly decreased spending on television and print advertising. The successes of advergames have led Chrysler to become the first advertiser to participate in a Nielsen Entertainment and Activision partnership program to measure how consumers interact with ads in online PC video games.

There are also very compelling side benefits to advergaming beyond increased awareness and cost efficiencies. First, an advergame provides an experience wherein technical and complicated information about a product can be explained without seeming forced, dry, or out of context. Second, marketers can use advergames as an experiential consumer research tool by monitoring which feature of a given product or service appeals most to each individual consumer. Third, the virtual consumer experience of an advergame can be reproduced in the real world to some high-impact and memorable experiential marketing. . . . one-to-one experiential marketing.

For instance, Chrysler has already incorporated its 2005 Jeep Grand Cherokee model into a game called Jeep Mountain Madness as part of its $50 million launch. The game featured the Jeep vehicles traversing off-road terrain through various harsh elements on challenging courses. The company took this thematic, an experience that is enjoyed by the player online, and took it to the streets. In support of the launch, teams in ten U.S. markets would park Grand Cherokees completely covered in mud around high-traffic city locales. Brand ambassadors would talk up the vehicle and take photos of consumers in front of the muddy trucks. The agency that created the campaign, GMR Marketing, based

147. www.clikz.com, July 28, 2004.

in New Berlin, Wisconsin, brought Chrysler's TV creative to life. Then Chrysler took it to a whole other level. To re-create the hyper-real experience of driving a Jeep in the virtual world—where the experience is amplified to allow the player to do almost anything possible—a Chrysler agency "drove" a Grand Cherokee up a skyscraper at New York City's 2 Penn Plaza and "parked" it in a vertical Jeep Only parking spot on the side of the building. The PR stunt—orchestrated by Clear!Blue—was an immediate hit. By hoisting a Jeep up a thirty-foot building and parking it there, the agency was certainly tipping its hat to the advergaming experience.

The success of the Chrysler suite of advergames has led the company to begin setting up gaming kiosks in its dealerships in North America, a practice already established by their Japanese counterparts. Daimler-Chrysler is also rolling out advergames to the "third screen"—the little one on all of our cell phones and PDAs. The company uses terms such as "invitation marketing" when it talks about sending games to an individual consumer, who is fully in control, deciding when and if the marketer appears on their cell phone screens. The idea is to motivate people to initiate the conversation with a marketer by opting into an advergame, and continuing with the dialogue for as long as they want. Much like the philosophy for online advergaming, invitation marketing on the cell phone capitalizes on the ability to mass-market a brand through an individual experience.

Making It Real

Nobody makes the game come alive better than the U.S. Army. While this statement can be construed to mean a number of very different things, the point for our discussion here is that the army's most vigorous recruitment effort has revolved around two very expensive advergames called America's Army: Operations and America's Army: Soldiers. The America's Army experience is an advergaming juggernaut, an empire that is looked to enviably by the rest of the advergaming nations. When a player comes to the game online, he and she step into the best-in-class advergaming experience. The graphics and speed are top-notch, the reality of the army's basic training courses and simulated combat is of console quality, and the authenticity of the experience is ensured right down to the individual caliber of bullets used in real army equipment. To put it in perspective, the typical top-end driving game, such as Chrysler's Race the Pros, would cost close to $1 million. America's Army: Operations, the first game developed by the army in late 2002, cost $7.8 million. According to an April 2003 story in the *Christian Science Monitor,* more than 1.3 million players had logged on more than 7 million hours of online play in eight months after the advergame's release. Between 15 and 30 percent of the roughly 35,000 people who play the game each day go on to check out the army's recruiting Web site.

The army did not rest on its advergaming successes, but chose to take the gaming experience to the streets, primarily by rolling out an experiential marketing campaign to large events and community gatherings. The traditional recruiting methods of accosting potential recruits were being transformed into more advanced and experiential methods, where one-to-one dialogue between a recruiter and a recruit was made possible in an interactive and experiential environment. The advergame made that possible. Unlike Chrysler, which placed its games on portal sites such as MSN, and Yahoo, where gamers congregated in a virtual environment, the army decided to place their games in a physical arena and went to places where their target recruits physically congregated and interacted. By taking their games to places where the recruits already expected a marketing presence—NASCAR and hot rod races, music concerts, extreme sports competitions—the army was able to allow the recruits to choose for themselves whether they wanted to participate in the experience.

Again, it was up to the "consumer" to choose to engage in the marketing experience. By turning their successes online with American Army: Operations into an experiential platform, and then rolling it out to highly targeted events for potential recruits to experience it, with a recruiter on-site to answer questions and comments one-on-one, the army was able to conduct one of its most successful recruiting and branding campaigns in modern history. But first, a little bit of background is necessary to get the whole story.

In 1999, when the army was still a place where one can "Be All You Can Be," the top brass missed their recruiting target by 17,000 soldiers. To the army, the shortfall was close to catastrophic. A $400 million request for proposal went out to marketing agencies to revive the "brand," which had staled with the younger generations, who saw the army not as a patriotic opportunity, but as a place to get tuition cash and bonuses. Out of this RFP, the Starcom Mediavest Group came up with "An Army of One," the first new campaign in more than two decades. The notion was to position the army closer to the mind-set of the new generations, one that focused on the individuality of the recruit rather than his or her role on a team. And whereas "Be All You Can Be" was driven by buckshot broadcast mass media, the new campaign divests itself into a number of codependent marketing disciplines. Media builds awareness, PR fuels outreach programs, and www.goarmy, where the games are located, drives interaction and information. But so far the biggest bang for the army's buck has been event marketing, which accounts for 10 percent of the total annual marketing budget. It's at events, where the potential recruit is most open to learning about the army brand, where the real victories are being scored.

Live marketing campaigns for the army are currently popping up all over the country though sponsorships, mobile tours, grassroots affairs, college tours, ethnic festivals, athletic endorsements, and spring break initiatives. A brand almost entirely powered by advertising before 2000, the army is now running one of the most aggressive event marketing portfolios in the business. The game may have made the army cool, hip, and sophisticated with the new generation of recruits, but by going to where they are most open to marketing and by delivering a marketing experience, the Army has hit its recruiting targets four years in a row, attracting more than 400,000 new recruits. (The military quagmire in Iraq has since contributed to the army missing its target for the first half of 2005.)

The army has created no less than ten major event marketing programs: sponsorship of the National Hot Rod Association, the Arena Football League, the U.S. Rodeo Association, and NASCAR; a proprietary All-American Bowl for high school football players; mobile college football tours; a spring break program; a number of third-party events; a fleet of customized Equally important to the reach that the army achieves with its event marketing is the depth it can garner during the events themselves. This is accomplished by the recruiters, who number two to ten at each event.

According to *Event Marketer* magazine, events "are the best opportunity for face time the recruiters have ever seen, as events create an exciting environment for them to tell (and sell) the story." Furthermore, the events fuel the rest of the marketing mix. "The army uses live programs to seed and feed other parts of the mix with what it calls 'event offshoots.' News, visuals, thematics, and buzz from events are used to literally feed the rest of the mix with content that makes it all more relevant."[148] Lastly, event marketing allows the army to go after the influencers to their target market—coaches, parents, older peers, friends, and relatives. Realizing that there are a steadily decreasing number of older folks who have served in the army, event marketing at school pep rallies and football games allow the army to educate the influencers so that they can talk about the army to the prospective recruit. By going to where the consumer is most receptive to the message, the army is using event marketing to *literally* influence the future of the country.

The army is strategic in determining where and when the mobile tours go, depending on the recruiting needs from year to year. In other words, the army wants to recruit where recruits are available and willing to experience the "brand." The college segment of the mobile tour, for instance, will present the "Go Army" brand experience—complete with climbing walls, interactive kiosks, private recruiting rooms, parachute simulators, video walls, and high-energy music—as an ideal place for postgraduate opportunities. It will position the army as high-tech and sophisticated. If 60 percent of U.S. high school students go on to college, the army reasons, then college campuses are where the army needs to be. In 2004 the army aimed their sites on two-year colleges and ROTC-supported four-year campuses. Mobile tour events at junior colleges are tailored for that specific market, as are high school events that concentrate more on the travel opportunities and job training that the army offers. The mobile tour hits two colleges per week, with four full-time brand ambassadors, one staff manager, and seven field reps who are hired at each local market.

148. "Hooah!" *Event Marketer Magazine*, January 21, 2004.

The cornerstone to the event marketing experience is—you guessed it—the army's ever-popular advergame called America's Army, as well as one-on-one sessions with recruiters. During events, potential recruits enter the gaming experience to team up and battle terrorists and other national threats. But unlike other video games, in this scenario a player who recklessly charges the enemy and fires wildly is destined to fail. The game factors in a player's stance, breathing, movement, and weapons mastery. Participants who accidentally shoot a fellow soldier wind up in a virtual brig. The goal is to provide a realistic idea of everything from basic training to combat. Not only do players get a fun and exciting experience, they also get as close to the real thing of being in the army as possible, without actually getting a buzz cut and general-issue fatigues. Furthermore, the army has been using the video game, and video game–like graphics, in their latest salvo of TV ads, so that when a potential recruit enters the event experience, he or she is most likely already aware of the army's brand positioning.

Call of the Mall

The look and feel of an experiential marketing campaign can closely mirror that of a brand's game or commercial, and can be considered a way to "bring the brand to life." This term can be used to describe any form of experiential marketing when the consumer enters a marketing world that he or she is already familiar with. This instantly gives a sense of context to the campaign. By "bringing the brand to life" at consumer intercepts such as that of the U.S. Army's tour, the consumer is reassured by and understands the marketing being conducted. The creative execution of that intercept event provides ample context for the consumer.

Another way to achieve that context is to conduct the marketing at a place where consumers expect it. It makes sense to conduct a marketing experience at a place where that marketing can be translated into a sale. The mall is like the big tent to a retail circus. Under the roofs of millions of square feet of retail space, a multiple-brand experience is already a given. Event marketing, hands-on trail, sponsored concerts, sampling events and innovative store design must enhance that experience. The mall, in effect, is a type of medium—like TV, print or radio—that can be leveraged for marketing purposes. But unlike other media, the mall is dedicated to selling something. It is a medium whose audience is both captured and in the mind-set to buy.

This makes the mall one of the best places to create a marketing experience, and an excellent example of successful marketing that is conducted where and when the consumer chooses. Staging events at this location is a natural fit. Consumers are prepared for a marketing experience before setting foot in the mall, and are most receptive to marketing when they are in the process of shopping. For marketers, event marketing at malls offer them the shortest distances among a consumer, a marketing message, and product purchase. Furthermore, malls allow them to achieve high volume with very little lead time and the ability to "target specific products to specific regions of the country."[149]

The target audience for mall marketing is predominantly the youth market—the consumers of the future, the same young audience that buys up video games at astonishing rates. In the past ten years, malls have become social centers as much as commercial ones for kids and young adults age twelve to eighteen. In some areas, the mall is the only point of shopping and entertainment for miles around. Kids instinctively flock to them, and spend a lot of time and money there. It has

149. Lorin Cipolla, "Location, Location, Location," *Promo Magazine*, January 1, 2004.

been a loosely held industry secret in the music business that boy bands and girl acts such as the Backstreet Boys, Britney Spears, and Aaron Carter were crafted, cultivated, and unleashed on the throngs of preteens through mall tours and in-store promotions. Malls are marketing nirvanas for reaching the teen set. Simon Property Group, one of the largest mall chain owners in the United States, has released startling statistics about the lucrative attraction that malls pose for teens. Teens visit Simon malls 325 million times a year and spend an average of $50 each time. Malls have thus become fertile ground for experiential marketing such as entertainment events, guerrilla marketing forays, sampling, couponing, or conducting market research through one-on-one interactions. They are a perfect place where teens can touch and feel a brand, then go across the mall aisle and buy it.

More importantly, in the age of teen apathy and oversophistication when it comes to knowing, discerning, and being influenced by brand marketing, nothing gets through to teenagers better than hands-on trial and interaction. And the mall is where they are most receptive to it. For instance, Nickelodeon's the N Network staged a multimall tour with Simon Property Group and General Growth Property called the Real Access Tour, to promote its *Real Access* series of television programming. The tour provided an interactive Hollywood experience, where each day a thousand to five thousand teens interacted with celebrity look-alikes and got personal massages as well as hairstyle and cosmetic makeovers. This environment was positioned in front of teencentric stores to ensure that their mall experience also included Nickelodeon. Nintendo got into the mall marketing experience with its Who Are You? mall tour in twelve markets around the country to showcase its new game lineups right before the Christmas season. Interactive gaming stations were set up in the environment, which saw more than four thousand teens pass through the mall experience.[150] A Nintendo exec was quoted in *Promo* magazine as saying that the company "[knows] that there's a lot going on during the holidays so we try to engage consumers on a one-on-one level and allow them to interact with our product and character franchises."[151]

Experiential mall marketing isn't just a pass-through endeavor. The latest trend for this type of marketing is to establish a permanent footprint in the malls. PBS Kids launched a first-ever PBS Kids Backyard in conjunction with Mills Corporation, another large mall operator. The PBS Kids Backyard is a 3,000-square-foot permanent playground that opened in November 2003 in a St. Louis Mills mall, which includes a PBS-themed shopping area, child-friendly stores and restaurant, full-size play structures, interactive computer kiosks, and a small theater for PBS character events. More than 200,000 parents and children showed up for the opening weekend.[152] PBS and Mills plan to launch the PBS Backyard environment in Cincinnati, Pittsburgh, and two other locations. In a similar vein, a marketing concept called Kids City has been raising eyebrows and turning heads ever since the first Kids City opened up in a Santa Fe mall in 1999. The 51,000 square-foot pavilion receives more than 820,000 visitors—kids and their families—each year. The concept behind Kids City is ingeniously simple and, according to some critics, overly commercialistic because its target market is kids two to twelve years old.

The pavilion is organized like a city, and within this city are areas and blocks that are virtual representations of real-life areas that are sponsored by a corresponding brand. For instance, every city should have an

150. Ibid.
151. Ibid.
152. Ibid.

airport, and the one in Kids City is sponsored by American Airlines. The hospital is sponsored by Johnson & Johnson; the supermarket is a Wal-Mart. Each area is kid-size: everything is miniaturized to accommodate the kids, and everything is also hands-on. Kids are able to "play" in a virtual operating room. When they are at Wal-Mart, they can play as either shoppers or checkout personnel. The airport, sponsored by American Airlines, has a scaled-down plane fuselage and cockpit for kids to get behind the controls. Kids can make minipizzas at the Domino's pizzeria, or learn how to make ice cream in the Unilever part of town. And, of course, there is a beauty salon sponsored by Pond's to give kids makeovers and new haircuts. In fact, the first Kids City has fifty-two marketing partners in total, and future Kids Cities planned for New York, Chicago, San Francisco, and Atlanta will have even more.

Pop-up Retail

The latest trend in experiential retail may never even reach the radar screens of the typical consumer. Outside the traditional stores, malls, catalogs, and Web sites, a new form of retail makes the act of just knowing where the store is an experience in itself. The concept is called "pop-up retail," and its increasing use is redefining the notion of when and where a sale can be made.

The original idea for pop-up retail took root with the fashionista and tastemaking urban youth in Tokyo and New York a few years ago. One of the oldest and more underground pop-up retailers is a collective called Vacant, "an exclusive . . . retail concept store and gallery opening for one month only in an empty space in major cities, including New York, London, Tokyo, Shanghai, Paris, Berlin, Stockholm, and Los Angeles, showcasing an exclusive range of one-off, hard to find, specially made, and limited-edition products."[153] These products include the latest shoe from Puma, the coolest gadgets from Sony, couture from a high-rising designer, thousand-dollar watches, hard-to-find vinyl LPs, vintage furniture, and the latest fashion accessories. The stores would feature highly coveted brands from around the world, as well as brands no one had ever heard of before. The stores act as entertainment spaces as well, with listening parties, product launches, fashion shows, magazine issue launch events, and live artist events enhancing the shopping experience.

More interestingly, however, is that not all products may be purchased, and limited quantities are available on specific items throughout the store. And here's the kicker: Vacant releases the address of the store location only moments before the store's opening. Even then, the store announces the location to a select list of customers. It is up to them to spread the word to others. Often the announcement is in the form of an e-mail or a text message. The communiqué is then forwarded to friends and family members, who then pass on the message through their social networks. The very act of getting an invitation to the store is an experience, as those with the inside scoop feel themselves privileged to be part of the in-crowd.

Pop-up retail seeks to combine retail with event marketing. It is also a cost-efficient way to build buzz and brand stature. Method, a seller of bathroom and kitchen cleaners and hand soaps, took over a vacant storefront in San Francisco's Union Square for about the same cost as it would spend on an outdoor billboard.[154] The company created a gallerylike display to showcase its wares, therefore bypassing the dogfight of getting its products on crowded supermarket and pharmacy

153. www.govacant.com.
154. Bridget Finn, "Why Pop-Up Shops Are Hot," *Business 2.0,* November 17, 2004.

shelves. For two weeks in August 2004, Purina opened its Meow Mix Café in downtown Manhattan, a gathering place and bistro for . . . cats. The café sold off Purina's new line of wet cat food (and some snacks for humans as well) by inviting cats and their owners to hang out at the pop-up store. Purina CEO Richard Thompson was quoted as saying that the $200,000 idea was "worth $10 million in publicity."[155]

These pop-up stores are necessarily experiential. There is no point in re-creating a typical retail environment. That's what big box stores and chain retailers are for. Pop-up retail seeks to surprise the consumer just by being there, and enhance the consumer experience through store design and consumer involvement. American Girl Place, at Forty-ninth Street and Fifth Avenue in Manhattan, is just such a place. The Wisconsin-based company, started in 1986 and since bought by Mattel, Inc., sells dolls starting at $80 and accessories that are equally high-end. More than 10 million American Girl dolls and 100 million American Girl books have been sold since then, and 650,000 girls subscribe to *American Girl* magazine. Fans of the dolls are not disappointed when they come into the store. At American Girl Place, there's a 135-seat theater and a doll hair salon. Girls and their dolls can also do lunch (or tea) together. Dolls get their own seat at the table and their own teacup. There are a number of boutiques in the store that sell different types of doll dresses and accessories, such as ear muffs and scarves. Some doll outfits come with matching girl outfits. Those retail at more than $100. More impressively, whereas the typical consumer spends about twenty minutes in a toy store, guests to American Girl Place spend over two hours. And the company does not advertise.

Target got hot with pop-up retail in the summer of 2004. After

155. Ibid.

rolling out an Isaac Mizrahi–designed pop-up store—a 1,500-square-foot temporary space in Rockefeller Center—Target set up a pop-up space in the Hamptons (a high-end vacation spot) for four weeks at the Bull's-eye Inn. Posters around Manhattan cajoled Wall Street execs to visit the store, a place to both shop and socialize during weekends away from the city. Even eBay got into the pop-up game. The company invited six interior designers to take over a posh Manhattan penthouse and, on a limited budget, style it with furniture and accessories bought only on eBay.com. The penthouse quickly grew in chic furnishings and reputation. All the items were then put up for auction for one week only, and the eBay Showhouse closed its doors for the summer.

Pop-up retail is a tactic being appropriated by nonretail brands. The Crown Royal Barber Shop popped up and opened its doors in New York City in the summer of 2004 to create a custom-tailored experience for its target consumers: young African-American males who like to keep their hair "fresh and clean." The Crown Royal Barbershop brings the typical American barbershop to life, but with a distinctly urban and hip attitude. The shop was open seven days a week, with three local barbers taking in consumers on a first-come, first-served basis. Michael Fernandez, the senior multicultural brand manager for Crown Royal, simply called the barbershop "an interactive billboard."[156] But it was much greater than just that.

Pop-up retail is a clear manifestation of the "experience economy." These temporary spaces not only surprise a target consumer base with their existence, they also provide them with an engaging experience. There is a sense of exclusivity to these pop-up retail sites because of the temporary nature of the stores, and the word-of-mouth

---

156. Jim Meskauskas, "Interactive Marketing . . . Offline," *Media Post,* October 21, 2004.

knowledge that is available to only a few consumers. Pop-up retail is also a manifestation of leveraging buzz to drive trial, and a way for retailers to experiment with design and product lineup. This trend will keep growing as upstart brands seek a way to reach their target consumers and as established ones try to reinvigorate their existing ones. And more importantly for this chapter, pop-up retail is a concept that accepts and embraces a basic premise of experiential marketing: it seeks to be part of the consumer's life when and where he or she wants or needs it the most.

For example, Target did not only provide a pop-up location for wealthy beachgoers in the Hamptons in 2004. On June 24 in Times Square, Target set up a one-day pop-up extravaganza called "Deliver the Shiver" and sold truckloads of air conditioners for $75 a pop. They gave away Bull's-eye carts for anyone who bought the unit to roll it home back with them. MTV Europe partnered with Adidas, Levi's, and Sony Ericsson in Germany to visit Berlin, Hamburg, Cologne, and Munich to establish one-week pop-up stores that will carry limited-item, exclusive, and cutting-edge products not available anywhere else in the country. All four brands knew that demand would be great for their sneakers, jeans, and footware. So they took them to the people. In a similar vein, fashionista mainstay Comme des Garçons spent only $2,500 to spruce up an old bookstore in the shabby-chic East Berlin district of Mitte, at about $700 a month in rent. The only advertisement for the store was about six hundred flyers posted around the area, and, of course, word-of-mouth. The store has a "shelf life" of twelve months, whether it turns a profit or not. The gesture was more important than profit. By going to an unfashionable section of East Berlin, Comme des Garçons thus became more fashionable. By not opening up another behemoth marble retail emporium—like the 20,000-square-foot Louis

Vuitton flagship on New York's Fifth Avenue—the small store made a big statement. Since then, Comme des Garçons has rolled out the pop-up concept to Barcelona and Singapore, with plans to open up one-year shops in high-demand and hungry markets such as Warsaw, Stockholm, Ljubljana, and Vilnius. Pop-up retail is here to stay.

If two-thirds of all purchases are unplanned, as consumer expert Paco Underhill contends, then why should retail be so static? Consumers want multiple points of access to their shopping needs, so retailers are trying to come up with unique shopping solutions to meet them. Even a power cyberretailer such as eBay has utilized pop-up shops to service its customers, spread buzz, and make more money. Pop-up stores also can benefit a community—Target donated all its New York pop-up profits to breast cancer charities—and acquire a kind of mom-and-pop familiarity in the neighborhood. This is a type of marketing that takes into consideration that consumers are interested more than ever at having their marketing appear when and where they are most receptive to it. The success of pop-up retail, when done with this consideration in mind, shows that this alone can provide a compelling experience for the consumer. Pop-up retail is also a major innovation for retailers and marketers alike. It takes a centuries-long practice into the twenty-first century, tailored for a new consumer in a fast-paced marketplace. If the consumer is evolving and progressing, shouldn't the marketing innovate itself as well?[157]

157. Clayton Collins, "You Want It? You Got It—Instantly," *Christian Science Monitor*, October 20, 2004.

| Chapter 7 | **Experiential marketing**'s goal is to succeed using innovative approaches and tactics to reach out to consumers in creative and compelling ways. |

D avid Polinchock has a great job. As founder and CEO of Brand Experience Lab in New York City, he is at the forefront of experiential marketing theory and practice. He's been talking about consumer experiences for a long time, back when experiential marketing was known as "experiential advertising." Polinchock started a company called CyberEvent Group in 1991, a company that used virtual reality technology for marketing campaigns. He called it experiential advertising because virtual reality allowed him to create experiences that would allow consumers to enter and interact with a marketing message. Since then he has expanded this directive into what Brand Experience Lab has become, namely "an agent of innovation that helps leading companies build and manage the most powerful, integrated brand experiences possible."[158]

Part of Polinchock's job is green-lighting some of the most interesting technology applications that help make marketing messages into marketing experiences. Brand Experience Lab is a tech incubator for experiential marketers. It's like the lab in all the James Bond movies.

158. From the Brand Experience Lab Web site: www.brandexperiencelab.org.

Here Polinchock oversees a portfolio of "transformational technologies" that are taking experiential marketing into uncharted realms of interaction and innovation. For instance:

· **Audio Spotlight.** This is an audio laser, a technology that allows marketers to put sound exactly where they want to put it, "whether it's swooping over an audience, whispering in a person's ear from tens of meters away, or putting an isolated directional beam of sound only on one spot." Originally designed with museums in mind, the audio spotlight has myriad marketing applications. Just imagine the possibilities of stepping into a branded audio booth in a crowded nightclub to get away from the DJs techno and chill out with a little jazz instead.

· **Video Messaging Kiosk.** Imagine a telephone booth that sends video instead of sound. Deployed at concerts, in-store, and at malls, sports events, and themed restaurants, the Video Messaging Kiosk acts as an "engaging, interactive communication and branding solution" that can record a short video message and deliver it via email anywhere in the world and viewed by the recipient in a customized and branded HTML message.

· **Ground FX.** Perfect for the retail and entertainment markets, the Ground FX technology "projects dynamic visual content onto virtually any floor or wall space and creates a full body interactive experience, literally allowing consumers to control an ad or game with their body motions."

· **Jam-O-Drum.** Want to get groups of people to make beautiful beats? This interactive drumming table is "inspired by experiences of communal music-making in non-Western cultures." This virtual drum circle uses real-time computer game play to "encourage users to create music as an ensemble[and] in a social setting." Talk about engagement!

· **Magic Mirror.** Another large crowd interaction comes in the form of this particular technology, which takes "live video of a group and then laying computer-generated effects, such as a huge ball and net [to play a huge game of virtual volleyball] over this image. Sensors that detect movement in the group allow audience members to physically affect the images they are seeing on the big screen."

There are many more interesting tech applications and platforms like these that are being incubated in Polinchock's lab. They are all thought of and spitballed from an experiential perspective, and all have innovative marketing applications. It's no surprise that Polinchock's clients are some of the most forward-thinking corporations in staging experiences. They are youth-focused, innovative, and global: Vodafone, AOL Time Warner, GlaxoSmithKline, Chase, the NBA, Mattel, Old Navy, and Toys "R" Us. Brand Experience Lab's research and product development are not simply technology-based, but are used to give clients technology solutions to create experiences. It is therefore imperative that the technology fits with the creative, social, and cultural forces that are influencing consumers each day.

This is a very important point to consider. Technology and the new products that enter the marketplace each day are becoming instrumental to savvy marketers' ability to reach the consumer. But they do not necessarily make the consumer experience better. A motion-sensing speaker imbedded inside a point-of-purchase cardboard cutout, or a plasma screen hanging in the corner of an office elevator, are both innovative marketing applications of emerging technology. But that does not make the technology innovative in improving the consumer's experience. Or as Brand Experience Lab states, the consumer "is accustomed to using technology in their daily lives" and so "to speak to them in their digital language, to delight them and engage them, you must find relevant new technology that helps your brand story better."[159] Of course, this innovation experienced by a consumer can come from all sorts of areas in a company: marketing, packaging, new products, promotions, etc.

Innovation can thus act as an experience enhancer. Continuous product innovation, like that exhibited by Apple computers and its peripheries, "increases the value of doing business with the company," according to Columbia Business School professor Bernd H. Schmitt.[160] More importantly, "innovation improves the lives of consumers and business customers by providing new solutions and thus new experiences."[161] These observations are spot on, and are as applicable to innovation in company product lines as they are to a company's lineup of marketing and advertising initiatives. "Since a desirable customer experience must be the ultimate goal of a business, a company seeking breakthrough innovation should incorporate the customer experience into the product development process."[162] This seems like stating the obvious, and needs to be taken a further step. Because a positive customer experience is indeed the ultimate goal of a business, so should the company incorporate experience into its marketing mix. The innovation

159. Ibid.
160. Bernd H. Schmitt, *Customer Experience Management* (Hoboken, NJ: John Wiley & Sons, 2003), p. 172.
161. Ibid., p. 173.
162. Ibid., p. 177.

it must embark on and continue is not restricted to product or packaging. It must be innovative in its marketing as well.

To do this, as Brand Experience Lab would contend, innovation should not hinge strictly on technology, but on the application of the technology in the context of cultural, economic, and social currents prevalent in the marketplace. For example, the tidal rise of digital video recorders (DVRs), TiVo, blogs, and mobile telephony technologies do not only present myriad opportunities for applying them in marketing initiatives. These technologies are the harbingers of a whole new media landscape. This means that they shouldn't just be integrated into the marketing, but that marketing needs to incorporate the emerging social networks and technological infrastructures into itself.

Take, for instance, the rise of mobile telephony and the wireless Internet. The rise of text messaging, location-based GPS, cooperative networks, and flash mobs is much more than an unparalleled opportunity for groundbreaking marketing. New-technology guru Howard Rheingold writes that "when you piece together . . . different technological, economic and social components, the results is an infrastructure that makes certain kinds of human actions possible that were never possible before. The 'killer app' of tomorrow's mobile infocom industry won't be hardware devices or software programs but social practices. The most far-reaching changes will come, as they often do, from the kinds of relationships, enterprises, communities, and markets that the infrastructure makes possible."[163] Of course, marketers are excited about delivering messages through SMS. But are they equally excited by—or even aware of—the new consumer who is emerging because of them? Rheingold continues to ring the bell for companies around the world

163. Howard Rheingold, *Smart Mobs: The Next Social Revolution* (Cambridge, MA: Perseus Books Group, 2002), p. xii.

when he predicts that "groups of people using these tools will gain new forms of social power, new ways to organize their interactions and exchanges just in time and just in place. Tomorrow's fortunes will be made by the businesses that find a way to profit from these changes, and yesterday's fortunes are already being lost by businesses that don't understand them."[164]

The first most radical change brought on by these new social structures is the growth of consumer empowerment. This empowerment not only comes in the form of greater connectivity, social networks, and the reputation systems that have made consumers both brand-aware and critical, but also comes in the form of determining when and where they want to be confronted with commercial messaging. Allowing the consumer this choice, or developing marketing programs that are sensitive to this imperative, is an integral part of experiential marketing. Adhering to this point allows marketers to transform the typical ad interaction into an experiential one. In this regard, and from a technological perspective, nothing addresses the rise of this empowerment more than personal digital video recorders (DVRs), and the most successful commercial rollout of this technology known as TiVo.

Death of Thirty Seconds?

The name TiVo is simply genius. This revolutionary moniker did one huge thing when the set-top box was announced to the world. It clearly conveyed that TV is no longer what it used to be. Early adopters would often remark that "it's not TV, it's TiVo." They were mesmerized by what they could do with the new technology, one main feature

164. Ibid., p. xiii.

being the unheard-of practice of skipping commercials. Of course, watching programs when they chose to watch them, as opposed to adhering to TV schedules determined by broadcast network and cable companies, was also a key component. But skipping ads is TiVo's claim to fame. Appropriately, TiVo's debut slogan in 1999 was intuitively powerful and clearly a call for empowerment: "TV your way."

Consumers responded in droves to the new promise. How could they not? The notion of a paradigm-shifting technology allowing them the ability to skip commercials or access programming they want when and where they want it is hard to resist. And it's not only early technology adopters who found this proposition so compelling. Speaking at a *Media* Magazine Forecast 2005 conference in September 2004, the COO of an online marketing research firm called Insight Express declared that "people who are using technology to take control are basically you and me, people who have very busy schedules, watch TV, rent movies, and have a lot of media options. This is a trend that is growing and is already here."[165] TiVo's philosophical cousin VOD, or video-on-demand, also has tapped into the consumer's desire for control and newfound empowerment. According to the Yankee Group, DVRs and VOD will continue to gain enormous footholds in the United States, with more that 32 million households being VOD-enabled by 2006, and more than 19.1 million DVRs rolled out to American households by the same year. By 2007, nearly one-fifth of all U.S. homes will be able to fast-forward TV commercials.[166] Clearly, empowerment is a good way to sell technology.

Take, for instance, the use of video-on-demand. A test case for cable operator Cablevision's Long Island, New York, market showed that in

165. David Kaplan, "How Madison Avenue Learned to Stop Worrying and Love the Remote Control," *Media Post,* September 24, 2004.
166. Paul J. Gough, "The End of the Thirty-second Commercial?," *Media Post,* May 6, 2003.

January 2003, customers accessed an average of 5.5 VOD programs. This average was compared to pay-per-view figures from twenty months prior to the test, which numbered only 1.4 times a month.[167] Cablevision must have seen the writing on the wall: 1.4 purchases of content when the broadcaster offers it, and 5.5 purchases when the consumer decides. It is no surprise, therefore, that VOD is seen by cable operators as the savior to their bottom lines in the future. And surely they must realize that the consumer's newfound power, and the innovative tools they may provide him to stoke it, constitute the only salvation of their viability.

It is indeed telling that in an innovationcentric economy like that of the United States or Canada, the major methodology for delivering mass media advertisements has not changed or evolved in more than sixty years. The thirty-second commercial is as archaic as the black-and-white TV sets that first broadcast it. Still it continues to limp along, unchanged in delivery or philosophy from the first time a commercial ever appeared on TV—a twenty-second ad for a Bulova clock broadcasted by WNBT New York during a game between the Brooklyn Dodgers and the Philadelphia Phillies in July 1941. (Bulova paid $9 for that first TV spot.) With an added ten seconds, the 30-second ad has since then been Madison Avenue's biggest profit engine. It is no surprise, therefore, that the top shops in New York and Toronto are in a confounding state of denial, anxiousness, and ignorance. Chuck Porter, the founder of new-kid agency Crispin Porter & Bogusky, explained this state of agency flux in a December 2004 interview with the *New York Observer*, stating that the major ad agencies "have a vested interest in the status quo, which up till now has been making thirty-second commercials. If that's what you do, you don't want the world to change. But the world is changing all around

167. Ibid.

them. Are they reacting more slowly? I would argue they are. But that may simply be because a revolution is not good for the ones at the top."[168]

Of course, Porter is a key player in his agency's explosive growth. This is the company that introduced Burger King's Subservient Chicken. It is interesting that this agency's first major breakthrough—Subservient Chicken—was based on allowing consumers to control a product icon. More than 12 million of them have visited the site, spending an average of more than six minutes interacting with a brand and marketing message. Perhaps the chicken is a harbinger of something greater. Perhaps the chicken is the new dog in town. Maybe the chicken is the first sign in the paradigm shift in power, from "the control of producers of product and the producers of media, into the hands of consumers of products and consumers of media."[169]

This control is thrilling and fun, much like the chicken. As the writers of *The Cluetrain Manifesto* attest, "companies that speak in the language of the pitch, the dog-and-pony show, are no longer talking to anyone." Marketing and ad executives cannot deny the chicken, and studies are beginning to show that even within the ranks of traditional agencies, the thirty-second spot is quickly losing its luster. The American Advertising Federation released a study of advertising industry leaders in November 2004 that showed 21 percent of respondents think that the thirty-second spot is in its death throes, up from 13 percent of the same respondents in a 2003 survey. Similarly, 13 percent of top ad execs thought that TiVo and DVRs were overhyped in 2003. Just one year later, only 4 percent thought the same way.[170]

168. Gabriel Sherman, "End of the 30-Second Spot," *New York Observer,* December 20, 2004.
169. Ibid.
170. "Nontraditional Formats and DVR to Shift TV Advertising Paradigm," Center for Media Research Brief, American Advertising Federation, November 23, 2004.

In a marketplace where 51 percent of TV watchers regularly channel-surf, 32 percent of them leave the room and 24 percent press mute when a commercial comes on TV, the ad execs better take notice.[171] The rise of DVR technology such as TiVo is only compounding the lack of effectiveness of the traditional thirty-second spot. In fact, a Magna Global survey points out that the longer consumers use DVRs, the more commercials they skip. Adding insult to injury, TiVo users actually watch more TV than non-DVR users.[172] Unfortunately for ad execs, that doesn't translate into watching more commercials. The prevalent attitude toward this phenomenon by advertisers and agencies is to combat it with product placements. If the audience doesn't want to see products and brands on the commercials, the only way they will see them is in the programming itself. This is a sign of regression. Before there were the TV commercials during programming, there were shows such as *Texaco Star Theater* which were sponsored by brands. Today, a show such as *The West Wing* incorporates more than twenty product placements into the scripting each week, instead of trying to embrace technology and innovation. The mass media industry feels comfy looking to the past for answers.

Conversely, more forward-thinking marketers are embracing DVR technology, and tech-smart companies such as TiVo are actively courting them. They recognize that a marketplace that is poised to accommodate more than 25 million digital recorders by 2008 will be the most empowered in history to tune out commercial messages.[173] To deny or ignore that power is futile. To embrace it is experiential. According to a *Business Week* story, less than 10 percent of TiVo's $141

171. *Media Post.*
172. Wayne Freidman, "DVRs Changing the Way Marketers Reach Consumers," *Media Post,* TV Watch Report, November 16, 2004.
173. Cliff Edwards, "Will Souping Up TiVo Save It?," *Business Week Online,* May 17, 2004.

million in revenues in 2003 came from advertising.[174] But that is the fastest-growing segment of TiVo's business. The latest offering, called Video-to-Video, is a major focus for the company, and smart marketers such as Ford, BMW, and a number of Hollywood studios are taking advantage of leveraging innovation and consumer empowerment to make watching television into an interactive experience.

Video-to-Video is the innovative answer—a compromise between marketers and consumer-empowering technology—to mass advertising's future. "More than 50 percent of people surveyed with a DVR say that skipping commercials is their favorite feature, according to Forrester Research. Because much TV programming is sustained by advertising, however, TiVo has a vested interest in protecting it."[175] With Video-to-Video, TiVo is delivering what has been promised to both consumers and marketers for years. Viewers are able to opt-in to their advertising by clicking on an icon at the bottom of the screen to watch a three-minute video that describes the products and services that interest them. These opt-in ads appear when TiVo users are skipping or fast-forwarding through the regular ads in their programming. TiVo says that nearly 70 percent of users use the video-to-video technology and watch the enhanced advertisements.[176] Compare that figure with those that show a third of regular TV watchers actually get up from their chairs and leave the room when an ad comes on.

The idea of commercial-free programming, enhanced with a more experiential ad format such as a minimovie, has already been tested on season premieres of shows such as ABC's *Alias* and Fox's *24*. Advertisers such as Ford got to broadcast a two- or three-minute minimovie before and after a show in exchange for an ad-free airing. Two things immediately occur in

174. Ibid.
175. Stephanie Olsen, "TiVo Looks to Tune in Advertisers," CNET News.com, March 23, 2004.
176. Ibid.

this format: the audience is more engaged with the ad and remembers it, and the content of the show is changed, too, as there is more time to develop the plot and prolong the audience immersion. It is also important to consider that the diehard audience for both these shows is young, media-savvy, and smart. The shows' scripts and plot lines are innovative and intricate. It makes sense that the marketing should be the same.

Eventually, TiVo will reintroduce a new way to watch TV, something the company is calling "telescoping." Let's say a consumer is watching a TV program and likes the main character's new car. He can click on that car in the program using a remote control to activate a vignette from the car's company, complete with product information, dealership locations, and even a link to schedule a test drive. He can then click out of the vignette to seamlessly return to watching the show where he left off. Importantly for this feature, and existing features such as Video-to-Video and Showcase (which gives advertisers disk space on TiVo to store long-form and sweepstakes information for on-demand viewing), TiVo's innovations offer advertisers a method to measure viewer interest in their products while also instantly presenting viewers the opportunity to get more detailed product information. Even more importantly for consumers, this technology allows them to choose when, where, and how they interact with the advertisements. This takes the TV viewing experience to the next level, something that is impossible to do with the current state of TV advertising.

Marketing firm Insight Express's COO Lee Smith has indicated that his company's research shows that 46 percent of consumers welcome advertising within interest categories "that they personally get to define." More than 37 percent are okay with advertising on interactive television, as opposed to 18 percent who like the traditional thirty-second commercials. "The reason is that if consumers have a hand in the marketing process, there's a willingness and acceptance to advertisers' message," explained Media Kitchen CEO Paul Woolmington to ad execs at a recent conference. "Help the consumer take control. Truly place consumers at the center of the communication universe. That's the ethos now." Experiential marketers have known this for a while.

Clearly, these TiVo technologies show that a consumer empowerment tool such as Video-to-Video does not need to be the end of TV advertising. Instead of worrying about how consumers skip past their ads, advertisers should instead look to these innovations as improving the consumer experience. Forward-thinking marketers from General Motors, Nissan, Lexus, Best Buy, Coca-Cola, Walt Disney World, and Royal Caribbean International have already jumped on board to take advantage of the screen tags that appear when consumers fast-forward the commercials, and many other advertisers are poised to do the same with the emerging technologies. In fact, while most TV and marketing execs look at the fast-forward button and the bane of the TV business (according to Forrester Research, 92 percent of TiVO users fast-forward through commercials), more astute marketers see a gold mine in the pause button on TiVo remotes.[177] That is another viewer-determined time when the interactive tags can be accessed by viewers and when interactive vignettes are activated. Lastly, the notion that marketers can know what brands and products viewers are interested in and interact with during their TiVo viewing allows ads to be as compelling as the programming itself. In short, the entire TV watching experience can be transformed to, incredibly, make both consumers *and* marketers very happy in the future.

177. Gina Piccalo, "If It's Not One Ad, It's Another," *Chicago Tribune*, November 22, 2004.

Measurable Interaction

Traditional marketing is hinging on an out-of-date medium for its survival: the thirty-second commercial. The faster all mainstream marketers understand this, the faster the consumer will embrace a panoply of new technologies that will change the marketing and advertising experience forever. Until media conglomerates and the agencies that serve them understand that the thirty-second commercial is only a few years away from being obsolete, new technologies and their correlating practices such as short text messaging (SMS), digital video recorders (DVRs), blogging, wi-fi computing, and virtual networks will be suppressed by the status quo entities to fit their mold of top-down messaging. Many traditional marketers call for a rethinking of the thirty-second spot and try to integrate it into these new technologies. This is a foolish notion. The TV ad as we know it is dead. It's time to consider the innovation and media habits that are influencing the way consumers are accessing marketing messages and media.

The overall paradigm shift that resolutely sounded the death knell for traditional mass medium advertising such as the TV ad has come in the form of mobile technology and Internet applications. In effect we are entering a whole new world where "large numbers of people in industrialized nations will have a device with them most of the time that will enable them to link objects, places and people to online content and processes. . . . Groups of people using these tools will gain new forms of social power, new ways to organize their interactions and exchanges just in time and just in place."[178] These groups of people, moreover, are not just the so-called early adopters or trend influencers. They are you and me. And we are all connected.

Obviously, the Internet has been a major driving force for this

---

178. Howard Rheingold, *Smart Mobs,* p. xii.

interconnectivity, and traditional marketers are beginning to use the tenets of online media to transform traditional media applications. The result is a greater emphasis on accountability and the tracking technologies that allow for greater measurement and targeting of media. According to Forrester Research, more than 90 percent of advertisers want new measurement tools for ad ratings and program viewing that are better and more informative than the existing panel-based methodologies employed by Nielsen Media Research, the standard-bearer of ad measurement. It is no longer sufficient to measure audience benchmarks such as the number of people who view an ad and for how long they view it. "That's a marked contrast from the meme of an established medium like television, through which companies typically aim commercials at a broad swath of consumers with certain demographics, then cross their fingers and hope that their ads sink in."[179]

TV advertisers are beginning to look earnestly at Internet networks as a substitute for delivering content and advertising outside the standard Internet fare such as pop-ups, banners, and interstitials. Of course, the advent of the Internet in the 1990s contributed to a gleeful appropriation of accountability through technology to monitor Web surfers' habits, click-thrus, and database targeting. It became painfully obvious that consumers were not clicking on the banners, were not volunteering personal information, and were not interacting with advertisers but actively avoiding them. In an attempt to grab attention, advertisers made online ads bigger, louder, and more intrusive. Consequently, companies that provided ad-blocking technologies prospered wildly.

Today, online advertising's biggest growth is coming from keyword search advertising, which places ads when people search for keywords

179. Stefanie Olsen, "Google-like Technologies Could Revolutionize TV, Other Media," CNET News.com, April 29, 2004.

related to the products and brands they are interested in. Google has now become the world's largest search-related ad network, which has shifted online advertising from impression-based measurement to performance-based advertising. Performance-based deals are quickly becoming the most-employed way to advertise on the Internet. In the fourth quarter of 2003, Web advertisers devoted 41 percent of their budgets to performance deals that delivered a click-thru or a customer, instead of paying for each time an ad is shown—namely, an impression. That is up from 26 percent during the same period a year prior. Impression-based ad deals dropped from 46 percent in the fourth quarter of 2002 to 40 percent in 2003.[180]

To say that this progression mirrors the state of TV advertising would be stating the obvious. The adherence to impression-based TV advertising is waning. This is clearly happening with tech applications such as TiVo, which allow advertisers to hypertarget their advertisements, and pay only when a consumer interacts with their marketing message. This type of new advertising paradigm will continue into other media formats, such as radio and billboards. Yes, billboards. New technology from United Kingdon-based company Hypertag allows consumers to point their cell phones at a billboard and download content such as product information, contest entries, coupons, and free ring tones. Not only do these Hypertags—which are infrared chips imbedded in the billboard—increase the measurability of the outdoor ad, they also increase brand awareness and interactivity exponentially. A UK campaign for Procter & Gamble in April 2004, for instance, got close to thirteen thousand consumers to interact with a billboard through their cell phones. Similarly, British cell phone company O2 was able to engage 25 percent of all passersby using this innovation.

180. Interactive Advertising Bureau.

As more and more home and cell phone devices enter the marketplace using Internet protocol technologies, advertising will be able to be delivered anywhere, anytime, and on demand when the consumer chooses. Innovation for marketing to consumers will thus be characterized by a melding of performance-based methodologies found on the Internet with interactive and engaging media such as TiVo. Certainly the phenomenal acceptance of video games into the media mix will further drive the consumer's desire for more innovative experiences when accessing and processing marketing messages and advertisements. Traditional ad agencies need to hire technology companies to not only deliver captivating content and messaging but also to laser-point the target audience and measure the effectiveness of their content and messaging. This is a dire necessity if they are still in the business of delivering meaningful and relevant experiences to consumers from their clients' brands.

Brands aren't waiting for their agencies to innovate and integrate, however. Why should they? They're losing share. The recent appointment of the new marketing chief at überbrand Coca-Cola aptly illustrates how marketing and advertising will be done in the future. In June 2004, Chuck Fruit was appointed CMO after leading the company's nontraditional marketing efforts. As senior vice president of integrated marketing, Fruit was instrumental in overseeing Coke's global sponsorship and event marketing as well as emerging media advertising. In announcing the appointment, Coke's CEO said that the promotion was in response to the need to "go beyond traditional advertising to connect with our consumers in deeper and more compelling ways."[181] In an internal company memo, the CEO also admitted that a company that has relied on TV advertising for the past fifty years needs to evolve,

181. Jim Lovel, "Thirty-Second TV Ads Lose Fizz for Coke," *Atlanta Business Chronicle,* July 2, 2004.

noting that "the impact has diminished" and that "thirty-second spots are not nearly as effective as they once were and can't stand alone."[182] It's no surprise then that a guy such as Fruit would get the top marketing job. After all, he was the one who came up with the idea of placing Coke products on *American Idol*.

Conversational Media

An astute marketer once told me that the traditional marketing paradigm is about persuasion and that the new marketing paradigm is about truth. In fact, the euphemism of persuasion is really concerned with control, the control of top-down messaging to the masses. Similarly, traditional advertising is impersonal. It's predicated on a brand purveyor trying to speak to everyone at the same time. Instead, what most forward-thinking advocates such as experiential marketers want to deploy and harness are individual voices—those of customers, brand managers, CEOs, associates, agency staff, freelance writers, consultants et al.—to carry on a daily conversation with consumers and customers. In effect, the manifesto point for the use of one-on-one interactions must be translated into the technology sector. It is not enough to physically connect in a personal and empathetic manner. Marketers must do the same in the cyber sphere as well.

One major recent online development has been the proliferation of personal Web-based logs, or blogs. At the tail end of 2004, U.S. dictionary publisher Merriam-Webster announced that the word "blog" topped the company's list of the ten words of the year. The blog, defined as "a Web site that contains an online personal journal with reflections,

182. Ibid.

comments and often hyperlinks provided by the writer," will therefore be so entered into the 2005 version of *Merriam-Webster Collegiate Dictionary*. Blogs are one of the many emerging uses of technology—in this instance, the relative ease by which anyone can post to, link, and update a personal Web site—that is giving outlets to hundreds of thousands of individual voices. By allowing these individual voices to connect with each other through hyperlinks, these voices are not shouts in the wilderness. They are a vital part of a massive online dialogue that is no longer controlled by media outlets or those in the "persuasion" industry.

Blogs are the first major emanation of conversational media, the avatars of an empowered consumer voice that cannot be ignored. Bloggers are today's "fact-checking, credibility-screening, gap-filling counterweights to traditional media."[183] One only has to recall the controversy brewed up by bloggers when they disproved and disclaimed a *CBS Evening News* story concerning President George W. Bush's National Guard service records. Within one day, the news cycle was awash with chatter about the bloggers who were disproving the claims, not chatter about CBS's so-called scoop. Certainly, seasoned journalists were caught off-guard when their research and reporting were discredited and immediately cast off by the "people's media" in twenty-four hours. They quickly learned their lesson, and marketers should do the same. In fact, "bloggers promise to hold marketers to new levels of accountability, impacting just about everything advertisers do, say and claim."[184]

If markets are conversations, as *The Cluetrain Manifesto* declares, then marketers cannot afford to ignore the chatter in the age of the blog, because this chatter is being initiated and propagated by consumers

183. Pete Blackshaw, "Advertisers Beware: Blog-Fortified Copy Cops at Your Doorstep," *Media Post*, September 23, 2004.
184. Ibid.

themselves. This empowerment is daunting to marketers who wish to keep tight control over their brand and product messaging, especially when confronted by studies that show consumers trust fellow consumers' opinions and responses to advertising more than the messages and efforts from advertisers themselves. In essence, a blog is a consumer-written diary or narrative that is logged "on a public, non-erasable hard-drive known as the Internet. A good percentage of blog content reflects consumer experiences with branded products or services. Because virtually all blog content is indexed on search engines, enabling ready access by other consumers, such narratives take on special meaning and importance."[185]

A 2003 study by Jupiter Research found that 2 percent of online users in the United States have created a blog, and about 4 percent read them.[186] These figures have certainly grown since the study was released. What is also becoming clear is that bloggers, and the people who read them, are most likely to be the so-called influencers or mavens to their peers and family members. "They're very opinionated and strong-minded. They do not want things forced down their throats. That's why they're turning away from traditional advertising. They're not watching TV."[187] They are also wealthy; the Jupiter study showed that 61 percent of bloggers live in homes where the total income is greater than $60,000. In an editorial column in *Advertising Age* in late 2004, the founder of Crain Communications wrote that "blog creators are influencers—people who pride themselves on knowing all kinds of arcane, insider details about the product, hence giving them credibility with consumers"[188] Furthermore, Rance Crain echoed what many savvy

185. Ibid.
186. Paul-Mark Rendon, "Blog Talk," *Marketing Magazine*, September 27, 2004.
187. Ibid.
188. Rance Crain, "The Growing Impact of Consumers' Web Publishing," *Advertising Age*, November 1, 2004.

marketers already know, that "advertising no longer has the luxury of being a one-way monologue. Consumers, much like voters, have the ability to not only absorb advertiser messages, but to change other consumers' minds about the message content and the product itself."[189]

Marketers are keenly aware that negative word-of-mouth spreads seven times faster than positive spin. Although studies have not yet been released, it is safe to assume that with the added components of instant online access and mass dissemination on the Internet, negative blog narratives spread at an even *faster* rate. It is clear that when compared to word-of-mouth agencies such as BzzAgent and their use of individual buzz agents to spread the gospel physically to friends and relatives about a brand or product, the buzz from individual bloggers achieves much greater exposure at a much quicker pace. The ability to hyperlink from one blog to another, as well as to be able to post replies to individual blog entries, makes blog buzz not only more viral, it makes it permanent as well. Remember, blog entries and narratives are easily searchable by engines such as Google and Yahoo. The more hyperlinks in the narrative, moreover, the more times the blog will show up in search results. And "in a world where your brand identity is basically the sum of your search results, a shelf space dominated by brand counterclaims and hostile consumer comments makes like very difficult for advertisers."[190]

So, can those TV and print ads touting a company's fabulous customer service really be effective when one blogger decides to embark on a personal-experience narrative about the company's terrible service? Remember, that narrative is being picked up from a search engine entry for the company's name, and the bad narratives are added and hyperlinked to every day.

189. Ibid.
190. Pete Blackshaw, "Advertisers Beware: Blog-Fortified Copy Cops at Your Doorstep," *Media Post*, September 23, 2004.

Thousands of cynical and disgruntled customers begin to voice their experiences, linking between each other, responding to horror stories, forwarding them to their friends. Can those now infamous pharmaceutical ads really gloss over the side effects—either through those sped-up voiceovers and the end of the commercial or the extra-fine print at the bottom of the page—when blogs are established overnight to post and share detailed lab reports and expert opinions with alarming counterpoints and dissent? Can any brand or company escape such scrutiny?

The daily adoption of more innovative technology such as camera phones poses even more problems for advertisers. A number of mobile phone blogs—called moblogs—are mushrooming at the same rate as text messaging and camera phones, especially with younger consumers. Instead of solely text narratives, mobloggers are able to post photos directly from their cell phones in real time to their online blog, with narratives composed through SMS (short text messaging) to caption the images. So what can a restaurant chain that boasts great food and high-end service do when a moblogger captures the dirty bathrooms or the nonhygienic conditions in the kitchen with a surreptitious click of a camera phone? If a picture tells a thousand stories, then we can only guess the amount of damage it can do to a company's brand. And it won't stop there. The latest round of technology is poised to take moblogs into the multimedia sphere, as video posts, called v-logs, take root. In short, consumer-generated media are poised to make marketing and advertising a more truthful place . . . finally. This is anathema to a lot of marketers, because "a company's fear is that a lone voice with an ax to grind will make up a truth as plausible as anything the marketing department has come up with."[191]

191. Rick Levine, Christopher Locke, Doc Searls, and David Weinberg, *The Cluetrain Manifesto* (Cambridge, MA: Perseus Books Group, 2001), p. 67.

So far, the blog discussion has focused on a pessimistic perspective. Obviously, a company's lack of attention to the consumer experience will be severely exploited, publicized, and disseminated. Blogs place the onus for positive consumer experience squarely on the shoulders of companies who are trying to sell to their customers. If consumer-generated media are poised to be a mainstay in the future of brands and marketing, then marketers and their agencies need to understand and appropriate not only the technology but also the ethos of new consumer empowerment. In fact, blogs and the open-source philosophy behind them can be a major salvation for marketers who are losing their edge and effectiveness. The key is to eschew the top-down control of messaging that marketers hold on to so tightly. If they can achieve this, then blogging can be "possibly, the most powerful type of corporate marketing per dollar spent ever invented."[192]

It's a simple premise, really. "Online markets will talk about companies whether companies like it or not. . . . Companies can't stop customers from speaking up, and can't stop employees from talking to customers. Their only choice is to start encouraging employees to talk to customers—and empowering them to act on what they hear."[193] Marketers need to take heed of this directive. In fact, many enlightened corporate execs and CEOs are already following it. By joining the blog revolution and opening up the channels of communications to achieve dialogue instead of monologue, they are making blogs into an experiential marketing tool.

Take, for instance, Jonathan's blog. Every four or five days, Jonathan posts easily readable and engrossing posts on a variety of tech subjects and recollections from his personal and professional history. The posts are filled

192. Rich Ord, "The Blog Marketing Explosion," *WebProNews,* November 5, 2004.
193. Rick Levine, Christopher Locke, Doc Searls, and David Weinberg, *The Cluetrain Manifesto* (Cambridge, MA: Perseus Books Group, 2001), p. 72.

with hyperlinks for easy reference to what Jonathan is talking about. Some recent post titles included "Every Customer Visit Is a Lesson," "Nothing Like a Good Conspiracy," and "An Open Letter to Sam Palmisano, CEO, IBM Corp." Jonathan's blog gets a lot of visitors, from hundreds of industry leaders and hundreds of thousands of customers, because this is Jonathan Schwartz's blog. He's the president and COO of Sun Microsystems.

Executives who blog do it for a number of reasons, many of which are the same as why they choose to speak at conferences and professional symposiums. Certainly, their personal profiles are elevated. They present themselves as forward-thinking and trend-conscious. They get a charge out of it, and some fun, too. But the primary reason for their blogs, or the primary effect from executive blogging, is their desire to reach out and connect to their customers *and* employees outside of the official channels of PR control and marketing department spin. More importantly, the blog allows customers and employees to respond to the exec's posts. These responses invariably open up into a genuine dialogue, and remarkably, a dialogue that the CEO or president cannot ignore. This is truly a revolutionary approach to CRM, when the head honcho of a multinational corporation joins in and encourages a conversation among all stakeholders.

Furthermore, this executive is instantly humanized, and by extension so is the company. By throwing out the corporatespeak and marketing spin, a blog narrative is entirely more believable than PR releases, TV commercials, and the like. We seem to know, intuitively, when something spoken, written, or recorded is sincere and honest—when it comes from another person's heart, rather than being a synthesis of corporatespeak filtered by myriad iterations of editing, trimming, and targeting. How different this type of interaction is compared to traditional marketing's imperative to stay "on message." And yet by opening up the dialogue and entering into personal relationships with all stakeholders, corporations may be entering a new era in marketing, advertising, and branding. As more and more blogs created by employees emerge for con-sumers to access, the company's consumers are instinctively drawn to visit them and strengthen their relationship with their products. For instance, Microsoft has for the past year—on Bill Gates's orders—actively encouraged their employees to build and update their personal blogs. The company has invested in providing them tools to allow a blog to be set up in mere seconds. This green light has inspired more than eight hundred corporate Microsoft employee blogs to be set up in less than a year.[194] Employees post pictures of the company's refrigerators, their favorite TV shows, insider jokes, and MP3s. More importantly, they blog about the products they are working on, their latest bugs and updates, and the inside dirt on new products coming from the company's labs. There are even long-standing debates on naming Longhorn—Microsoft's eagerly awaited and long-overdue operating system—Longwait instead.

Customers can read all of this and respond. They add their concerns and opinions, as well as offer tech pointers and lines of code to make the products better. This quickly accomplished two things for Microsoft: they can help drive product innovation while simultaneously creating a loyal audience for these blogs. Furthermore, the more truthful these employee blogs are, the more valuable they are to their customers. This is a key point, one that the traditional corporate structure is finding hard to accept. A *Business Week* story in the summer of 2004 warned that "it's only a matter of time before some workplace pundit spills a trade secret, unwittingly leaks a clandestine launch date, or takes a swipe at a CEO that turns into

194. Michelle Conlin and Andrew Park, "Blogging with the Boss's Blessing," *Business Week Online*, June 28, 2004.

slander."[195] Exactly! It's time to let go of the reins. If employers try to co-opt their employees' blogs, or even try to exert control over consumer blogs, the ramifications to the company's profile will certainly be dire.

Consumer-generated media will invariably win over corporate messaging. Remember Apple and "Apple's Dirty Secret"? The Neistat brothers' blog garnered more than 15 million visits from around the world and forced Apple to change their iPod battery. If Apple had allowed their employees to blog about the iPod before its release, perhaps they would never have had to deal with their own dirty secret.

Stoneyfield Farms has so fully embraced the blog revolution, they present four blogs from their Web site. The New Hampshire–based dairy producer uses these blogs in a combination of employee-generated narratives, product news, and information blogs, and customercentric dispatches as well. The blog titles are indicative of their intent: "Strong Woman Daily News," "The Bovine Bugle," "The Daily Scoop," and "Creating Healthy Kids." Marketing blogger David Burn points out that "The Bovine Bugle," for instance, is written and maintained by a Stoneyfield supplier, a dairy farmer in Vermont. "The Daily Scoop" is written by employees of the company's yogurt division. Each blog presents an authentic and genuine voice of the company, one that is committed to social responsibility, health, and the environment. Combined, these blogs are a greater branding tool than any amount of TV advertising can accomplish.

Thumb Nation

It was just a few short years ago that text messaging—also called SMS—was just gaining a foothold in North America. Europe had already

195. Ibid.

embraced the cellular phone service fully, in a marketplace where local landline calls were twice as expensive as cellular calls. Youth especially were head over heels with excitement when SMS came out. It was an ideal way for them to communicate cheaply without relying on a parent phone plan and keep in touch with their friends clandestinely as they punched in their messages with their thumbs under the dinner table. In North America, the mobile phone operators decided to charge both sender and recipient for an SMS exchange. Furthermore, up until only a year or so ago, none of the phone companies would acquiesce to an interoperability protocol, so that an AT&T user could not text message someone on a Sprint network.

Every marketplace other than North America collectively decided on one single protocol, and in doing so, pushed cellular usage and growth leaps and bounds past those in the United States and Canada. For instance, only 65 percent of Americans have cell phones, compared to more than 90 percent of Britons. *Emarketer.com* estimates that only about 30 percent of U.S. users send text messages, compared to 80 percent of the UK population. And while European cell phone companies get 12 percent of their total revenue from mobile entertainment such as ring tones, games, and photo/video capabilities, U.S. carriers get only about 3 percent from these services. "Cellphone gaming, still a nascent market in the United States, is already a $2 billion-plus business in the Asia-Pacific region, where, in many countries, cells outnumber people. . . . [and] while In-Stat/MDR expected U.S. users to spend $146 million on ring tones in 2004, the global market was $3.5 billion, according to Arc Group (about 10 percent of the global music market)."[196] So why hasn't the North American market embraced the mobile revolution as

196. Jonah Bloom, "Why SMS Marketing Will Soon Matter in the US," *Advertising Age,* January 10, 2005.

fully as our European, Asian, and Middle East counterparts? And more importantly for this chapter, why haven't marketers here jumped at the chance of using such highly interactive and personal technology to reach their customers and support their brands?

The first reason is that carriers have only recently allowed marketers to deploy cellular campaigns across all wireless-service providers and their networks. No campaign could be effective when constrained to just AT&T users, excluding all others from Telus, Sprint, or Bell. Secondly, consumers in North America have for a long time presumed that cellular technology was a voice-to-voice platform. Carriers didn't do much to convince them otherwise. By almost exclusively concentrating their marketing efforts on price wars for talking minutes and long-distance charges, carriers in North America ignored the social connectivity and new interactive technology that cell phones presented and made possible. In hindsight, this was a colossal mistake. Cell phones are not just phones without a wire. They are empowerment tools that use an entirely new form of medium, and the weekly releases of new and exciting innovations for mobile telephony make their use perfect for experiential marketing campaigns.

My former company had been working for cell phone carriers in Canada since 2000, when we were hired by Fido to help them introduce SMS capabilities to students and educate them on usage. Yes, that's right, in the year 2000. Whereas the European marketplace was already awash in millions of kids text messaging each other, students in Canada were much slower to adopt the technology. We developed a mobile tour of the eight biggest campuses in Canada to roll out an experiential marketing campaign that made headlines:

Branded vans pull on to the campus quad during Frosh Week and a uniformed team jumps out, megaphones in hand to bark up people for the "Pickup Lines" competition on the quad. A large stage is set up right on campus. Models—three beautiful women and three studly guys—are introduced to the crowd, while student peers in Fido T-shirts and visors walk around the crowd with cellular phones for the audience to use. Every model guy and girl has a Fido phone number emblazoned on their T-shirts, and participants are urged to send their best pickup lines to the girls or guys. An emcee announces the pickup lines to the crowd, and an elimination round for the date begins, after which the model chooses who will have the opportunity to have dinner with her or him at a local restaurant that night. Other prizes included WWE tickets, bungee jumping, front-row seats to a hip-hop show, a night out at The Beaches, etc. The winning guys and winning girls were also handed a prepaid Fido phone to keep in touch with their friends during the date and report back using text messaging. Since kids in Europe used SMS to flirt and date, we felt that Canadians would do the same. More than three thousand students used a Fido phone to text-message a pickup line to one of the models and go on a date, and more than fifteen thousand students witnessed a new way to communicate through SMS.

This new form of communication also has an entirely new vocabulary. Expressions such as *lol* (laughing out loud), *brb* (be right back), *cul8r* (see you later), and *lmao* (laughing my ass off) are the early manifestations of a new language that's evolved from SMS conversations. Each oral and written language in societies with prevalent SMS usage has a parallel cell phone and chat vernacular as well. When Rogers AT&T came to us to activate their customers in the Quebec market, we knew that a province with fierce language issues and a pride in their culture would need their own SMS dictionary. Through a French-language site (www.texto.ca) we created and maintained the first-ever Quebecois dictionary for a youthful SMS culture and community in Quebec, and rolled out a promotional campaign with music network MusiquePlus. In just over a month we had collected more than twelve thousand SMS terms in Quebecois and published the terms in promotional materials distributed at grassroots events and concerts.

My company also developed special text message underground parties for carriers in Canada desperately trying to turn on the youth there as they were turned on in Europe and Asia. We called them the "If It's Too Loud, You're Too Old" parties, where the music was so loud in the bar or club, you needed to text-message your drink order to the bar. Similarly in the United Kingdom, Diageo sent out SMS messages to participants in its Guinness promotion to get them out drinking on a quiet Tuesday night. Their phone was sent an SMS message with an address of a pub where a free pint of Guinness was waiting for them as soon as they showed the barkeep their phone and message. Again in the United Kingdom, Nestlé launched a huge promotional campaign for its Kit Kat brand, utilizing SMS code on 80 million packs. A unique code printed on the inside of the wrapper translates into Kit Kash currency, which consumers add to their accounts with SMS messaging. The accumulated Kit Kash can then be used to bid on prizes online such as cars, vacations, or a walk-on part in a TV show. *Advertising Age* reported on an incredibly interactive SMS campaign created by Kellogg and its agency Starcom in Dubai. Called "Arabian Rally," it's an interactive TV show that gets kids to race against each other live on TV by controlling their cars with their cellular phones.

This interactive application of mobile telephony is a harbinger of a new conversation between marketer and consumer. Greater innovation will only result in greater depth of conversation. Phone manufacturers such as Nokia and Samsung have already released handheld units that can stream video from Major League Baseball or the National Basketball Association, and a subscription service called MobiTV streams live television stations such as Fox and TLC to the palm of your hand. The result of this type of innovation is that mass marketing can become delivered as an individual experience.

Traditional marketers, together with agencies and tech companies, are already calling mobile telephony the "third screen." The first screen is television, the PC screen is the second, and now the miniscreen that more than 171.2 million U.S. consumers view every day is the third.[197] It's quite indicative that these traditional marketers would consider the cell phone a media receiver versus a communication tool. When SMS technology first came into the fold in about 1998, marketers were doing cartwheels thinking about coupons and promo text that could be delivered to individual consumers. When GPS (global positioning service) was added into the mix, marketers were hyperventilating from the thought of sending an individual consumer a coupon SMS message when he's within one mile of a Dunkin' Donuts: if you come in to Dunkin' Donuts at 534 Main Street within fifteen minutes, get one free donut with a coffee purchase! And now, with the advent of rich media and video delivery to the cell phone screen, the promise of a traveling pocket TV and a walkie-talkie for marketing messages is finally here. You can now make custom-made television shows and commercials for one person at a time.

This interactive application of mobile telephony is a harbinger of a new conversation between marketer and consumer; a revolution is being conducted in the new conversation between consumers themselves. To become part of this conversation is the new paradigm of marketing and branding.

197. Nat Ives, "Marketing for the Third Screen," *The New York Times,* November 8, 2004.

The Flash Mob

The first reported incident came from New York City late in 2003 and was described in the United Kingdom's *Guardian* newspaper. In a relatively obscure SoHo bar, and in four other similarly nondescript bars in the neighborhood, a group of a hundred twentysomethings gathered for no particular purpose, in no particular order, and for no discernible reason. A few days prior, they were all virally e-mailed or text-messaged a set of specific and top-secret instructions that guided them all to the same bars in SoHo. No one knew each other at the bar, being culled from dissimilar social and professional strata, but all shared a certain furtive excitement of doing something daring and new. The e-mail or text message had given them the same instructions:

"By 7:00 P.M., based on the month of your birth, situate yourself at [one of the bars] and buy a drink. A representative will arrive and give you further instructions."

The reps arrived at exactly 7:00. People at each bar were given a slip of paper with further instructions, as well as a directive to act out a persona described in the note:

"Leave the bar at exactly 7:16 and go to the Otto Tootsi [an expensive but relatively unknown shoe boutique] *by 7:18. Act out your persona. Disperse by 7:23."*

Everyone did what they were told, and by 7:17, more than a block surrounding the shoe shop was swarming with total strangers bent upon a common mission: to be part of nonpolitical grassroots social activism based primarily on "not giving a shit" absurdity. By 7:23 the congregation effortlessly dispersed as quickly as it arrived.

This is what's called a "flash mob." Since the first reported incident, the frequency and size of flash mobs in New York and London have grown with each inexplicable (dis)appearance, while cities such as Minneapolis, Berlin, Amsterdam, San Francisco, Vienna, Boston, and Chicago are witnessing their own flash mob phenomena. Hundreds, if not thousands, of people have gathered at department stores and asked the clerks for new rugs, a phalanx of yuppies have played "Marco Polo" in a Cineplex, groups of people flocked to Grand Central Station and broke into applause on cue, mobs have appeared on street corners and shouted into their cell phones—purportedly for the sheer fun of it.

Participants in flash mobs generally state that their actions are apolitical, lacking any agenda, and without social criticism, which makes participation in this "movement" that much more appealing to members and new recruits. But the ramifications for the popularity of a social trend such as "flash mobbing," the very ability to get people to anonymously gather in the streets, are as political—and marketable—as it gets. Flash mobs are just one of the latest social trends that catapult word-of-mouth, grassroots, and viral pass-along from simple *mots du jour* to powerful and highly accessible tools for social mobilization and, more importantly, social and economic action.

Howard Rheingold, author of *Virtual Reality* and *Smart Mobs: The Next Social Revolution,* defines the term "smart mobs" as "people who are able to act in concert even if they don't know each other." Using the Internet, pervasive computing technologies, and mobile communications, smart mobs are subtly reshaping the way societies organize, interact, work, buy, sell, and govern.

Clearly, the flash mobs that are popping up around the globe are prototypical, albeit inane, manifestations of this quiet revolution. And from this readership's perspective, the tidal rise of flash mobs is both justification and motivation to continue to pursue viral marketing strategies. My gut tells me that this is in fact the future of marketing. If a guy can get a thousand unrelated New Yorkers to squawk like birds in Central Park by sending out five e-mails, what can marketers create by sending out fifty?

In essence, most retail marketing strives to get a lot of people to do the same thing at a specific time. That's not too much different from the modus operandi of a flash mob. And if we as marketers are indeed here to push the boundaries of our industry, flash mobs and the advance of the smart mob armies offer prime vantage points into successful viral and grassroots campaigns, not to mention more time-tested forms of marketing.

Let's look at flash mobs as taking the concept of chat rooms into the real world, or a literal embodiment of a "cc" list. Right now, the flash mob appeal comes from the sheer surprise and frivolity of the action itself—not unlike a brand parody ad or other such "fwd:" content. Flash mobs are regarded by their proponents as purely grassroots, untethered by corporate, commercial, or government machinations. But just like parody ads, frivolity and subversiveness can be creatively leveraged by a brand for incredible viral results. Sometimes it's necessary to walk away from a brand's established positioning and creative guidelines, and dive into the viral world with something wholly new and extraordinary.

Refer-a-friend functionality alone will rarely spark a viral stampede. Smart incentives that "speak" the targeted consumer's language should re-create the visceral attraction for something daring and new that flash mobs represent. Flash mobs also show that successful viral and grassroots marketing is not necessarily based on mass. Rather, it's based on exclusivity, a sort of velvet rope passport into coolness for the chosen few.

Marketers have to be acutely aware of the consequences when smart mobs turn against brands, products, and retail establishments, because in the near future, the mob rules. The power of the flash/smart mob cannot be underestimated. Although most flash mobs are based on absurdity or frivolity of the act itself—such as squawking in Central Park—they also can be based on much more serious actions. Not only can the collective power of flash mobs topple brands, they already have been harnessed to topple governments.

On January 20, 2001, Philippine president Joseph Estrada was forced out of office by a flash mob. More than a million Manila residents assembled in the same square at Epifanio de los Santas Avenue, known to locals as "Edsa," prompted there by a series or coordinated text messages to their cell phones: *Go 2EDSA, wear black*. This wasn't the first time that a flash mob mentality and corresponding tools were used for a political cause. In September 2000, a government-sanctioned rise in gasoline prices outraged so many Britons that groups of them would use mobile phones, e-mail and SMS to coordinate dispersed packs of demonstrators to block fuel delivery at gas stations throughout the country. A simple thing such as message forwarding made both protests possible. With only a few thumbstrokes, an individual can disseminate a received message to everyone is his or her address book. The compound effect results in a text message traveling from one to millions in hours.

Rheingold considers flash mobs to be part of a new social paradigm called "mobile ad hoc social network." The term "describe the new social form made possible by the combination of computation, communication, reputation and location awareness."[198] All urbanites are mobile; just look at how many of us have the cell phone tied to our heads, or how many kids are tapping away at their two-ways. The ad hoc nature of these networks comes from the fact that most people use their mobile technology to organize themselves informally and on the fly, the way young urbanites text-message among themselves on a Friday night

198. Howard Rheingold, *Smart Mobs,* p. 170.

when looking for a party. Each of the individuals in this network is a "node" in a web of social "links"—channels of communication and social bonds—to other individuals. These nodes and links are the fundamental elements of social networks made by humans, as well as the operating elements of wireless technology. "In some sense, an ad hoc mobile information system is the ultimate peer-to-peer system. It is self-organizing, fully decentralized and highly dynamic."[199]

Clearly, modern marketers are acutely aware of the importance of peer-to-peer interaction in growing business for their brands, products, and services. The rise of P2P social networks has had massive repercussions for marketers worldwide, and for new technology thinkers who see a whole new way of human interaction. These new paradigms are equally important for experiential marketers, who look at innovation as a way to not only reach consumers with a relevant message, but to engage them in it as well. For instance, the spread of wireless and Bluetooth technology now allows our portable devices to literally talk to each other and exchange information about their owners. When two people meet, their mobile devices can mediate and enhance the social encounter by comparing personal profiles and automatically alerting participants in the face-to-face interaction about each other's mutual interests or common friends that they may or may not know they share.

Imagine the effects this may have on experiential marketing, which holds personal interaction between consumer and marketer as an instrumental aspect. If the consumer wishes to share information with the marketer, that interaction will be greatly enhanced. A marketer may be alerted that a particular consumer is not interested in the pitch, and won't bother the time-crunched individual. Or the consumer's device

199. Ibid., p. 171.

may indicate that he is willing to talk to the marketer, to see how the brand can help his life, how the marketer can answer questions on a particular subject, or who of his friends already enjoys the product or service.

Ad hoc social networks also get groups of people to collectively take action very quickly and decisively. Rheingold compares individuals in an ad hoc social network to individual "fish and birds (and tight-formation fighter pilots) [who] school and flock simply by paying attention to what their nearest neighbors do. The coordinated movement of schools and flocks is a dynamically shifting aggregation of individual decisions. Even if there were a central tuna or pigeon who could issue orders, no system of propagating orders from a central source can operate swiftly enough to avoid being eaten by sharks or slamming into trees."[200] This type of perspective is extremely valuable for experiential and traditional marketers alike. First, it posits that social networks are immune to top-down corporate messaging and brand control. Second, it clearly shows that tapping into the network to influence a few individuals in the flock can get the entire flock moving in a different direction. The first point is a hard pill to swallow for traditional marketers. Brand control is all they know, but they'll have to let go eventually. The second point is integral to experiential marketing: to get individuals engaged enough to turn their flock with you and not against you. It means tapping into the collective consciousness of your consumers and allowing them to make collective purchasing decisions.

Enhancing the Personal Experience

Some forward-thinking marketers are willfully entering into these ad hoc social networks to get closer to their customers, mostly through

200. Ibid., p. 176.

SMS marketing, as described earlier in this chapter. So far, most attempts have been relatively tame. For instance, ski resorts send SMS messages early in the morning after a particularly good snowfall, driving more guests to the slopes sooner. Summer resorts similarly alert golfers of last-minute open tee times. Or a real estate agent can automatically send information to a client about homes that just came on the market. But these efforts are not really experiential. There is no personal interaction or deep consumer engagement. There is clearly a benefit to the individual consumer, but will it do anything to move the flock? A truly compelling flash mob campaign has yet to be rolled out by marketers, but consumer-populated sites are using this technology for experiential marketing all by themselves.

Take, for instance, www.dodgeball.com. The New York City–based company is a social networking site built specifically for mobile phones and their users. The idea is remarkably simple: users tell the site where they are, and the site tells users who and what is around them. The site will "ping" the friends in a user's address book to tell them where he is, lets him know when friends of friends are within ten blocks of him, and allows him to broadcast content from his phone to people within that ten-block radius or blast messages to groups of friends. Here's an example the site gives its users: "Okay, so you're having drinks at Luna Lounge. Send us a text message telling us where you are and we'll send out a text message telling all your friends where you are *and* send you back a message letting you know if any friends of friends are within ten blocks. If you have a camera phone, we'll even send you their picture."[201]

The site is different from online social network sites because it allows people to connect while they are out in the world, not tethered to their

201. From the Web site: www.dodgeball.com.

computer screens in the basement. It's meant to enhance the individual's experience while out and about as they are having fun or looking for some. It is meant to connect people while they are in their natural habitats, alone or with their friends, doing what they do naturally. Why wouldn't a marketer such as Bacardi offer the same service for consumers who are going out to bars? Why wouldn't Alliance Atlantis or Universal Pictures get people connected to go see a movie? People don't like to go to the pictures alone. Why not connect someone to people who also want to see a particular movie? What about shoppers who need a second opinion about a dress from a friend or a peer? If one is within ten blocks, she can come to the store and help her friend make a purchase decision.

In this regard, experiential marketers seek to enhance not strictly the marketing experience, but the overall experience of each individual consumer. A flash mob network such as *dodgeball.com* does just that. It enhances the individual's lifestyle experience through a unique approach to leveraging the power of flash mob elements. It is not enough to rely on technology to reach the consumer with marketing. The technology must enhance the marketing experience.

David Polinchock wrote to me warning of the tendency to rely on technology for the sake of technology itself. "In the tech world that we live in today, we have a tendency to get all caught up in what can be delivered while losing sight of what the experience is supposed to be," he wrote. "There's a huge amount of discussion today about how rich media will save the online advertising industry, but no one is talking about the fact that the online advertising industry is having problems because of the poor quality of online advertising. It doesn't add to the online experience at all. It interferes, distracts and rarely gives us valuable information. It's a bad experience! It rarely compels any word-of-mouth advertising other than 'why do we have to put up with this stuff?' "

Furthermore, technology cannot replace the personal interaction. From an experiential marketing point of view, it can't be used in the same framework as mass media. It can't mirror the top-down delivery of mass advertising. It must allow for personal interaction instead. Nothing can really replace the human interaction, and those marketers who think an SMS blast will engage their customers are dangerously wrong in their assumptions.

"I just went to my first grocery store that had the self-service checkout system. If you haven't seen this system, it's pretty cool. Even my wife, who doesn't get as excited about all of this new technology as I do, had a great time with this system," writes Polinchock. "But you know what? I know the grocery store will use this as a chance to fire staff, rather then figure out other ways to use people—not unlike ATM machines, which were originally marketed by banks in terms of the cost savings that would be passed on to customers. Now they're charging for ATM withdrawals—and deposits. No matter how cool this system is, it will never replace a great cashier who knows how to say hi and make you really enjoy your shopping experience."

Exactly.

Chapter 8	**Experiential marketing** will make—or break—the brands of the future.

Not many are familiar with the term *jumping the shark*. It has yet to make it into the *Oxford English Dictionary*. But it's certain to make its mark soon as it speeds through the Internet to the tipping point where the *OED* will take notice. Case in point: it won't be long before *tipping point* is added to the *OED*, after the huge popularity of Malcolm Gladwell's book and the Internet buzz that comes from it. In fact, the expansion of the World Wide Web has contributed to the more than ten thousand new words and terms added to the *OED* since March 2000. Similarly, *jumping the shark* has its roots in the Internet, with an eponymous Web site dedicated to this weird and catchy saying.

The site defines it as "a moment, a defining moment when you know that your favorite television program has reached its peak. That instant that you know from now on . . . it's all downhill. Some call it the climax. We call it jumping the shark. From that moment on, the program will simply never be the same." The best example of this moment, and the reason the term was invented in the first place, comes to us from the television program *Happy Days,* which ran on network TV from 1974 to 1984. Although pop culture pundits can point to many moments during the sitcom's run that could be construed as the climax of the series, the jumping the shark moment came when Fonzie—the übercool greaser in a leather jacket played by Henry Winkler—water-skied off of a ramp to actually jump a shark (never mind that *Happy Days* was based in Milwaukee). Some viewers knew that from that absurd moment on, the show was going nowhere but downhill and would simply never be the same again.

Marketing as we know it jumped the shark in 2004. Most marketers didn't even notice. Indeed, a jumping the shark moment doesn't necessarily mean that it's obvious, or that the moment will have immediate repercussions. In fact, *Happy Days* aired for many more years after Fonzie put a life preserver over his black leather jacket and flew over a great white. Indeed, jumping the shark is a moment perceptible to few, and it may take years if not decades before the occasion is recognized by the rest of us. But for those who do see it immediately, the moment can signal a profound revolution.

So how did marketing jump the shark in 2004? To answer this question, I need to posit two paradigm shifts in the marketing industry, which have been alluded to often throughout this book:

- Mass media no longer serves—nor holds—the interest of the enlightened and highly empowered consumer.

- The industry paradigm of the propagation and sustainability of "brand" and "brand essence" is over.

Wait a minute: corporate obsession with the brand is passé? Mass media such as television, radio, and magazines are soon to be relics of the past? Well, yes . . . and no. The corporate blind drive for branding, and marketing's dependence on mass media, won't disappear immediately, but the existing paradigms are certain to be permanently altered if not totally jettisoned in the near future. Our view of marketing will never be the same again. The sharks have been jumped.

Mass media jumped the shark when a little-noticed column in *Advertising Age,* penned by its editor Scott Donaton in October 2004, announced that for the first time in history, communications spending by U.S. consumers surpassed ad spending. According to a study by Veronis Suhler Stevenson's Communications Industry Forecast, consumers spent $178.4 billion on movies, music, cable, Web, video games, and other entertainment, compared to $175.8 billion in U.S. ad spending. If you throw in spending by consumers at work and not just at home, the gap widens between the $331.5 billion spent by consumers and the $316.8 billion spent on marketing services and advertising combined. This isn't just an aberrant blip on the marketing radar screen; this is the start of a consumer-led revolution against big media. According to a source in the column, "for years the consumer went along with a model of intrusion perpetuated by the networks, advertisers and ad agencies. The consumer has decided to take over." In fact, this glossed-over revolution is bound to expand. The same study predicts that consumer spending on communications will continue to grow at a 6.6 percent compound annual rate over the next five years, while advertising and marketing will grow at a 6.2 percent clip.

Many marketing pundits and antimarketing zealots like to contend that mass media jumped the shark when TiVo gained critical mass with an enthusiastic consumer base. In 2004, major TV broadcasters extracted their heads from their collective posteriors and came to realize that TiVo is a major threat to their comfortable existence. With more than 16 million users predicted for 2005 and 20 percent market penetration by 2007, TiVo will once and for all prove to lazy ad agencies and

TV execs that the thirty-second commercial is passé, and so may be their jobs. TiVo and the next generation of Internet-enabled media hardware all have ad-skipping technology. So far, studies suggest that consumers definitely use this feature. The company says that 80 percent of all TiVo users skip the commercials when watching TV. To the mass marketer, the bells may indeed be tolling. But for future marketers, the advent of TiVo and ad-skipping technologies in DVD players and TVs themselves is merely one more marketing battleground to successfully launch revolutionary campaigns.

Smart marketers and agencies are realizing that the nature of marketer/consumer communications is changing, with power shifting more to the consumer. Consumers will be the ones who control what they watch and when they watch it. Writing in *Wired* magazine, Frank Rose predicts a world where brands interact with the TV viewer one on one. "With technology giving time shifting and programming control to the consumer, current media brands such and ABC, NBC, and Fox will become irrelevant. What will become very important are individual networks; channels created and programmed solely and individually by the consumers to suit their specific viewing needs."

Branding and the notion of the brand were ready to jump the shark after Naomi Klein published her antibrand opus *No Logo* in 2000. For me personally, brands flew off the ramp and over the shark when Kevin Roberts, CEO of Saatchi & Saatchi Worldwide, published his passionate ode to brands called *Lovemarks: The Future beyond Brands.* There might be absolutely nothing surprising about a Saatchi & Saatchi head honcho waxing poetic about brands. His ad agency practically invented the idea of the brand, although Roberts posits that it was his former employer Procter & Gamble that first championed and rode hard the concept of the brand in the 1970s, even though P&G's brand gurus codified the brand management system in 1931. No, a Saatchi & Saatchi brand man paying tribute to branding isn't surprising at all.

What is surprising, however, is his notion that "brands are out of juice." The consummate brand maven has lost faith in brands. Roberts makes clear that brands are worn out from overuse; brands are no longer mysterious; brands don't understand the new consumer; brands can't compete; brands are formulaic; brands have been smothered by caution and risk-aversion. "The great journey from products to trade-marks and from trademarks to brands is over," he declares. Instead, Roberts wants the marketing world to start looking at brands as *love-marks,* which are defined as "brands and businesses that create genuine emotional connections with the communities and networks they live in." Lovemarks would have to meet a couple of criteria to transition from the lowly concept of a brand. Lovemarks must connect companies, their people, and their brands; lovemarks must inspire loyalty beyond reason; and lovemarks must be owned by the people who love them. In other words, "lovemarks could not be constrained by the world defined by brands and marketing."

Roberts presents an interesting premise for the future of brands, and in the process might have augured a double shark-jump. I'm not sure which jump is more powerful—the notion that brands as we know them are obsolete, or the fact that a devout brand man such as Roberts and a brand-pushing company such as Saatchi & Saatchi need to come up with a term and concept such as *lovemarks* to keep themselves rele-vant in the new consumer-dominated economy. In either case, the per-ceived demise of the brand, and the traditional notions of branding, is clearly at hand. In fact, a general maxim of branding holds that when a brand has run its course, it should be reinvented and reinvigorated to become another brand. Certainly it sounds like lovemarks is just another type of brand repositioning, mandated by the need to come up with something new after the predecessor has "run out of steam." With the introduction of lovemarks it's obvious that brands are going nowhere but downhill.

And if the notion of lovemarks doesn't jump the shark for brands in 2004, perhaps the Black Spot sneaker can accomplish it even better. At the tail end of 2003, *Adbusters* magazine—the definitive voice of the culture-jamming, anticorporate, and brand-bashing movements—announced the upcoming launch of the Black Spot sneaker to be sold to jaded consumers in 2004. The Black Spot is *Adbusters*'s own concocted brand, a running shoe meant to be a subversive brand alternative to the much-hated Nike brand behemoth. And so, in a coup de grâce to the antibrand movement, alternative culture bought into the mainstream obsession with branding. This move wasn't just jumping the shark. It was more like jumping the entire ocean.

The Mark of the Brand

So where is the notion of "branding" heading? To fully figure that out, it makes sense to see where brands have been. As famed *New York Times* columnist William Safire pointed out in a column on the subject, the word "brand" first made the scene a thousand years ago as a mark burned into the skin of an animal as a sign of possession, or on the skin of a criminal as a mark of infamy. In the nineteenth century, the burned-in mark was being applied to wooden casks of wine or beer. This "brand mark" became a "trademark," and by the twentieth century "the designated item so labeled became a 'brand.' "[202] By 1950 the brand was

202. William Safire, "Brand," *The New York Times Magazine*, March 10, 2004.

being proselytized by David Oglivy in the form of brand image, a way of thinking that tried to persuade the consumer that "brand A, technically identical with brand B, is somehow a better product."[203]

Brand image is what advertisers and marketers have been selling us for decades. Brand image is also how companies have been structured and run ever since Ogilvy's creation, or at least since the likes of Leo Burnett and Bill Bernbach introduced the idea of branding as an irrational, emotional, and creative exercise. The playful, right-brained, and lateral thinking in creating brands was cornered by marketing and advertising agencies, who have grown and been consolidated to form a global monopoly on branding. Six agency conglomerates—Omnicom, WPP, Interpublic, Grey Group, Havas and Publicis—control and re-create most of the world's brands. These six companies, for instance, control more than 60 percent of the billions of dollars spent on advertising and marketing in the United States each year.[204]

These firms and their offshoots help brand managers to reinvent and tweak existing brands, create new ones, and provide justification for killing off some. In fact, according to James Woudhuysen, professor of forecasting and innovation at De Montfort University, "brands are more central to capitalism than ever before."[205] He quotes marketing guru Philip Kotler, who foresaw that "most manufacturers eventually learn that the power lies with the companies that control the brand names. . . . perhaps the most distinctive skill of professional marketers is their ability to create, maintain, protect, reinforce and enhance brands. A brand is a name, term, sign, symbol, design or combination of these, which is used to identify the goods or services of one seller or group of sellers and to

203. Ibid.
204. David Leonard, "Nightmare on Madison Avenue," *Fortune*, June 28, 2004.
205. James Woudhuysen, "Brands: Don't Buy the Hype," *Spiked Essays*, August 25, 2004.

differentiate them from those of competitors."[206] In other words, capitalist power "does not lie in the productive, wealth-creating resources of every firm, but in the eye of the consumer, in the intangibles that distinguish one firm's offering from another."[207]

It would seem obvious, therefore, that branding may be more important than ever. And it is. But most marketers view branding and brand management as a form of risk management. The proliferation of brands is a direct consequence of a company's aversion to risk. Brands are a relatively low-cost way to achieve short-term profitability. Today's marketplace is all about the shareholders' demands on profitability, and creating new brands or brand extensions is an easy way for businesses to appease the wolves at the door. Rebranding a tired old brand with a new tagline and/or sexy celebrity spokesperson is nothing more than a regressive tactic. It's meant to keep consumers from leaving the brand. Advertising agencies aren't trying to get new consumers, they're trying to keep as many consumers from jumping ship as possible. This is exhausting work, and the creativity shows it. Using brands as tools risk management for quick and easy results is a de rigueur marketing practice for far too many businesses. The current state of brands, it seems, is much more about protecting market share than growing it. Keeping loyal customers is much more important than winning over new ones. The main role for brands is nothing more than keeping the status quo.

How else to explain the lingering death of General Motors' Oldsmobile brand, for instance? For years, Oldsmobile's brand managers tried to keep the brand alive by repositioning it through ever-changing slogans such as "This Is Not Your Father's Oldsmobile" or "A New

206. Ibid.
207. Ibid.

Generation of Olds." But neither campaign did anything to attract younger consumers to the brand, and in 2000 GM announced that Oldsmobile would be phased out. So then why did GM take so many years and so much money in efforts to resuscitate a tired brand and brand image? Why couldn't these brand managers redirect youthful consumers to GM's other brands? Why couldn't they take the money wasted on tired marketing and instead launch a totally new target-specific brand, as Toyota did with Scion? In an article printed by *Harvard Business Review* titled "Customer-Centered Brand Management," the authors use the Oldsmobile example to explain this defensive nature of branding and the risk avoidance of brand managers. "It's because in large consumer-goods companies like General Motors, brands are the raison d'être. They are the focus of decision making and the basis of accountability. They are the fiefdoms, run by the managers with the biggest jobs and the biggest budgets. And never have those managers been rewarded for shrinking their turfs."[208] Brand management over-powers customer management in most large companies.

This overwhelming focus on growing brand equity is inconsistent with the goal of growing customer equity. For companies to become geared toward growing consumer equity, they need to replace traditional brand managers with a new position—the customer segment manager. Companies must target brands to as narrow an audience as possible and develop the capability and the mind-set to hand off customers from one brand to another within the company. They should also change the way brand equity is measured by basing calculations on individual, rather than average, customer data. To grow customer equity, therefore, a number of experiential marketing tenets emerge. If

208. Roland Rust, Valerie Zeithaml, and Katherine Lemon, "Customer-Centered Brand Management," *The Harvard Business Review,* September 1, 2004.

the new role of branding is to escape the equity-building trap and go after consumer equity instead, then experiential marketing will be a key component to connect with the new consumers.

Brand managers will have to work extra hard to accomplish this, because the role of the individual consumer—the prosumer—has acquired groundbreaking clout. As pointed out in the beginning of this chapter, and throughout this book, the consumer is now firmly in control of how brands break through the ad clutter to reach them. Because of the growing media fragmentation, and the proliferation of submarkets and niche consumer segments, mass advertising and marketing can no longer effectively deliver a monolithic brand message. It follows, therefore, that a monolithic brand image is impossible to achieve in the modern marketplace. Brands are too many things to too many people. This desperately worries the risk-averse brand managers. In response, forward-thinking marketers are focused on establishing mass consumer cults around experiences instead, which can engender a sense of shared insight and belonging for the consumer.

That's why marketers are looking at experience providers such as Apple, Nike, Starbucks, and Harley-Davidson as avatars of building cults around brand experiences, versus "older" companies such as Coca-Cola, Microsoft, and Nokia, who still play the brand image game. Nike allows consumers to design their own sneakers, and consistently sponsors grassroots efforts to reach out to and interact with the core consumer. Apple allows consumers to design their own marketing for the iPod brand, for instance, and uses its stores to position the brand through space design and one-on-one interactions at the Genius Bars. Every Labor Day, hundreds of thousands of consumers gather in Milwaukee to celebrate Harley-Davidson and mingle with like-minded evangelists. Can you think of any other brand that gets tattooed on the bodies of thousands of consumers each year? These brands are able to build brand cults because they offer the individual consumer a sense of customization, interactivity, and community. These elements are all integral to the ethos of experiential marketing.

The individual is not just empowered as a consumer; the individual is also empowered as a brand. Calvin Klein, Martha Stewart, and Ralph Lauren have been able to transform their personal name, character, and lifestyle into a brand, one that gives consumers a clear idea of the nature, outlook, image, and essence of their products—be it shirts, perfume, linens, or silverware. In the same vein, athletes, actors, and performers are brands in themselves as well. The Internet, moreover, opened up the brand to anyone. Suddenly individuals started to brand themselves as unique individuals and therefore unique brands. Just think of www.craiglist.com or even Malcolm Gladwell and his tipping point "franchise." And the explosion of blogs started in 2004 is certain to drive the notion of the individual as a brand even more.

The extension of the brand into the everyday spheres of society, down to the individual herself, has greatly contributed to the meteoritic rise of the antibranding movements of the past decade. The leading opponent of global brand hegemony is Naomi Klein, whose book titled *No Logo* positioned brands as dominating and detrimental forces that victimize workers, citizens, and consumers. Brands, she argues, accumulate their vast power in a "branding economy" because they are able to exploit their workers (usually in Third World countries), forego job creation in the name of profits, and co-opt youth culture to pursue ever-aggressive and "edgy" branding. It is brands and the companies that seek to proliferate them that are restricting creativity and expression. Branding is a colonization of physical space, and of mental space. "When brand awareness is the goal shared by all, repetition and visibility are the only true measures of success," she writes.[209] It is no surprise, therefore, that the brand has been propped up and sustained by the many forms of mass marketing and advertising, from millions of direct mailers to never-ending banner ads, pop-ups, and the almighty TV spots.

Brand protesters are closely tied with the antiglobalization movement. The organization called Adbusters (www.adbusters.org) is the beacon for anticorporate, antiglobalization, antimedia, and anticonsumption forces that are growing every day, their ranks swelling with media-literate youth and fed-up consumers. Adbusters is the most recognized and prolific antimarketer in the world, and while most average consumers are not familiar with the group, for those who are charged with creating, growing, or protecting a brand, Adbusters is a force to be reckoned with. But the antiglobalization swell—especially evident within the ranks of the new consumers entering the market—has not really affected branding per se. Protests and acts of civil disobedience may have brought some brands down off their pedestal—McDonald's, Microsoft, and Wal-Mart come to mind—but the overall dependence of branding has only been strengthened, as existing brands and upstart ones have begun branding themselves eagerly around the notion of ethical corporate practices and social responsibility.

Klein's missives against the branded world's singular vision of making money at the expense of people may have struck a raw nerve with consumers—and may have dealt a body-blow to major brand marketers—but they did nothing to change the way brands are controlled and propagated today. Companies have simply introduced corporate responsibility into their brand image. Ironically, brand managers "have identified antiglobalization people themselves as an

209. Naomi Klein, *No Logo,* p. 45.

important market segment, making up 13 percent of consumers worldwide, and reinforcing the need for brands to display social responsibility."[210] Even antibrand zealots can be branded.

So the idea that experiential marketing must deliver a meaningful benefit to the consumer is not too far off from this new movement in branding, one that is propelled by antibrand pundits and antiglobalization consumers. This new direction in branding is also supported by the directive for experiential marketers to empower the individual and activate their campaigns at the grassroots level, all the while being authentic and relevant to the consumer's needs and desires. If antibrand activists are alarmed by the loss of individualism and individuality because of a deluge of brands, and the co-opting of culture and social values because of the growing power of branding in the capitalist world, then the experiential marketing directive for engaging consumers through one-on-one interactions must also be a welcoming development in the brand marketing world.

Kinetic Theater

The most profound impact that experiential marketing will have on brands, however, will center on the control of the brand itself. Brands such as Jeep, Volvo, and Nike have certainly used functional messaging to push their products, but they also have infused their marketing with the goal of building a relationship with their consumers and making them feel like they are partners with the brand. They have taken the brand away from brand managers and opened it up for their customers. "The smarter marketers have an alliance with their consumers,"

210. James Woudhuysen, "Brands: Don't Buy the Hype," *Spiked Essays*, August 25, 2004.

explained Douglas Atkin of Merkley & Partners on a fabulous PBS special called *Frontline: The Persuaders*. "They're not trying to do things *to* consumers; they're trying to do things *with* consumers. In fact, there are examples of brands now where the brand manager has to just let go. When I worked at Procter & Gamble, the organigram, if you like, of brand marketing was definitely one of command and control. If you think about it, the terms they use in marketing are all about military campaigns. You run a campaign, you have a target, you try and penetrate a particular category. It's a very aggressive, very controlling vocabulary. Nowadays, many brands have a life of their own, and a brand manager has to just learn to let go, allow consumers themselves to create meaning and communities around their brands."[211]

But what allows them to do this? Certainly the Internet provides the tools and access to create meaning and build communities around a brand. No other medium does it so well. But it is hampered by its virtual nature. Experiential marketing, on the other hand, is the physical medium to create meaning and communal affinity for a brand. In the modern marketplace, some of the most pressing challenges for brand marketers are the ability to truly understand what emotional messaging is internalized by the individual consumer, and how this messaging affects the perception of the brand. Equally challenging is the ability to identify what changes are required to steer the brand's defining equity in the right direction, when to do it, and how to ascertain if the new direction is right. Experiential marketing campaigns are the forums in which that brand equity gets put to the test by the consumer and where brand marketers can address these challenges through firsthand observations.

Swivel Media's Erik Hauser views experiential marketing as a form of

211. Frontline: The Persuaders, www.pbs.org.

"kinetic theater." Each time a consumer encounters a brand through an experiential marketing campaign, he or she participates in an ever-fluid performance not far removed from improve or avant-garde theater, where the audience is an active and integral member of the performance itself. Every performance is slightly different, depending on the level of audience—or consumer—participation. And much like a good play or piece of theater, an experiential marketing campaign will take the audience to a different place, a branded place where the senses are heightened and emotion overtakes reason. Experiential marketing can achieve equal suspension of disbelief, as a good movie can.

According to Atkin, a "sense of mystery happens with people's experience of a brand, just as someone's experience of religion is often very personal in that sense of mystery. . . . When I talk to Harley-Davidson riders, they would talk about their experiences of riding a motorcycle in the same terms as someone describing the transcendent moments of their religion. It took them out of the everyday. Their experience was on the edge. They felt transported to a different place. That's where the mystery lies. There can be no mystery in how we communicate to consumers. The mystery has to come from the experience of the brand."[212] This personal mystery and a consequent personal relevance are part of the spark of magic that happens during a successful experiential marketing campaign, or during a single experiential marketing interaction between consumer and brand.

The key to fostering brand mystery is to allow the individual consumer to experience it firsthand and personally. In other words, the mystery arises out of the individual's brand experience, and not from the brand itself. It is therefore becoming increasingly clear that the

212. Ibid.

future of branding lies in allowing consumers to participate in the brand experience itself, and not relying solely on brand propagation and command/control messaging. It's the difference between experiencing brand marketing such as the Potty Palooza campaign versus seeing a Charmin commercial on television. The brand is no longer contingent on controlled branding; it is a unique and memorable part of every individual consumer who experienced it.

Much to marketers' chagrin, brands have escaped from the control of brand managers and the agencies that serve them. In the hands of experiential marketers, brands come to life for each individual consumer through meaningful branded experiences. Hauser sees the future of branding as a form of "kinetic theater." Australia-based marketing guru Johnnie Moore likens today's interaction between consumers and brands as "the dance." To him, the word *brands* isn't anything close to being concrete; it's "an averaging out of all the different stories in each of our heads about what an organization means. You can influence these stories by what you do and say, but you can't control them. . . . But the interesting stuff is what isn't controlled."[213]

Letting Go of the Brand

As I write this, the word *blog* has certainly reached tipping point. Admittedly, I started my blog (www.experiencethemessage.com) rather late, in January 2005. The year before saw an absolute explosion of blogs. I had heard the term first in 2003 from a group of young writers and journalists who were not only interested in publishing their work, but also in reacting and working with the feedback that fellow bloggers would

213. From the Web site: www.johnniemoore.com.

publish about it. Blogging is a two-way street. The most-read and most-admired bloggers aren't talking to their audience; they're talking with it and engaging it. More than any other mass medium on this planet, the notion of the blog and the action of blogging are based on a conversation. It is simply the easiest and most accessible way for an individual voice to be heard in the din. It is also fast becoming the best way a company can listen to its consumers, react with them, and give them the keys to drive the brand. That in itself would be a groundbreaking marketing experience.

Here's one way to let go of the reins: a company called Marqui in Portland, Oregon, paid twenty bloggers to write about the company, a software outfit that automates marketing communications. The company made it clear that the bloggers would be paid even if they bad-mouthed and trashed Marqui on their blogs. This wasn't a publicity stunt, nor was it an age-old and useless "even bad press is good press" mentality. The company wanted to become part of a conversation, and understood that sometimes you have to hear ugly truths from your friends to get better.

Even a behemoth such as Microsoft is secure enough with its largesse to open up with *msdn.mircrosoft.com,* a blog where more than a thousand employees are dishing out their daily experiences and knowledge base about the Microsoft business. Developers, customers, and curious geeks can tap into this talent pool to ask esoteric questions about complex software issues, operating systems, new product development, and what the Redmond, Washington, campus cafeteria serves on Thursdays. Internet provider EarthLink has started a blog to address issues about Web security—spam, spyware, wi-fi, identity theft—on www.protection-blog.net. Not only does this make their customers feel comforted and empowered with valuable security information, the blog also helps keep

EarthLink's servers free of security-related problems caused by uninformed and naive users.

The blog and its variant future extensions are mainstays in Western media. The popularity of blogs, and the speed to which individuals gravitated toward them, is certainly unrivaled by the growth of the Internet, television, or radio. Each day, a brand new weblog is created every eleven seconds, according to Technocrati, Inc.[214] *Business Week* reported that in December 2004 there were 5.4 million blogs created. In January 2005 that number grew to 6.6 million. A month later it was at 8.7 million blogs total. Here are some more startling figures: a Pew Internet and American Life Project survey found that 7 percent of the 130 million American *adults* who use the Internet had set up a blog of their own. More than 8 million people are actively publishing blogs in the United States, and the numbers are growing. By the end of 2004, more than 32 million Americans were blog readers.

The blog revolution will rival the world's appropriation of the Internet as a community-building tool. It may prove more revolutionary than Gutenberg's press and Marconi's radio. Blogs will empower individual voices like no other medium invented. And this will profoundly change the way consumers are marketed to. One significant change is already here. In April 2005, Weblogs, Inc., the largest publisher of professional blogs on the Internet, launched a service to its advertisers called Focus-Ads. For the first time ever, consumers were given the choice to publicly comment on an ad or about the product being advertised on banner ads and pop-ups on several of Weblogs's densely populated blogs such as *AutoBlog.com* and *Engadget.com*. Readers on the blogs can click on links at the bottom of the ads to post public comments, and

214. From the Web site: http://blog.teledyn.com/node/1482.

read other readers' posted comments as well. All comments are then forwarded to specific advertisers such as American Suzuki Motors Corporation, Subaru and ABS Computers, who have been first to sign up for Focus-Ads. The advertiser can then choose to not respond to the comments, publicly respond to them, or send a response directly to the individual reader by e-mail. This simple exchange allows consumers to gain enough knowledge through other testimonials to better decide about engaging the advertisers. It also allows the advertisers to acquire insight into their messages and product to consistently adjust their marketing and therefore improve their bottom line. David Harris, e-marketing manager for American Suzuki, said through a press release that his company is "in a new marketing environment that is based on consumer empowerment, and blogs are at the forefront of that movement. Focus-Ads allow us to reach auto enthusiasts and gain valuable insight on how they perceive our products and the way we promote them."[215]

Blogs, and the blog ethos of individual voices being heard above the din, are also a pivotal arena to reach the influentials, those consumer enthusiasts who are key to sparking buzz and recruiting brand evangelists. The Pew Internet and American Life Project survey also found that bloggers are young, 48 percent of them under age thirty. They are, unsurprisingly, Internet veterans: 82 percent have been online for six years or more. Bloggers are closer to the top of the wealth pyramid, as 42 percent of them live in households earning more than $50,000. Thirty-nine percent of bloggers have a college or graduate degree. Bloggers are informed and vocal. They take pride in commenting on articles and other blog entries, posting their own tips and tricks for others, enaging like-minded individuals, and sharing their experiences with products

215. Sean P. Egen, "New Banner Ads Let Consumers Talk Back," *iMedia Connections,* April 11, 2005.

and media messages among other groups of bloggers. Many bloggers are already experimenting with video logs (vlogs), RSS (really simple syndication) feeds, and podcasts as alternative ways to acquire content they are interested in. All these tools combine to allow the individual consumers to release their own content extremely quickly and easily. If marketers were worried that media fragmentation would hamper their ability to reach consumers with their messages, the rise of the blog revolution transforms this worry into a tolerable nag. Citizen-generated content is replacing mass media with every new blog on the net. Influencers are now more important that ever, because they simply need a laptop for the whole world to hear what they have to say, with or without the participation of marketers.

If the blog revolution will make individual voices heard, then the thumb culture of mobile telephony will make individual action possible. The rise of the flash mob phenomenon and the concurrent proliferation of mobile text messaging will empower the consumers to act immediately on information received on their handheld communication devices. Mobile technology can topple a government in the Philippines, and it can get a hundred New Yorkers to spontaneously squawk like birds in Central Park. The increasing capabilities of handheld devices to deliver rich, medialike video will only expand the thumb culture. What is certain is that the little screen in the palm of our hands is a delivery tool for a very personal media experience. This screen can now deliver any desired content anywhere and anytime. No other device can boast this power. The tumb culture is prevalent in front of the television as well. Instead of pushing number keys, consumers are punching the ad-skip feature on their TiVo remote controls. An Arbitron and Edison Media Research survey released in March 2005 found that an estimated 27 million Americans owned one or more on-demand media devices. Seventy percent of digital video recorder (DVR) owners skip the commercials.

The status quo mentality of branding is unsustainable in this emerging marketplace. The accepted notion of the brand is a direct outcome of the rise of the television medium, and this medium is quickly becoming irrelevant to the empowered consumer. New technologies such as the Internet, blogs, DVRs, video-on-demand (VOD), podcasting, and RSS are making the mass media giant obsolete, or at least vulnerable enough to be taken down. According to Nielsen, network television audience has dwindled an average of 2 percent each year for a decade, while the U.S. population has increased by 30 million people. The cost of reaching 1,000 households with a TV commercial has increased from $7.64 in 1994 to $19.85 in 2004. In 2000, Americans watched TV an average of 866 hours each year, and spent 107 hours on the Internet, a ration of 8 to 1. For 2005, it is predicted that Americans will devote 785 hours to TV and 200 hours to the Internet, a ratio of just slightly less than 4 to 1.[216] Mass marketing is predicated on low cost per thousand, on the ability to reach people cheaply. When television becomes expensive, however, mass media no longer seems as attractive as it used to.

The problem for brand marketers today is simple. The basic value to a mass medium such as television lies in its ability to deliver marketing messages through reach, frequency, exposure, and cost per thousand. It is a medium devoted to reaching as many eyeballs as possible, at the least cost available. It is based on economies of scale. It is a perfect medium for a mass marketing consumer, except that the consumer no longer responds to mass marketing. Marketers can no longer effectively sell to a massive and anonymous crowd. They must now forever

216. Bob Garfield, "Bob Garfield's Chaos Theory," *Advertising Age,* April 13, 2005.

sell to individuals instead. Even Procter & Gamble's global marketing officer, who oversees over $5.5 billion in marketing budgets, thinks the current mass marketing model is broken.[217] If marketing messages with billion-dollar budgets behind them can't compete with a small cadre of bloggers with a $19.95 per month broadband account, then certainly there is something broken. For instance, when comedian Jon Stewart appeared on CNN's *Crossfire* and got into a heated argument with the hosts, the show probably had about 400,000 viewers that day. After the altercation was copied onto the Internet, the segment was seen more than 5 million times by viewers from around the world. CNN execs didn't release it on the network's site, however. Consumers with simple digital editing software did it for them.

This is why major corporations are moving away from the broken model. *Advertising Age* reported that Procter & Gamble launched its Prilosec OTC with 75 percent of its marketing budget away from television. American Express uses more than 80 percent of its marketing budget for nontelevision initiatives, and the new Pepsi One campaign used no television spots whatsoever for its launch. A 2004 study from Sanford C. Bernstein & Co. predicts that ad revenues from narrowcast media such as the Internet will grow at 13.5 percent a year from 2003 to 2010, while mass media stutters at 3.5 percent. By 2010, marketers will spend more for advertising on cable ($27 billion) and the Internet ($22.5 billion) than on network TV ($19.1 billion) or magazines ($17.4 billion).[218]

Ad critic Bob Garfield wrote in *Advertising Age* that "as more control has been placed in the hands of the consumer, the consumer has shown every intention of exercising it." He predicts a period of chaos among

217. Ibid.
218. Anthony Bianco, "The Vanishing Mass Market," *Business Week*, July 12, 2004.

advertisers and marketers as they and their brands deal with "the total democratization of media, combined with the total addressability of marketing communications." He sees a future marketplace where "we, the people, cease to be demographics. We become individuals again."[219] The chaos arrives when mass marketers begin to eschew the notion of economies of scale, and instead begin to focus on what one new marketing exec calls "the economics of reaggregation . . . which is how do you get 10, 20, 30, 40 thousand people instead of taking in 250 million? How do you reaggregate one at a time into the tens of thousands?"[220]

Get Them with Experience

The above heading answers this question. An increasingly fragmented and heterogeneous marketplace requires much more one-on-one communication, instead of the one-to-many format, such as mass advertising and marketing. Experiential marketing is the methodology that can provide a bridge between the old status quo of brands based on mass marketing, and the future of marketing that is based on personalized messages delivered to a consumer who can choose to engage the brand on his or her own terms. Marketing will have to become relevant enough to be welcomed by the consumer at times and places where she is most receptive to it. The mass market will not entirely disappear, nor will mass media. But in the upcoming times of chaos, major companies will fail or succeed depending on how well they accept and adapt to a fading mass market and an emerging era of micromarketing.

According to Rishad Tobaccowala, president of Internet media agency Starcom IP, this transition will be manifest in the increased use

219. *Advertising Age*, April 13, 2005.
220. Ibid.

of experiential marketing strategies and tactics. He sees in the near future a move to a lot of event- and store-based marketing, for instance. Referencing a company such as Starbucks, he expects consumers to move completely away from electronic media to more experiential media. That's right: an Internet guy is touting experiential marketing. And why not? The experiential marketing tenets espoused in this book are tailor-made to a consumer base transitioning from traditional mass marketing. Experiential marketing is predicated on a one-on-one inter-action between consumer and marketer, in direct antithesis to mass marketing. It seeks to empower the individual consumer to engage the companies that are trying to reach her, and to provide a marketing experience that is relevant and memorable. Experiential marketing should be conducted when and where the consumer is most receptive to it, exactly as today's consumer demands. It seeks to use innovative tactics and technologies to converse with the consumer and keep pace with his or her personal media delivery preferences. Experiential marketing campaigns are conducted on a grassroots level, in places and domains that traditional mass marketing cannot reach. And experiential marketers hope to provide a clear benefit to the consumer with their campaigns in ways that a TV commercial or magazine ad can never accomplish.

Experiential marketers understand that the traditional command-and-control model of brand marketing is outdated and ineffective. Renaming the term "brand" with "lovemarks" does not accomplish much for the consumer. It is just another name for an agency to use to propagate the top-down approach of traditional marketers. Just because an agency calls them lovemarks doesn't mean that consumers will actually love them. To accomplish this, marketers need to forget going after eyeballs; it's hearts and minds they should be after. The focus should rest squarely on how consumers *experience* brands, not on how they *perceive* them.

Take Starbucks again as an example, this time as both a brand and an experience. As Lewis Carbone writes in *Clued In*, "if you are considering how you feel *about* Starbucks, you are thinking about the Starbucks brand. If you think about how *you yourself feel* as a result of a visit to a Starbucks, you are relating to the experience. . . . What customers value is the experience. And that's what they associate with the brand (brand association)."[221] In this regard, experiential marketing is poised to change consumer perceptions about a brand by influencing the experience they have with the brand at various touch points beyond mass media. Traditionally, brand managers and the agencies they hired to market their brands have tried to establish an emotion to attach to the brand. Conversely, experiential marketers, look to establish and enhance an emotion felt by the consumer. In other words, traditional branding is based on creating a consumer emotion about the company, not the emotions that consumers actually feel when engaging with it. "Brand very often is an expression from an *organization* out: the business wants to deliver a message that it controls and leave an impression that it believes will favorably position it in the consumer's mind." Conversely, an experiential approach is "customer-back: it starts by identifying emotions *customers* want to feel as a result of an experience (which recognizes the customer is in control), then works back to what the organization has to do to get to that emotional end frame."[222] This is exactly how experiential marketers approach the new marketplace, and how a directive to provide a clear benefit to the consumer through marketing could be successfully championed in marketing circles.

The "customer-back" approach to marketing fits snugly with the

---

221. Lewis Carbone, *Clued In: How to Keep Customers Coming Back Again and Again* (Upper Saddle River, NJ: Financial Times Prentice Hall 2004), p. 44.
222. Ibid., p. 49.

notion of consumer empowerment. Branding can no longer become a form of corporate ownership; brands cannot simply be renamed lovemarks just because agencies say so. A brand is by its very nature a tightly controlled projection of a company's ego. It is controlled by the company that originated it, not by the customers who interact with it. This practice is unsustainable in the near future. Not only do consumers no longer respond to the media channels that have for decades propped up the notion of a brand, they also no longer accept the one-way control that companies have over them. Companies need to acknowledge that their brands no longer satisfy the emotional needs of consumers, who instead find value in a brand through the various experiences they have with it. It is the job of experiential marketers to ensure a great experience at all touch points the consumer may have with the brand—packaging, point of sale, retail, promotional marketing, events, guerrilla marketing, interactive, viral, mobile marketing, and PR. This is the only way to sustain a brand these days.

A study by retail-industry tracking firm NPD Group found that nearly half of those who described themselves as highly loyal to a brand were no longer loyal a year later. Another study found that just 4 percent of consumers would be willing to stick with a brand if its competitors offered better value for the same price. Consumers are continually looking for a better deal, moving, sharing, accepting and rejecting brand messages at every turn and at every media touch point. For instance, in 2002 Nokia was the sixth most valuable brand in the world, with an estimated brand worth of more than $30 billion, according to Interbrand. The very next year, the company failed to release a clamshell phone that customers were demanding. The cell phone company lost customers in droves to the competition, and sales plummeted. In one year, Nokia lost $6 billion in brand equity. Clearly, having a strong brand does not guarantee security for a company. If a company must constantly deliver new value to its loyal customers just to keep them, those customers aren't loyal at all, which means brands have little or no value independent of what a company actually does.

The brand is no longer paramount to the new consumer. The experience with the brand is. This development has led to the rise of experiential marketing at the expense of mass marketing. Because experiential marketing is based on a deeper interaction between a marketer and a consumer than traditional marketing and advertising, it allows for each consumer to enter into an experience with the brand. "In the aftermath of the interaction, the way people remember and value an experience emotionally will have everything to do with their ultimate commitment to the organization or brand, says Carbone.[223] In other words, customer loyalty in the future will be based more on the experiences consumers have with brands than what they rationally think about individual products or services a company offers. If brands in the future will be built on individual consumer experiences, why shouldn't successful marketing campaigns be built on the same foundation? This is at the core of experiential marketing.

The Brand as Experience; the Experience as Brand

Experiential marketing is the next marketing methodology that can bridge the disconnect between consumers' increasing demand to engage marketers and brands on their own terms, and the slow-footed reluctance of traditional marketers to move away from mass media marketing and the one-way, command-and-control ways of building brands

223. Ibid., p. 66.

they have been accustomed to for decades. Traditional marketers continue to contend that mass media is still relevant to the consumer, especially when launching a new brand. But as is evident by the launch of Scion, a brand doesn't need mass marketing to be born and grow. An experiential approach to launching a brand may be more effective and relevant than anything that television ads can offer. In Australia, Absolut launched a brand called Cut through a strictly experiential marketing point of view. Using public relations, point of sale, online, and event marketing, Absolut was able to cut out traditional advertising altogether, something unheard of when launching a spirits brand. In a rather astounding bow to experiential marketing over mass marketing, Absolut also leased two bars in Sydney and Melbourne, and put on DJ sets, band concerts, and photo exhibitions in these spaces. Visitors to the Absolut Cut bars get a free bottle of Cut, and consumers are given a chance to contribute their photos to the exhibits, generating what Absolut hopes will be a viral element to the campaign. The campaign flies in the face of traditional ways to launch a brand. Instead of using mass marketing to blanket the millions to reach the few, Absolut chose to target the few to eventually reach the masses.

The same is true for Pabst Blue Ribbon beer, a brand that has witnessed a twenty-year span of sales declines and loss of market share. The brand's marketing budget couldn't compete with the likes of Budweiser, Miller, or Coors. So instead of continuing marketing the brand with traditional mass media, brand managers at Pabst decided to take an experiential tack and began sponsoring subcultural events in the same vein that Scion went grassroots to reach the influentials. Pabst would support subculture events such as scooter rallies, dodgeball tournaments, fashion shows, bike messenger races, and art exhibit openings. All of this was done on a shoestring budget. Pabst didn't underwrite these events, but merely donated beer or a few thousand dollars to print flyers and posters for the events. Eventually, influencers who were organizing their own grassroots events began to approach Pabst directly to be involved. According to Neal Stewart, senior brand manager at the suds brewer, the brand was able to connect with the younger, ad-savvy consumers precisely because it didn't advertise on television. "They literally said to us, 'I love your beer but the minute you advertise on TV, I'm done with you.' They felt like they discovered it, and there was a sense of ownership."[224] Using experiential marketing instead of traditional mass media, Pabst reversed that twenty-year sales decline. After losing 90 percent of its volume between 1978 and 2001, Pabst was in the positive numbers in 2004, with a 15 percent volume lift. So not only can experiential marketing tactics launch a brand without mass media support, it can rejuvenate it as well.

Brand managers need to take note of these experiential successes. A strong brand can no longer shield a company from competition, nor can it ensure that customers stay loyal to it. Product differentiation is no longer a viable strategy for creating value in the mind of the consumer. Products are reverse-engineered almost as fast as they can be developed, making product enhancements a short-lived advantage. Products are also becoming congested with too many features, making it difficult for the consumer to distinguish one product from another. According to Brand Central Station's Mike Bawden, this environment forces brand managers to find new ways to create and maintain a relationship between their product or service and the customer in a way that makes their brand be more than just a fancy nameplate on the front of a product. Experiential marketing is the new way.

For decades, the strength of a brand ensured that its brand extensions

224. Jennifer Nasty, "How Pabst Blue Ribbon Reversed a Twenty-Year Sales Decline with Underdog Event Marketing," *Marketing Sherpa,* November 15, 2004.

would also prove successful, an easy way to respond to consumer fickleness and profit pressures. Since 1991, the number of brands on U.S. grocery store shelves has tripled. In 2004, the U.S. Patent and Trademark Office issued an incredible 140,000 trademarks—100,000 more than in 1983. But in a surprising survey of 22,000 cases of brand extensions, Research International found that brand extensions are actually more likely to fail than new products. Clearly, brands are not as strong as brand managers and traditional marketers claim. In fact, the proliferation of brands is not a sign of strength, but one of inherent weakness. The larger the number of brands in a company's portfolio, the greater the overlap of brands on consumer segments, positioning, price, and distribution channels. Many brands in a portfolio end up competing against each other rather than against those of the competition. A larger brand portfolio also means lower sales volumes for individual brands as they are divided among the total market. Brand extensions also tend to take up a lot of a company's time and energy, as brand managers within the company jockey for ad dollars and other resources. For instance, Diageo sold 35 brands in 170 countries in 1999, but just 8 of its brands accounted for 50 percent of its sales and 70 percent of its profits. Unilever had an astounding 1,600 brands in its portfolio in 1999, but more than 90 percent of its profits came from only 400 brands. The rest of the brands posted either losses or marginal profits.

Perhaps this is why some leading companies are choosing to forgo brand extensions for something more experiential. As empowered consumers are increasingly demanding better products and services, and thereby disproving the notion of brand loyalty, brands are beginning to team up with each other to offer consumers a new type of brand that answers this demand. It is now no longer surprising to see two, three or four separate brands combine their core competencies to launch a "branded brand." For instance,

Jim Beam bourbon teamed up with Starbucks to launch Starbucks Coffee Liqueur. Philips Sonicare partnered with Crest to launch IntelliClean, a power toothbrush and liquid toothpaste dispensing system. Beermaker Heineken coupled itself to coffeemaker purveyor Krups to come up with the BeerTender, a professional-grade beer tap for the home. More than 1.4 million units of the BeerTender were sold in the Netherlands in less than a year, and now the BeerTender is available for Heineken-owned brands such as Amstel and Stella Artois.

These examples are not exercises in brand extension. Rather, they are an indication that brand managers are becoming aware that the consumer is demanding a better *experience* with the brand, and by bringing different brands and their core competencies to the table, brands are able to enrich this experience. The same applies to experiential marketing as well. Quite often an experiential marketing campaign will align a number of partnering brands to enhance the marketing experience. DaimlerChrylser brings in dozens of brands to enhance the Camp Jeep marketing experience. When conducting a ski hill campaign, we partnered with North Face clothing and Rossignol to make the experience that much more authentic and relevant to the skiers we were trying to reach. Imagine trying to do this with a television ad! Imagine watching a commercial where three or more brands are being hyped simultaneously. Experiential marketing can meet consumers' demands for quality marketing experiences in a much more compelling way than traditional marketing can muster. These experiences combine to drive buzz about a brand, and the more experiential the marketing, the better the buzz.

Of course, a person's feelings about a company can be shaped by something as simple as word-of-mouth. Typically, though, it's the product of a series of direct and indirect experiences, each adding or subtracting from perceived status. In effect, a brand is the sum of the customer's experiences with the relevant product or company. It is transmitted in every interaction with the customer over the lifetime of the relationship. So why would traditional marketers continue to support their brands with marketing interaction that the consumer no longer responds to? Consumers are more skeptical than ever about marketing and advertising, and often tune out marketing messages completely. This only serves to magnify the imperative for brand managers to find out and appreciate how their brand is understood by the empowered consumer, and how consumers are interacting with them differently than before. By engaging in experiential marketing campaigns, brand marketers are able to gain valuable insight into this realm by interacting directly with consumers outside of the mass media landscape. If consumers can now respond directly back to the advertiser through links on banner ads and pop-ups, experiential marketing allows them to respond directly to a brand ambassador during the marketing intercept.

The primacy of the brand in marketing is over. Brand managers are losing control over them to an empowered and proactive consumer base. Instead of a consumer economy in which success is determined in large part by name, it's now being determined by performance. The element of product performance is a key component to experiential marketing campaigns today. Just think of the Maytag "try it before you buy it" stores, or the twenty-four-hour test drives being offered by car manufacturers around the world. Brands are now also being driven by the consumers themselves, through experiential elements such as Converse's cocreation marketing and Scion's cultivation of brand evangelism. The marketing industry is being radically changed from a mass media landscape to more individualized, fragmented, and personal media choices. If brands are to survive in the near future, they need to appropriate experiential marketing tenets to deal with this transformation.

This requires more effort than the typical brand manager or traditional marketer is often willing to expend. It requires a rethinking of
how to personally engage consumers and how to open dialogue with
brands—a rethinking that hasn't been possible with the instinctive
dependence on mass media that has characterized marketing and advertising since the late 1940s. As I write this, General Motors—the ultimate
American superbrand—has announced that it will lay off twenty-five
thousand workers by 2008 as it tries to reduce costs and improve quality.
Packaged goods companies are desperately trying to deal with their
inability to achieve premiums and raise prices. Increased prices for raw
materials, coupled with the Wal-Mart effect of consumers demanding
ever lower prices, are certain to force many companies to kill off their
brands by the hundreds if not thousands.

The new forces emerging in the marketplace focus on consumer experience as paramount to doing business. There is no such thing as advertising anymore. Advertising has *jumped the shark*. Everything is marketing
now. And marketing must be based on the consumer experience. Just
think of JetBlue. Skyrocketing costs of doing business have virtually dec-
imated profits for airlines such as Delta, United, and American. Yet Jet-
Blue has shown profits every quarter since its IPO in April 2002. Why? In
one word: experience. The company's vice president of sales and marketing, Andrea Speigel, makes sure that the JetBlue brand is shaped by
customer experience, everything from flight uniforms, food served on
the flights, and interior design to customer service technologies. In a
CMO magazine interview from the summer of 2005, Speigel was asked
what made JetBlue profitable in an industry woefully struggling to stay
solvent. The answer was the consumer herself. "I think that customers
understand we are completely focused on them and their needs. We really
try to keep it quite simple but with a little irreverence and personality,"

she explained. "But at the end of the day, it's really giving customers what they want. In certain markets at certain times we may be $2, $3, $4 higher than some of our competitors, but our customers still come back because of the experience that they had with us. They know that they're getting a constant, reliable and very enjoyable experience."[225]

It's not rocket science, really. JetBlue does the little things right to provide a consistent experience. They don't nickel-and-dime the consumer; headsets and snacks are free. Flight attendants are renowned for their friendliness and helpfulness. When the weather slows down or cancels a flight, customers get a flight credit right away, often without even asking for it themselves. At JFK International Airport, for instance, JetBlue operated two "cafés" where delayed passengers can relax and get free refreshments, and harried parents can watch their kids frolic in Jet-Blue play areas. In smaller airports, JetBlue empoweres their managers to be proactive in servicing customers, going so far as to order pizzas from the local restaurant to serve to hungry passengers. It's no wonder that JetBlue is ranked at the top for best service in the airline industry.

These actions and business practices are clearly reflective of the tenets laid out in this book for marketers and brand managers. The business successes achieved by focusing on customer experience are exactly why experiential marketing is becoming increasingly important to any company's marketing mix. It may be a modest percentage now, but it will inexorably grow. Companies will soon be forced by the consumer to adopt experiential marketing tactics and strategies in order to reach them. Instead of relying solely on advertising, brands will seek out events where the consumer can physically interact with them. Marketing campaigns will need to deliver clear benefits to consumers, allowing causal

225. Constantine von Hoffman, "Nothing but Blue Skies," *CMO Magazine*, July 1, 2005.

marketing to take a more prominent role in a company's marketing plans. Consumer engagement and empowerment will become instrumental in driving sales. The Internet is already making this a reality. For instance, 80 percent of Hyundai consumers currently go to the Web to choose their vehicle, even before they step into a showroom.

Marketers will have to find niche markets for their brands, and mass media advertising will not be able to help them. Instead, going grassroots with marketing programs will prove to be even more necessary than in the past. Communications planning will be taken to the next level. No longer will a network television buy be as effective as determining when and where the consumer is most receptive to marketing messages. Marketing will have to deliver context to its messages. This makes a methodology such as product placement as something less than the panacea that traditional mass marketers hope it will be. Marketers can no longer afford a "one size fits all" approach to mass media. Each campaign's creativity will have to be tailored to accommodate the media vehicle—television, Internet, mobile telephony, word-of-mouth, face-to-face, etc. Look at the gaming industry and its experiments with advergaming. This may hold clues to the immediate future of advertising, where, again, contextual experience is king, because a mass, buckshot approach without it is no longer viable.

More far reaching is what experiential marketing holds for the future of our everyday experiences with brands and services. Experiential marketing can make brands important again. Instead of marketers spending their time on new products, line extensions, or new and improved packaging, they should concentrate on their existing marketing strategies to see how they are engaging, benefiting, and empowering their customers. If they do this, they may just stumble on "the next big thing." They may invent a product or a service that can actually change our lives—change the quotidian into the extraordinary. Think iPod. Think Jeep. Think JetBlue. Think American Apparel. Then think of the chapters in this book:

- Experiential marketing campaigns should clearly deliver a meaningful benefit to the consumer.

- Experiential marketing will be predicated on one-on-one personal interaction between a marketer and a consumer.

- Experiential marketing will be authentic. This will mobilize the marketplace.

- Experiential marketing is based on engaging people in memorable ways.

- Experiential marketing will empower the individual consumer and unleash the power of grassroots evangelism.

- Experiential marketing will deliver relevant communication to consumers only where and when they are most responsive to them.

- Experiential marketing's goal is to succeed using innovative approaches and tactics to reach out to consumers in creative and compelling ways.

- Experiential marketing will make—or break—the brands of the future.

The tenets espoused in this book are just as much applicable to experiential marketers as they are to traditional marketers. These tenets may hold the answer to birthing and growing brands in the immediate future. As a marketer, I see this future as filled with great reward arising from the ability to take great risks. As a consumer, I see a marketplace where my voice matters, and where my personal experiences with brands drive my purchase habits and loyalty.

If you want to stay in the game, you have to play by a set of new rules. Game on.

Acknowledgments

For Bertrand Russell "the main things which seem important on their own account, and not merely as means to other things, are knowledge, art, instinctive happiness, and relations of friendship or affection." While I continue to pursue and develop the first three things, I am ever so grateful to have known great affection and friendship in my life, none greater than for my wife Summer. She is my best friend and my true love. And although I'd like to say that it was my passion and perseverance that made this book possible, it was really Summer kicking me out of bed in the early morning.

She had help with the kicking, of course. My editor at McClelland & Stewart, Chris Bucci, has a size-12 shoe. Philip Turner at Avalon Publishing has an editorial black belt. Together (if I can squeeze in another metaphor here), they are like a literary Bruce Lee and Chuck Norris super-tag-team main event combo.

I've made great friends writing and researching this book. Steven Finder, an Argentine scholar with whom I share my alma mater, gave me insight and knowledge I could not have found with anyone else. That goes double for all my colleagues and fellow "nonners" at the International Experiential Marketing Association, and the free-thinkers and new marketers on the Experiential Marketing Forum.

I'd also like to give a big shout out to my erstwhile partners at Gearwerx, Adam and Jonathan Starr. Ten thousand miles driven in a branded Hummer: $3,000. One hundred thousand miles flown from city to city to spot-check campaigns: $50,000. Starting and running an agency for an entirely new marketing paradigm: priceless.

To my marketing comrade Robert Finkelstein— the Sancho Panza to my Don Quixote or the Don Quixote to my Sancho Panza—I offer my thanks unreservedly for your marketing genius and really bad sense of humor. You, my friend, make me look real good.

To Craig Silverman, who has always been a keen and avid caller of b.s., most often exercised during my out-loud musings on the state of marketing, pop culture, and media.

And what would an acknowledgment be without an incredibly heart-felt thanks to my agent Don Sedgwick at the Transatlantic Literary Agency, and his wife, the one and only Shaun Bradley. You two are the very best. I couldn't have done this without you. Really. I couldn't.

To you all, I hope you had as much fun as I did. And I hope we can have a lot more of it in the years to come.

Give thanks and praise.

M.L.
Chicago, Illinois

Index

Index

....

Index

Index